Stateless

Stateless

Chen Tienshi Lara
Translated by Louis Carlet

NUS PRESS
SINGAPORE

© 2024 Chen Tienshi Lara
© 2024 Louis Carlet (translation)

Published by:
NUS Press
National University of Singapore
AS3-01-02
3 Arts Link
Singapore 117569

Fax: (65) 6774-0652
E-mail: nusbooks@nus.edu.sg
Website: http://nuspress.nus.edu.sg

ISBN 978-981-325-232-5 (paper)
ePDF ISBN 978-981-325-233-2
ePub ISBN 978-981-325-271-4

All rights reserved. This book, or parts thereof, may not be reproduced in any form or by any means, electronic or mechanical, including photocopying, recording or any information storage and retrieval system now known or to be invented, without written permission from the Publisher.

Cover image: 1972 family photo (author's personal collection)

Typeset by: Ogma Solutions Pvt. Ltd.
Printed by: Integrated Books International

Contents

List of Images vii
Prologue ix

Chapter 1 Lara of Chinatown 1
Chapter 2 Living in the Crevice between Two Countries 11
Chapter 3 Assimilating into Japanese Society 20
Chapter 4 Venturing Out into the World 31
Chapter 5 Off to Hong Kong, Off to America 56
Chapter 6 Learning about Statelessness 87
Chapter 7 Asians and Statelessness 103
Chapter 8 Applying for Naturalization 117
Chapter 9 Statelessness in other Countries 140
Chapter 10 Launching the Stateless Network NGO 160
Chapter 11 Not Someone Else's Problem 177
Chapter 12 State-Engendered Conceptual Boundaries:
           Nationality, IDs, Xenophobia and COVID-19 195
Epilogue 219

Bibliography 224
Index 228

List of Images

My parents married in Taiwan in 1953	4
A 1960s family photo with my grandparents who were visiting Japan	6
Chinatown's Bruce Lee (age 4)	12
A Japanese re-entry permit	22
My goateed paternal grandfather	40
Passport control at an airport	116
Interior Ministry Citizenship Authorization Certificate issued by the ROC on September 28, 1972	126
The word "stateless" on my driver's license	134
Stateless family near the Thailand-Myanmar border	140
Stateless Network	163
Students formed "Stateless Network Youth" and their activities were covered in *"The Japan News by the Yomiuri Shinbun,"* February 26, 2016	179
Picture book about stateless people, published in July 2022	180
Phê and her one-year-old daughter	188
Mama with her ID cards. One of the ID cards labeled her as "stateless", another labeled her as "Taiwanese"	190–1
Stateless children in the Sulu and Celebes Seas	199
Dr. Eugene Aksenoff, 1924–2014	203
Zeid Mahmud's ID had "Undefined" in the nationality field	213

Prologue

In the springtime of the year that I was 21, I found myself stuck at the border between two familiar countries, unable to enter either. I had never felt my statelessness so keenly. Rejected by the Republic of China (Taiwan), which I had long considered my homeland, I was told that I could not enter Japan, the country of my birth and upbringing.

For the first time in my life, I experienced the terror of international limbo, unable to enter any country. What would happen to me? Would I be trapped forever in an airport?

To be stateless is to be someone without citizenship, a national of no country. Around the world and for myriad reasons, people fall into conditions of statelessness. Little is known about their experiences.

That year, the long Golden Week holiday running from late April through early May was over. The day that we left Japan, Tokyo's Haneda Airport was pretty much empty. A few travelers were taking it easy. A handful passed through the departure gate. A Ministry of Justice passport inspector at the exit customs, perhaps relieved the holiday rush was over, spoke to us with a kind voice.

"Going on a family trip *after* the holidays? Must be nice!"

My father answered affably. "Yes, I'm taking my wife and youngest daughter to a gathering in the Philippines." Mama and I smiled. Basking in excitement, the three of us passed the gate without incident.

My family lived in Yokohama's Chinatown. Mama and I were accompanying Baba to a gathering of overseas Chinese in the Philippines. We were in the Philippines for four days. Because the return flight home to Japan stopped over in Taiwan, Mama suggested we meet one of my elder brothers who was working there. It was also an opportunity to briefly visit the country that my family also considered home. Born in mainland China, my parents had moved to Taiwan after World War II, then later migrated to Japan.

We landed in Taipei around midday. Deplaning, the three of us heard spoken Chinese and smelled the stale, humid air. At that point in my life, I referred to travel to Taiwan as "returning to Taiwan" (*hui Taiwan*). Of our family of eight (two parents, six kids), I was the youngest child, and the only one that had been both born and raised in Japan. I had never lived in Taiwan. But since childhood, my parents had taught me to "live proudly as a Chinese national," so I naturally called the Republic of China (ROC) my home country.

Although they too were technically stateless, my parents carried identification that verified their official Republic of China family registry, since they had previously lived there. Walking ahead of me, they sailed through customs. On my turn, I handed over my Republic of China passport to an immigration officer in her early thirties.

Taiwan's nationality law is based on *jus sanguinis* and regards ethnic Chinese living abroad as emigrant compatriots, or *qiaobao*. A special law in force from 1972 through the early 1990s accommodated overseas Chinese, regulating their citizenship and stipulating passport issuance at overseas diplomatic missions to those without citizenship. Although I was officially stateless in Japan, I had been issued a Republic of China passport and used that whenever traveling abroad. I naturally expected that the passport would gain me entrance to Taiwan.

The immigration officer flipped through the pages of my Republic of China passport, then sucker punched me.

"You cannot enter without a visa."

"What? I have a Taiwanese passport. Why do I need a visa?"

I tried to explain my situation, but she just shook her head. I insisted. A few other immigration officers came over and glanced at my passport. They wouldn't budge.

My parents were staring over at me with growing anxiety about what was going on at the other side of the border. All I could do was shout to them that I couldn't enter the country.

"They're saying I can't go through!"

Bewildered and confused, my parents were unable to return to my side to ask what was happening, since they had already completed the immigration process and officially entered the Republic of China. The immigration officer hurried them away from the immigration checkpoint. I had to board the next flight to Japan.

I later discovered that my parents' family register didn't include my name, since I had been born in Japan and never lived in Taiwan. Before I was born, my parents and siblings had lived in Taiwan for more than a decade. They all had a family register and identification papers to prove it. Because of this, the procedures for my entering Taiwan differed from those for my parents. Despite my ROC passport, because I was not listed on the family register, I was officially considered to be *a visitor from abroad* who needed a visa to enter.

Refused entry to what I considered to be my homeland, I had to board the next plane back to Japan, heartbroken. After landing alone at Haneda Airport, all I could think of was getting home as soon as possible. Our parents had called ahead to my elder sister, telling her: "Tien-shi will be going back to Japan by herself." She was waiting for me at the arrivals gate. Anxious to see her, I hurried towards customs.

A stateless, permanent resident of Japan must present a re-entry permit and alien registration card every time they enter Japan. The immigration officer looked puzzled when examining mine. Told to wait at a bench in the back, I had a sinking feeling that I would be refused entry.

A few foreigners sat nervously on the bench with me. The long customs queue dwindled over the next hour. Then, one at a time, we were called over to an office. I entered. The agent got straight to the point and told me to *go back to Taiwan immediately*. I could not enter Japan because my re-entry permit had expired.

"I am a permanent resident and live in Yokohama. I just came back to Japan because I could not enter Taiwan."

The immigration officer expressed indifference; it was not his concern.

"Even a permanent resident cannot enter Japan with an expired re-entry permit. If you leave the country without renewing your re-entry permit, it means you have no intention of returning to Japan."

Were the ties that bound me to Japan so frail and transitory? It was as if I were a mere particle of dust swept away by a broom. Not only did nobody care if I existed; they preferred my *not* being around as the tidier option. Frustration and anger swelled in me, making it tough to remain calm.

"Where am I supposed to go?"

"I don't know. But you cannot enter Japan with these documents."

I was on the verge of bursting into tears when other agents just finishing their shifts entered. One of them turned to me:

"Hey, aren't you the kid who left a few days ago with your parents? Is that your sister outside?"

Waiting outside the gate, my sister had noticed something wrong. She had apparently spoken to the agents, asking them to let me through, saying she could vouch for me.

"Did you come back all alone?"

It was the same friendly inspector who had handled our family's exit customs when we left for the Philippines several days earlier. I kept quiet, not knowing where to begin.

"I'm sending her back right now," the stricter official said.

"Why? What happened?" The friendly inspector looked surprised.

"Her re-entry permit is expired."

"What? No way!"

The friendly inspector stared at my brown re-entry book, wide-eyed. My re-entry permit had already expired by the day of our departure, the day that agent had facilitated our exit from Japan without noticing my permit's expiry date. My interrogator pressed the inspector.

"Wait a minute. Weren't you the one who didn't check the expiration date and let her leave with an expired permit?"

The agents left the room, then returned with a heavy file. They rifled through the documents.

"Oh, good, good!" the friendly inspector said. He pulled out my exit document from the week before, took out a stamp, recalibrated the date, then used it to retrospectively stamp the file and my re-entry permit, *thwomp, thwomp.*

"Luckily, no one has applied at this office for re-entry permission since you left that day." I had no idea what was happening. "I'm issuing you a one-time re-entry permission backdated to the day you left the country. You can enter Japan now. That'll be 3,000 yen."

I paid the fee and went through the gate. My sister, who had been waiting in the arrival lobby, ran up and hugged me.

"What happened? I was so worried!"

On our way home, I explained to her what had happened, although I was still confused. I was also exhausted from frustration at the pointlessness of the ordeal. Even to this day, I feel uncomfortable when I hear someone say they will return to Taiwan or return to Japan.

Where do I belong? What is my nationality? With that traumatic travel experience, I felt my identity begin to crumble, as if I had been transformed into a speck of dust, easily swept away, needed by no one. In one day, I learned firsthand how nation, nationality, and national borders can exclude people.

I had a painful lesson about what it means to be stateless that day. Afterwards, I shut my shock away deep into the recesses of my heart. I told no one. I figured that few people would understand, and to be honest, it made me feel somehow inferior. In conversation, I tried to avoid the topic. Many days, though, I could not avoid coming face to face with my statelessness. When asked to show my ID to rent an apartment, open a bank account, or the like, I would reluctantly pull my ID card out of my wallet. The face of the person asking me invariably turned gloomy upon seeing the word *mukokuseki* on my Japanese ID card. They would furrow their brows, screw up their face as if they were having trouble hearing me, and ask, "what does it mean that you are stateless?" They would then usually ask me for supplementary documentation in order to demonstrate that I was a trustworthy person—such as proof of a bank balance or proof of my school attendance.

I was studying international relations, and decided to take a hiring test at the United Nations, which was the very international body that was supposed to support and protect stateless people. Surely, the UN would be a good place for me to work. My heart leaped when I was notified that I had passed the documentary stage of the vetting process. But when I went to New York for an interview, I discovered that I had been naïve. At my interview, I was told that they could not consider hiring a stateless person; I could reapply to the UN after getting Japanese citizenship.

This was yet another example of the social reality that emerged because of the creation of nation states. Being stateless brought with it extra trouble and required endless patience. The frustration that I felt then later drove me to research stateless people and ultimately become active in supporting them.

Ten Million Worldwide?

In my research on and by speaking with stateless persons, I found that the reasons that people became stateless and the situations they found themselves in varied quite a bit. Stateless people have no legal connection to any nation state and no citizenship. They are not considered full members of any country, nor do they have the corresponding rights and obligations of citizens. There are even people who are effectively stateless, who despite holding identification that indicates citizenship are still denied the rights of citizens. Whereas stateless people can obtain residence rights in Japan, in other countries they may not have access to registration or residence rights. Those without residence rights are often an invisible underclass whose very existence is officially denied.

The reason for a person's stateless designation can depend on a number of factors, including their birth nation's circumstances, international relations, and that person's particular narrative. As with the former Soviet Union or former Yugoslavia, the collapse of the nation state and changes to territorial rights might cause statelessness, or statelessness can be caused by diplomatic agreements or changes, in cases such as my own.

Some children fall through the cracks of different nations' nationality laws, as a result of international marriages or migration. This is true for the many Amerasians in Okinawa as well as for out-of-wedlock children who have been born to a Japanese man and to one of the growing numbers of Filipina women. Since the 1990s, these women have come to Japan as Overseas Filipino Workers (OFW), many of them are dancers. Adding to these, there are many Rohingya persons who become stateless due to ethnic discrimination and a large category of people who fall stateless due to administrative errors.

The United Nations High Commissioner for Refugees (UNHCR) is known mainly for aiding refugees, but they also have expanded their work to provide aid to stateless persons. The number of stateless persons around the world was estimated at 10 million in 2016, 3.9 million in 2018, and 4.2 million in 2020, according to a UNHCR poll. These wildly fluctuating numbers raise serious questions about the validity of such data collection. Researching and proving a negative (a lack of citizenship) is quite a formidable task, so it's no surprise that figures are not reliable.

The UNHCR has led a campaign to reduce to zero the number of stateless persons in the world by 2024. To that end, the UNHCR has called on countries to sign both the Convention Relating to the Status of Stateless Persons (1954) and the Convention on the Reduction of Statelessness (1961). Japan has ratified neither of these treaties, although some of its residents are stateless.

I was stateless for more than three decades, and my experience led me to research stateless persons for two more decades. Modern society seems to accept the concept of nationality with neither qualms nor questions about the defects and discriminatory practices inherent in the system itself. However, outmoded ideas of nationality can no longer accommodate the changing conditions of modern lives. In this era of globalization, we must now more than ever deepen our understanding of the meaning of citizenship and take ownership of the problems engendered by such constructs.

Nationality tends to get discussed from a legal perspective, leading many to conclude that it's a thorny issue. There's even a push to eliminate statelessness based on the idea that human rights are better protected because nationality and citizenship exist. This book will look at nationality from an anthropological perspective. I would like to consider and gain an understanding of nationality—which is deeply tied to our identities and daily lives—from a perspective of personal accountability. This book will focus on stateless persons themselves, recording through interviews show how they came to be stateless, what each of these individuals has experienced and thinks about those experiences, and how they identify themselves. I will explore the nature of statelessness through these personalized, individualized perspectives. It's difficult to change the core aspect of the issues, such as the relevant laws. But by deepening our understanding of nationality from the softer aspect that is the experience of fellow human beings, I aim with this book to speculate on the nature of humans, society and new global bonds.

1 Lara of Chinatown

Born in Chinatown, Yokohama

The midday sun blazed high above Chinatown on that day in August 1971, when in a Yokohama hospital, I was born, the sixth child of Chen Fu Poo and Chen Chang Pa Chun.

Baba operated a café and a confectionery in Chinatown. He simultaneously served as secretary-general of the Yokohama Overseas Chinese Association, a sort of neighborhood community association and non-governmental diplomatic agency for Chinese living in Yokohama's Chinatown. He was tall at 183 cm (6 feet), with straight posture. He wore suits and drew people's attention just walking down the street. A gentleman to all, he smiled often and spoke unhurriedly. Although Baba managed the shops, Mama ran them. A career woman who had worked at the Bank of Taiwan until moving to Japan in 1963, my mother had a better head for business than my father, who was more the academic type.

Saddled with five kids and speaking broken Japanese in the unfamiliar new world that was Yokohama, my parents struggled to run their business. It sometimes felt as though they were running in a three-legged race with no idea where the finish line was. They often said that their children's smiling faces kept them going.

When Mama brought my sisters and brothers to join Baba in Yokohama, he had already been living there alone for a time as an international student. While he was away, Mama had raised the kids in Taiwan with my paternal grandfather.

Baba hailed from Heilongjiang Province, Mama from Hunan Province. In the vast expanse of China, it is hard to imagine how one person from the northernmost province and another from the southern end of the country found each other. Their generation lived through the war: Baba was born in 1922, and Mama ten years later. My maternal grandfather served as a general in the Kuomintang (Nationalist Party of China). War was personal for my mother. Each time she sent her father off to war, there was nothing to do but wait, wondering when he would return.

No sooner had China celebrated their victory after World War II, then the country—having learned nothing from war with external powers—lurched right back into it, this time into a civil war that pitted the Kuomintang against the Chinese Communist Party (CCP) in a bid for political supremacy. The CCP quickly gained power, leading to the birth in 1949 of a new China, the People's Republic of China.

The Kuomintang regime retreated to Taiwan, where they set up the provisional government of the Republic of China. They set forth goals: Prepare during year one; fight back during year two; mop up during year three; and succeed in year five.

Many Kuomintang supporters and those who feared Communist Party rule left their hometowns for the new island sanctuary. These migrants were not native to the Taiwan province, but rather provincial outsiders (*waishengren*) born on the mainland.

My parents too left their homes for Taiwan.

My then 17-year-old mother left her village determined to meet up with her parents, who had departed earlier. She traveled alone via Hong Kong, staying there with her aunt, before reaching Taiwan. Her parents had settled into their new lives at Beitou, a mountaintop district known for its stunning scenic beauty.

Baba left his hometown Mudanjiang and headed south, passing through Shenyang, Jinzhou, Beijing, Shaoxing, Ningbo, Xiamen (Amoy), and Zhangzhou. After nearly three years, he boarded a ship at Xiamen and sailed to Taiwan. He lodged at Beitou, where Mama lived with her parents. The mountains of Beitou boasted hot springs and drew urban dwellers who wanted to leave the city for vacation. This allowed mainlanders to rent the many homes that became available during the off-season.

My parents were "neighbors" in the sense that they lived in the same village. Baba's and Mama's families, as well as many mainlanders, longed to return to their hometowns. They missed their families, the homes and possessions left behind. Unaccustomed to Taiwan's climate and food, these *waishengren* dreamed of the day they could return to their homes. That day never came. Instead, day by day they adapted to new lives in a new land. Facing this new reality, more mainlanders started up new families in Taiwan.

"I Know a Really Nice Young Man for You"

Mama's uncle introduced my father to her. They started dating soon after. They shared their life stories, fell in love, and married in 1953. Baba worked for the Ministry of the Interior; Mama worked at a bank. They lived happily enough with their children, but they got to think about their outsider status (*waishengren*) and about their future.

My ambitious father wanted to study abroad. At that time in Taiwan, the affluent tended to head to Europe or the US to study or live. It was the *de rigueur* career path for elites. My father couldn't afford to migrate to either of those continents. He had too little money to study abroad, but he managed to find a way. He took an exam to win a government-funded study-abroad scholarship granted to civil servants. He chose Japan since he could speak Japanese from his time living in Manchukuo (State of Manchuria), then under Japanese rule. My father's efforts paid off, and he won the scholarship; so, at age 34, he began his studies in Japan. Mama had no interest in living in Japan, and so she stayed behind with the kids.

Year after year, Baba continued his studies alone in Japan. After Baba moved to an area that housed Japan's ethnic Chinese community, he decided to bring the family over. Mama decided that although she hated the idea of living in Japan, she would do it, if only to be reunited with my father. Her parents, unsurprisingly, were vehemently opposed to my mother's moving to Japan, and when she refused to change her mind, my grandfather struck her.

This Kuomintang general wasn't about to let his daughter migrate to a former enemy country. As a father, he must have felt anxiety over the trouble he anticipated my Mama's family would experience in a foreign land, and anger at her leaving behind a stable job and life in Taiwan for a bumpy road abroad. My mother's decision to move, overriding their concerns and objections, must have tormented my grandparents.

Mama brought five children to Japan, and the family of seven lived in an apartment of about 12 square meters. The kids at first felt frustration at living in a tiny Japanese home, but they cherished the happiness they felt being reunited with their father.

At first, people taunted my mother, sisters, and brothers who could not speak the language. A maid working in a nearby Chinese home called my sisters and brothers *kojiki*, or beggars. Not understanding, Mama smiled and uttered the only Japanese word she had learned from Baba: "*arigato, arigato*" (thank you, thank you). How mortified she must have felt later when she understood what the maid had been saying. Perhaps this and other encounters caused her to regret immigrating, abandoning her career, and starting over in a foreign land.

My parents married in Taiwan in 1953

But there was no turning back. She had already made her way to Japan in open defiance of her father's heated opposition. She resolved, come what may, to show him that she had made the right decision.

With help from Chinese friends and her saved earnings, my father and mother opened a Chinese confectionery, and worked there morning till night. The children grew up watching their parents work hard.

Eight years after my mother and siblings arrived in Japan, the family had overcome their initial poverty, and they began to have a bit of money to spare. Then, good news—Mama was pregnant. This would be their first child born in their new country. The sixth Chen child, I was born when Baba was 50, and Mama 40.

I arrived 17 years after my eldest sister and eight years after my youngest brother. My mother suffered three days of painful contractions before a difficult childbirth. Her physician had warned her from the start that childbirth would be dangerous, and she had contemplated ending the pregnancy. But her close friend, who was not blessed with children, encouraged her: "Everyone loves your wonderful children. Don't give up on your baby. Go for it." Mama braced herself for an agonizing birth and had me that August.

Baba witnessed my birth. My grandfather in Taiwan had hoped for a boy, but my sisters and brothers were delighted to get a new baby sister. With my arrival, the Chen household filled with excitement and energy. Baba came to the hospital every chance he could get to attend to Mama. The damage to my mother's body was more severe than anticipated. Her post-partum recovery didn't go well, and she had to stay in the hospital for a month. Afterwards, she suffered a variety of adult-onset conditions.

My elder siblings banded together to help Mama. After school, my two big sisters took care of the café our parents ran at the time, and my three big brothers divided household chores. They took turns visiting the hospital. When their new baby sister was brought out for viewing, my siblings pressed their foreheads to the glass to see this addition to their family. They were delighted to see the expressive face of their little sister crying and laughing. The five of them pooled their savings to buy me a rubber doll set. Each of the four dolls represented a different emotion: joy, ire, misery, and mirth. They apparently bought them because the dolls' round eyes and wheat-colored skin reminded them of me. That was the first present I received in my life.

I was named Tienshi (天璽), which means "treasure sent from heaven." The day I left the hospital, I was taken straightaway to our Catholic church. The priest baptized me *Clara* after Saint Clare of Assisi, whose feast day is in August. My Christian name *Clara* was immediately shortened to *Lara*.

A 1960s family photo with my grandparents who were visiting Japan

Back home, I was the topic of Chinatown, including among our Japanese customers.

"I went to see sister Chen's baby today! Can't say this too loudly, but unlike her older siblings, she's kind of ugly."

"Hey, at least she was born healthy."

I was an affable, affectionate child, and grew up being cuddled and coddled by countless customers at our café. They called me *Lara-chan* (Little Lara).

At the time, Yokohama's Chinatown was less touristy than today. In addition to the many Chinese restaurants run by Chinese, Japanese grocers, fish stalls, and candy counters lined the streets. Multiple cultures coexisted in the same neighborhood. Everybody knew everybody— white-uniformed chefs buying vegetables and fishes; kids out of school and running around; people moving to and fro. People communicated well with each other in broken Japanese or Chinese, and sometimes we'd hear someone burst out laughing. The neighborhood was a tight-knit community, full of familiarity and boisterous energy. One of my favorite places was the Ichibadori market street, in a side alley just off the main thoroughfare. I would trail close behind my mother as she bought a great deal of groceries to feed her family. Mama would always smile as she listened to my selfish demands:

"I want oxtail soup. I love your boiled chicken feet too!"

The butcher would call out to my mother: "How can I help you today, Mamasan?" Then add, "Ooh, Lara-chan's with you today!"

These memories make me smile even today. The town's mélange of nationalities and cultures felt natural and comfortable to someone like me, born and raised in Chinatown. If someone asked me where my hometown is, I'd say Yokohama's Chinatown without hesitation. It was neither China nor Japan, but rather a town that mixed both cultures and peoples.

Normalization of Sino-Japanese Relations

I was a year old when it happened—an event that would profoundly affect the lives of Chinatown's residents. On September 29, 1972, Japan and the People's Republic of China (PRC) normalized diplomatic relations.

Prime Minister Kakuei Tanaka visited Beijing, and his hardy handshake with Premier Zhou Enlai changed the course of history. China gifted Japan with giant pandas—Lanlan and Huanhuan (Jp: Ranran and Kankan), attracting long snaking lines of parents with their children waiting to see them at Ueno Zoo. This "panda diplomacy" made Japan feel close to China for the first time since World War II.

This new relationship led Japan to make another dramatic decision—to sever their longstanding diplomatic ties with the Republic of China (Taiwan). Foreign Minister Masayoshi Ōhira abrogated the Sino-Japanese Peace Treaty.

Shock waves coursed through the overseas Chinese community in Japan, but reactions were mixed, depending on each person's political stance. Japan shuttered the embassy of the Republic of China in Azabu, Minato Ward, Tokyo, later reopening it as the embassy of the People's Republic of China. ROC consulates around the county were also closed. The Chinese community in Japan underwent great turmoil over land and assets belonging to the government of China. Those who sympathized with the PRC led by the Chinese Communist Party (CCP) unfurled the emblematic five-star red flag and celebrated their ideological victory. Those who supported the ROC/Taiwan led by the Kuomintang felt up against a wall.

Many political and economic changes had taken place in China and Taiwan, including the civil war; the PRC's founding; the Great Leap Forward, which led to mass starvation; the Cultural Revolution; and Taiwan's economic development. With loyalties split between the PRC and the ROC in our overseas Chinese community, each change contributed to the rise of differing forms of Chinese nationalism and shook the foundations of our national identity.

This time, however, the Japanese government forced the Chinese community in Japan to make a consequential decision—choosing citizenship—with little time to even gather our thoughts. We were all Chinese, but with no way to know even what the word *Chinese* meant, since the Japanese government had now changed the definition.

We could now put PRC or ROC citizenship under the column for China on our alien registrations. Unlike the Chinese who came to Japan after World War II with ROC passports, few who had arrived in the late nineteenth and early twentieth centuries had carried government-issued passports that documented their citizenship as that was an era of lax passport control and vague notions of citizenship. They and their descendants felt little need to choose citizenship despite Japan's policy decision over which China would be recognized as a nation state.

Those who came to Japan after World War II with ROC passports anguished over the question of citizenship. They were forced to choose from among three options: (1) Keep their ROC passports and live in Japan as citizens of a country with which Japan had no diplomatic relations; (2) switch to a PRC passport and live as a citizen of a recognized state; or (3) naturalize and live as a citizen of Japan.

The Japanese government fast-tracked citizenship applications. Many people ended up choosing to naturalize, change their names to Japanese-sounding ones, and for all intents and purposes become Japanese. Some switched to PRC citizenship. Some abandoned their lives in Japan and immigrated to other countries like the US.

Fear spread among the Chinese community regarding how the Japanese government would treat those with ROC citizenship who remained "Chinese" on their alien registration papers without switching citizenship to the only China recognized by the Japanese government. Anxiety spread as no one knew what to expect.

Choosing Statelessness

The shockwaves reached our family too. Baba was forced to make what, given his background, was an impossible choice.

He was born in Manchuria. As a boy, he got caught up in the Mukden incident, perpetrated by the Japanese military in order to bring about the establishment of Japan's Manchukuo puppet state. He still remembers the Japanese military shutting down his school. He also remembers walking down ruined streets in abject fear.

My father's family owned a lot of land that they rented out. With the CCP gaining strength in the civil war just after World War II, the tide turned against landowners and capitalists. With no time even to change their clothes, my father, grandfather and uncle found themselves fleeing their hometown and heading to Taiwan.

Considering my father's memories of the war against Japan and his ideological differences with the CCP, taking on either Japanese or PRC citizenship would mean humiliation.

My parents discussed the dilemma until late every night. My eldest sister suggested acquiring Japanese citizenship since they planned to continue to live in Japan. Baba struggled, concerned over how that might impact his children's futures. Mama was adamantly opposed to taking on Japanese citizenship. Baba anguished over the decision for several days before arriving at the final decision that we would choose neither Chinese nor Japanese citizenship. Instead, we chose to become stateless.

The Kojien dictionary says that the Japanese word *kokuseki* indicates "qualification to belong to a particular country." Citizenship is thus a legal relationship that designates a person as a member of a country. A state creates a system of citizenship to regulate its citizens and define their rights and obligations.

Throughout and after the war, my father and his family were tossed about by the notional vicissitudes of the word *nation*. He thus chose *no* citizenship, refusing to confine his identity within a national framework and, thus, voluntarily entered a state of statelessness. Nobody could know then what consequences this decision portended. Baba mumbled to himself that no citizenship (*mukokuseki*) is itself a type of citizenship (*kokuseki*).

While deciding what to do about citizenship, including querying friends and looking up the law, Baba discovered that stateless persons are in fact protected by international law.

In 1954, the United Nations enacted the Convention relating to the Status of Stateless Persons. It includes the preambulatory clause: "Considering that it is desirable to regulate and improve the status of stateless persons by an international agreement…."

The Universal Declaration of Human Rights stipulates that "everyone has the right to a nationality" and "no one shall be arbitrarily deprived of his nationality nor denied the right to change his nationality."

In 1961, the UN enacted the Convention on the Reduction of Statelessness.

Perhaps these treaties led my father to believe that his and his family's fundamental rights would be guaranteed even if Japan's national government offered no protection.

The United Nations High Commissioner for Refugees (UNHCR) has called on all nations to ratify these treaties, but as of February 1, 2023, only 96 countries had acceded to the 1954 convention, and only 78 to the 1961 convention.

With the announcement of the normalization of relations with the PRC, the date for the closing of the ROC embassy fast approached. Ethnic Chinese waited in long lines at the soon-to-close embassy in Azabu, Tokyo, as well as the consulates in Yokohama and elsewhere to renounce their citizenship and obtain a Certificate of Loss of Nationality (CLN). States do not usually let their nationals give up citizenship, once conferred, without a very good reason. But even taking the action of switching from ROC to PRC or Japanese citizenship would first require renouncing ROC citizenship and thereby becoming temporarily stateless. Chinese residents wanted the CLN as a bulwark against every eventuality.

A citizenship official in the Ministry of the Interior noted that "more than 20,000 ethnic Chinese residents lost their ROC citizenship after the termination of diplomatic relations." Some of these people later obtained Japanese citizenship, and others changed to PRC citizenship.

Precise figures are impossible to get, but Japan's Ministry of Justice Civil Affairs Bureau estimates that more than 930 residents were stateless in 1971, a figure that jumped to more than 9,200 in 1974 before dropping back down to around 2,900 by 1977. We can probably attribute these dramatic shifts to Japan's overseas Chinese residents.

Baba was in one of those long lines.

In September 1972, all eight members of my family became stateless, holding citizenship in no country. In the black-and-white baby photo affixed to my CLN, I am wrapped in a cotton blanket, sleeping soundly. I had just turned one.

2 Living in the Crevice between Two Countries

Haiya!

I was Bruce Lee. A regular kung fu master, I wore jeans and a denim jacket with an eagle embroidered on the back. I thumbed the side of my nose, in classic Bruce Lee style. I walked atop Chinatown's guardrails, balancing myself as if on a tightrope. I brandished plastic *nunchaku*. Passersby complimented my mother for her "spritely young boy." Nobody thought I was a girl.

I wanted to be a boy. When people teasingly asked if I was a boy or girl, I would open my eyes wide, lower my voice, and growl, "I'm a boy." I used the little boy's room.

My parents converted their café into a Chinese restaurant. A decade or so had passed since immigrating from Taiwan, and they had grown accustomed to doing business in Japan. But transforming a modest café into a full-fledged restaurant required a bit of determination. We had to secure ingredients, hire chefs, and design seasonal menus. Where to start?

For my Chinese parents, opening a Chinese restaurant in Chinatown was not mission impossible. But juggling business and family can be a challenge when you have many children running about. A Chinese restaurant enabled my parents to run a business and cook for us kids. They apparently went with the restaurant business so we would never go hungry.

Two years had passed since our entire family became stateless. Our lives didn't change abruptly just because we became stateless. All that really changed was that on our alien registration cards, re-entry permits, and other government-issued documents, the word *Chinese* that had once been written under nationality was gone, and the documents now read *Stateless*.

Chinatown's Bruce Lee (age 4)

My two sisters—who were a year apart—had already graduated from Japanese high school and entered university in Taiwan as *qiaosheng*, Chinese students returning from abroad. The Japanese equivalent designation would be *kikokusei*. My eldest sister went to National Chengchi University; my other sister studied at National Taiwan University. While my sisters were away studying in Taiwan, I was surrounded by three brothers back in Yokohama. This environment intensified my tomboyishness.

My international kindergarten sat atop a hill. I spoke to teachers and friends almost exclusively in English. When I spoke English at home, my parents scolded me: "You are Chinese; don't lose your ability to speak Chinese." I think my Chinese identity began to form at this stage, and I began to notice the distinguishing traits of my American, Korean, and Chinese schoolmates.

My kindergarten had always held a stage performance at the yearly graduation ceremony. Each child donned his or her country's traditional clothing to sing and dance. My mother embroidered the blue sky, white sun flag of Taiwan on the chest of my black kung fu uniform, and I channeled the ghost of Bruce Lee.

Honorable Entrance Exam

In my childish innocence, I wouldn't have understood that my parents thought carefully about what kind of education I should get. Mama wanted to send me to an international elementary school, likely hoping to raise a daughter capable of living abroad, free from the stifling limitations experienced by Chinese residents of Japan. Even if they had grown up in Japan and spoke fluent Japanese, Chinese faced discrimination in the job market.

Many Chinese residents in Japan grew tired of the discrimination and migrated to Europe or the United States. Gaining Japanese citizenship was trickier back then, which didn't encourage Chinese residents to see Japan as a permanent home or as their own country.

A friend of my mother suggested sending me to a certain well-known Japanese private girls' school. That would ensure I got a good education and secured a stable future. Mama was open to that as an option. Baba wanted to educate me as a Chinese person but yielded to Mama's judgment.

But I couldn't just want myself into the school. The entrance exam was highly competitive and given in Japanese. Since I went to an international school, I required a tutor to help me prepare. My tutor instructed me in an empty banquet room in our restaurant, using a dining table as a study desk.

I learned the hiragana syllabary in a fun way, as if we were playing cards. I enjoyed learning reading and writing. In no time at all, my Japanese exceeded my parents' level. Arithmetic was my favorite subject. Every night, I tackled Mama's arithmetic puzzles while soaking in the tub. When the family went shopping or to a café, I would calculate and pay the bill, enabling me to bask in an aura of quasi-adulthood.

I preferred learning through experience rather than just sitting at a desk. I appreciate my parents for creating such an environment for me. If they had made me sit alone at a desk with my nose in a book, a mischievous kid like me would surely have dozed off with my head plopped down on the pages of my textbook.

Things got weird on the day of my entrance exam. Looking back, I realize that this was the first day I had ever strayed from my beloved Chinatown to venture into Japanese society, at least in microcosm.

The integrated elementary-through-high school was for well-off girls. Parents led their well-behaved, well-bred daughters by the hand to the testing site. Most of these princesses had long hair, tied with a ribbon. I too wore a navy one-piece and white knee-length socks that my mother and sisters had prepared for me. I had no choice but to slip them on in the morning. Wearing ladylike clothes marked a dramatic break from my previous tomboy image. I loathed them. The garb made me so self-conscious walking down the street that I could look nowhere but downwards.

After everyone had entered the classroom, the exam began. I breezed through the Japanese language section, which was the top concern of those around me. The hardest thing was writing my own name. Despite multiple attempts, I couldn't fit in the allotted space the 19 strokes of the Chinese character 璽 (*shi*), from my given name *Tienshi*. I had to erase my scrawl over and over before managing to squeeze it in.

I made quick work of test questions in my favorite subject, too. *How many apples are there? Add up all the flowers.* Finishing early, a bit of time remained, so I looked around at other students and the proctors overseeing our exam. All the other students sat up straight, diligently applying themselves to the test. Somehow, they all looked the same to me, as if I was the only child out of place. I looked around restlessly, and the proctor quietly approached me. Thinking I might be scolded, I sat up straight and faced forward. The teacher peeked at my answer sheet, grinned, then continued.

After the written portion came the in-person interview, with my parents expected to attend. Many Japanese families waited in the classroom until told to move to the hallway for the final stretch. Something about the other parents seemed different. Mothers in their twenties and thirties carried a handbag in one hand and a handkerchief in the other. They clutched the handkerchiefs in front of their mouths when they spoke, the picture of refined elegance. My mother wasn't like that. When my parents spoke in Chinese, the assembled parents glared at us. We were out of our element.

Our turn came to wait in the corridor. A student led her parents in every five or ten minutes. Our turn to go in finally came, and I entered the classroom with my parents. We were received by the principal and a crew of sober-looking interviewers. I sat between my parents. After confirming our names, a teacher who seemed passionate about education asked me, "Do you like studying?"

"Yes, I love studying."

"What subject are you best at?"

"Arithmetic," I answered with confidence. The questions were extremely simple and ended far too soon. My parents' turn came. Baba answered the questions in Japanese with a Chinese accent. Questions to my parents dragged on interminably.

Why do you want to send your daughter to our school?

Won't there be any language issues?

What is your thinking regarding how different she will be from the other students?

After some time, an interviewer turned to me and said:

"Tenji-chan [Japanese read my name as *Tenji*], you can leave now. Wait out in the corridor."

The chilly corridor made me feel forlorn, as I waited 45 minutes for my parents to emerge, while observing the waiting teachers and families.

Later, I learned that the interview with my parents revolved around debate and questioning on the issue of our citizenship.

Why is she stateless?

What do you plan to do about her citizenship in the future?

Aren't you concerned your daughter might be bullied because she is a foreigner?

The school representatives decided that my admission carried a great number of risks. At the end of the interview, the principal said,

"We have never admitted a stateless student. We cannot start now."

Chinese School

I ended up going to Yokohama Overseas Chinese School, a minute's walk from my home. Baba's determination to get me a Chinese education only intensified after the unsuccessful interview at the private primary school.

"A Chinese person should know how to speak proper Chinese. We should send you to a Chinese school."

Baba had always wanted me to go to Chinese school, so he was ultimately rather relieved that I had failed to make it into the Japanese elementary school.

He had first come to Japan in 1956 as a graduate student at Meiji University. After finishing his master's degree, he began graduate work at the University of Tokyo. The Yokohama Overseas Chinese Association offered him the position of secretary-general, so he left school and became active in the growing Chinese community.

Yokohama's Chinatown was designated as a foreign settlement after Japan opened its ports in the closing days of the Edo period (1603–1868; aka the Tokugawa period). Chinese compradors and servants migrated to Japan and came to be called by the Japanese pronunciation of the Mandarin word *huaqiao* (華僑), which is *kakyo*. Those from the same province came together to provide day-to-day mutual aid. In the prewar chaos, few received a high school education.

After the war, Chinese residents planted deeper roots in Japan and began to deal more directly with Japanese people. They increasingly wrote materials in Japanese, including business contracts and documents submitted to the government.

The Chinese community needed someone who understood the position of Chinese residents and was able to speak and write documents in Japanese. Baba stood out as the obvious choice since he had studied in Japan, worked as a civil servant, and was skilled in document preparation and dealing with government bureaucrats. As he volunteered for the community, he gradually came to believe that Chinese residents needed to insist upon a certain level of dignity, if Sino-Japanese relations were ever to deepen. Such dignity required Chinese language skills. He believed parents had a duty to ensure that their children learned the language of their mother country.

Baba was ecstatic that I would get a proper Chinese education. At that time, Japan had five Chinese schools: two in Yokohama, and one each in Tokyo, Osaka, and Kobe. Overseas Chinese placed great emphasis on educating children in their mother tongue and raised funds through donations to build their own schools. One such school had been in place for more than a century. To a greater or lesser degree, Chinese schools could not avoid being influenced by the politics of China. Undeniably, some schools had certain political biases.

Yokohama-Yamate Chinese School leaned toward the PRC and so taught simplified Chinese characters. But the pro-ROC Yokohama

Overseas Chinese School taught traditional Chinese characters. Different flags flew at the two schools. The popularity of China early in the twenty-first century inspired many Japanese parents to send their kids to Chinese schools to learn Chinese.

I attended Yokohama Overseas Chinese School, in a cozy little schoolhouse located right there in Chinatown. Its few students thought of each other as siblings, with the school itself like one big family. The integrated K–12 school also had a nursery school. During my time there, most grades had only one section of at most ten students, but we were the first year of the boomer generation, so I had a whopping 13 classmates.

Classes were taught in Chinese; we even had to learn science and math formulas in the mother tongue. We used history and geology textbooks published in Taiwan. We learned three languages in total—including Japanese, beginning second grade, and English conversation taught by a native speaker, beginning third grade. The school drew Chinese kids from the suburbs of Yokohama and Tokyo in addition to us Chinatown children. Extracurricular activities included learning the traditional lion, dragon and other folk dances. We gradually cultivated a Chinese identity.

Caught Between Two Histories

One incident in first grade at Chinese school will always stay with me. I was still more or less a boy. When the recess bell rang, I would storm out of the classroom faster than anyone. I had to be the best at everything, whether it was kicking the can, dodgeball, or kickball. I didn't mind being covered in cuts and bruises all the time.

One sunny day during lunch break, I bucked my usual practice of running around outside and instead headed to the library where Chinese-language books lined the shelves. As a first grader, I was so short I had to stand on a chair to retrieve books off the top shelf. But the thick book that caught my eye was on the bottom shelf on a rack in the corner. It was a struggle to pull the book out, heave it over to the desk, and plop it down. The book smelled of dust, as if no one had read it in ages.

I flipped open the blue cloth cover. It was full of records documenting the history of the Sino-Japanese War. Graphic and lurid photos showed the bodies of dead Chinese as well as uniformed Japanese soldiers standing next to a Chinese man who had his hair in a queue and was being buried alive. I could not read the descriptions, which were written in Chinese characters that I had yet to learn. But even my juvenile mind comprehended the savagery of this Sino-Japanese event.

Distraught, I bolted out of the library and scampered home. In my mad dash home, I plowed into someone on the street but couldn't bring myself to push out the words *excuse me*. All I wanted was my Baba and Mama.

Reaching home, my inconsolable sobbing prevented me from explaining myself to my parents. All I could tell them was that I had seen scary pictures. Over and over, I screamed at them in anger, demanding to know:

"Why are we in Japan?"

Why had my Chinese parents come to Japan, a former enemy country? Why had I been born in this country? Why did we live here? Yet my parents insisted I get educated and raised Chinese. I could not understand. I pressed my parents, releasing a child's raw, unadorned emotion.

Baba took me into his arms as I choked on tears. In his large embrace, my tears began to subside. He propped me up, gazed into my eyes, and in a low voice said,

"Lara, we live in this country to conquer that history."

Not grasping his meaning, I just sniffled.

"Going through the war, I came to understand that person-to-person relationships reach deeper than bilateral relations between nations. Mutual understanding prevents conflict. That's why we raise you as Chinese residents in Japan. I want you to grow up to transcend national identity."

It was tough for a little kid to grasp. All I knew was that Baba had somehow assigned me a sort of mission. My identity juxtaposed a deeply ingrained sense of being Chinese and belonging to China against my day-to-day intimacy with Japan, the country of my birth and upbringing. The fact that these two countries shared such a wretched history of mutual loathing made me despondent. I did not want to believe that the war had happened. How could I ever get over my newfound knowledge of it?

Usually, I waited for the restaurant to close at nine in the evening, returned home with my family, and sat up gabbing about events of the day, with the TV playing in the background. When they came home that evening, however, I was already tucked in and sound asleep, probably exhausted from sobbing. I wonder what my parents thought watching me sleep like that. Looking back, I regret saying such harsh things to them that day.

I thought of a nation as a cohesive union. The world map I had studied at school assigned a different color and name to each country, and the televised Olympic Games divided athletes up into individual nations they represented. Thus, my grade school kid perspective on the notion of nation had its limits.

Yokohama Overseas Chinese School taught me that I was Taiwanese and belonged to the Republic of China. Each morning, we sang the national anthem and saluted the national flag. We were taught to be proud of our people and culture. But that country existed far away somewhere. The country I knew and lived my life in was Japan.

My parents often took me to Taiwan to see my grandparents, who lived there, and my brothers, who studied there. I came to feel a closeness to Taiwan, in addition to Japan. During my third-grade spring break, my eldest sister, 17 years my senior, married a former college mate. We prepared to travel to Taiwan, where the wedding was scheduled.

Yokohama Immigration Bureau issued us a re-entry permit. For a foreign resident like me leaving Japan, a re-entry permit served as a visa enabling me to return. Even if you lived in Japan, you could not get back without it. The ROC government had special overseas agencies in lieu of its former embassies, and an agency that is now called the Taipei Economic and Cultural Representative Office issued us ROC "passports" and *hui tai jia qian* (回台加簽; signed returns to Taiwan), in effect visas for overseas Chinese, required to enter the ROC. I was just eight but still remember processing those documents with my parents.

The Immigration Bureau handed each of us a brown re-entry permit, a pamphlet that bore a passing resemblance to a passport. Inside, I saw my picture affixed, with my name, date of birth, citizenship, home address, and visa status—all handwritten. Under citizenship was written: stateless. As instructed, I wrote my name in Chinese characters and signed it in English, as the adults did, exhilarated to have joined the ranks of adults who sign government-issued certificates. I spared not a thought to the import of those three little characters 無国籍 (*mukokuseki*, stateless) under the heading of citizenship.

3 Assimilating into Japanese Society

The Nation State—New Walls to Scale

During my middle school years, I became aware of how odd it is to exist in a state of statelessness. I became engrossed in volleyball, but Yokohama Overseas Chinese School had no gymnasium. So, we used lime to draw lines for a volleyball court on the gravelly, pebbly playground, stringing our own net. Our team practiced hard. I was the outside hitter and a spiker from the left. During our 45-minute lunch break, we ran intense practice sessions under a hard-nosed coach. I had to find other times to eat lunch.

My school life came to center on training. This included partnered setup drills while lying prone on the ground and refining my barrel-roll digs in the mud. We were fired up about the sport. We practiced every day and at summer camp, developing a strong sense of team unity. Seeing our growth inspired the coach to redouble her coaching efforts, and she suggested we take on other teams. She made us uniforms and arranged matches with other schools.

But ethnic schools like Yokohama Overseas Chinese School were not permitted to participate in sports activities and tournaments organized by local municipalities. We could play matches with Japanese schools arranged by coaches through their personal connections, but at official games we were admitted only as observers. We could participate in tournaments and beat other teams, but we would win no prizes and our hands would never hold trophies.

Despite this constant frustration, we teenagers had little choice but to resign ourselves to outrageous discrimination and contradiction. The experience drove home to us the reality that we were different from Japanese children. Students attending Japanese schools and overseas Chinese schools often felt friction with each other out in the world. After practice, my teammates and I would go to fast-food joints in Motomachi or Isezakicho, munching and chatting.

One of us would make a comment in a mix of Chinese and Japanese.

"*Jintian bisai ni-no tosu saiko datta-yo* 今天比賽你のトス再高だったよ." [Your setup during today's match was outstanding.]

Another would respond:

"It worked! And *ni-no* [Sino-Japanese construction meaning *your*] spike was *hen li hai* [awesome] 你のスパイク很厲害."

We code-switched in what had come to be called *kakyo-go* 華僑語, overseas Chinese language. As girls approaching adolescence, our voices rose along with the excitement of our banter. We still wore our uniforms with *Yokohama Overseas Chinese School* emblazoned on the chests.

Japanese students sitting at another table quickly realized that we attended a school for ethnic Chinese. They would whisper and furrow their brows. Sometimes they would gossip about us, making us uncomfortable and leading to quarrels. Each time, it made me feel that Japanese society had no place for me.

Even though we were born and raised in Japan, people still refused to recognize us as belonging to the country. Every time I faced this fact, my heart filled with frustration, and I yearned to go somewhere that would accept me; I became determined to leave the country one day.

The whole team's hard work paid off, and our volleyball skills improved day by day. Our principal realized we would get little opportunity for a real match in Japan, so he arranged for us to play friendly matches with middle schools in Taiwan.

In the spring of my sophomore year of middle school the whole team left for Taiwan. In my bag were my ROC passport, issued by the Taipei Economic and Cultural Office in Japan, and my re-entry permit, issued by the Japanese government.

The flight from Narita Airport to Taipei took about three hours. I had visited Taiwan with my family many times, but this was my first time with my teammates, and it felt different. I had to fill in the entry card and other papers for immigration on my own.

I chatted with friends while waiting in line at the immigration gate. My turn came, and I submitted my ROC passport and the entry card to the inspector.

He looked at my documents then glared at me.

"What do you mean *stateless*?"

While asking this, he tapped his finger multiple times where I had written the word *mukokuseki* 無国籍 on the entry card. I couldn't understand his attitude. I showed him my re-entry permit, issued by the

A Japanese re-entry permit

Japanese government, and explained that I had written *mukokuseki* on the entry card because that is what was written on my re-entry permit.

He refused to listen to me. Instead, he grabbed a ballpoint pen and brusquely crossed out the word *mukokuseki* from my entry card and ordered me to "write *Republic of China* here."

During this interaction, my friends had already cleared the gate. Some of my closest friends worried upon seeing my anxiety. Unconvinced and with an ineffable sense of offense, I dutifully took the entry card and wrote *Republic of China* just above the now-effaced characters for *Stateless*. I passed through and beyond the entry gate. I had managed to enter the country, but with a bitter aftertaste in my mouth.

On the other side, my friends listened to me gripe about what had happened. All they could do was nod. To be honest, we didn't know what the hell was going on.

We took out and compared passports and certificates. Some of my friends had naturalized and carried Japanese passports; others held passports issued by the ROC government. I was the only one who had both an ROC passport and a Japan-issued re-entry permit. And the permit said I was stateless, making my situation unique among my friends. That is why, without thinking it through, I had written *stateless* on the

ROC entry document in line with what was written on my Japan re-entry permit. This is why I had been stopped at the gate in Taiwan.

I didn't get it. What was the problem? Why did he so aggressively order me to rewrite my entry card? Apparently, the document issued in Japan didn't pass muster in Taiwan. The reality that your identity and status can vary depending on the country you are in made me feel indignant.

Japanese High School Entrance Exam

In the spring of my third year in middle school, my close friends began attending *juku* cram schools to prepare for their high school entrance exams. They also talked about the uniforms of the schools they hoped to get into. They sat at the desks lined up against the classroom windows, showing each other school brochures.

"Yo, look at this high school uniform, with a checkered skirt. So adorable, right?"

"Yeah, but I prefer this one with the ribbon."

"Yeah, but that's an all-girls school, isn't it? I want coed."

I was all about volleyball, and I couldn't care less about other school uniforms or my next stage of education. I intended to advance to Yokohama Overseas Chinese School's high school. Among the dozen or so of my classmates, only two or three were preparing to test and switch over to a Japanese high school. But the classmates that were looking to switch over were my good friends, so I too began reflecting on my schooling options.

I considered three options for high school: (1) Continue on at Yokohama Overseas Chinese School; (2) return to the international school where I had attended kindergarten; or (3) transfer to a Japanese high school. After thorough reflection, I decided to sit for the exam to get into the international school. I loved English and wanted to improve my proficiency. My elder siblings and their friends were off studying in Taiwan and the US, with the occasional trip home to Yokohama. They seemed so cool to me, and I wanted to emulate them.

I came up with the idea of eventually going to an Australian university. I spent an hour on the train to get to the Australian embassy to research my options. At school, I blabbed so much about Australia that my friends started calling me *Koala* and joked that I bore a passing resemblance to the marsupial.

At the time, I didn't want to go to a Japanese university. In the mid-1980s, during the heady days of Japan's bubble economy, most people thought Japanese college students did little but mess around. Looking back, maybe I was already keenly aware that, even after growing up I might not be fully accepted into Japanese society and might therefore have to live overseas. As I didn't plan to go to a Japanese university, I didn't try to get into a Japanese high school.

My father, however, had different ideas: "Take the entrance exams for Japanese high schools too." He knew ethnic Chinese schools were not recognized as Article 1 schools under the School Education Act. My school was considered to be an "ethnic school," technically listed as an Article 34 miscellaneous school. Graduating from an ethnic Chinese high school alone was insufficient for eligibility to sit for a Japanese university entrance exam. For that, these graduates had to take a separate qualifying exam, called a *daiken*, which was akin to a high school equivalency test.

Baba was less than ecstatic about me harping on about college in Australia. He tried to persuade me to reconsider narrowing my options too early by shutting the door on Japanese college while still in middle school. I was in my rebellious phase and kept saying *iyada* (no way) to taking the Japanese high school path.

We hammered out a compromise. I agreed to take the entrance exam for Japanese high school in addition to the other entry exams I wished to take. I had not budged on my desire to go either to a Chinese or international high school. I vowed not to go to the Japanese high school even if I passed the entrance exam.

I submitted my exam application to Tomioka High School in Kanagawa Prefecture on the last possible day. I got back my examinee number, 678, the last candidate of the year.

I was struck by a curious feeling on the day Tomioka High School announced the exam results.

Why should I care if I pass the exam to a school I don't even want to attend?

Baba and I walked several dozen meters from the high school's front gate to the bulletin board where results were posted. The walk seemed longer than I had anticipated. Baba hurried me along.

"Let's go see the results."

"Who cares?"

I glared at my swift-paced father's back while straggling behind him. I had mixed feelings and dreaded looking up at the bulletin board. It was almost as if I *did* care about what was posted there.

The last number on the list of successful applicants was 678. The moment I saw it, I jumped up with a glee that unexpectedly swelled up in my heart. Why was I ecstatic about passing?

Passing the Japanese high school entry exam exacerbated my anxiety about the next stage of my education. Baba doubled down on me going to

Japanese high school. He arranged several meetings to discuss my future with teachers at Chinese schools. Their opinions were divided.

Some teachers recommended remaining in the overseas Chinese school, agreeing with my repeated objections that "even if I were to go to the local prefectural school, I have no intention of going on to a Japanese university."

But my two most trusted teachers opposed my stance. They personally visited me at my home to convince me.

"Tienshi, you can still study abroad at those universities you want to go to, after studying in a Japanese high school. But you won't be able to get into Japanese university if you remain in our Chinese school or transfer to an international school. You will be limiting your own options."

These teachers tried to sway me just as my father had. I got a bit uppity with my father, perhaps, but I just could not obediently accede to his insistence. But after anguishing over his and my trusted teachers' advice, I came around and, in the end, decided to go to the Japanese high school.

Japan, Knock, Knock!

It was April and the day of Tomioka High School's entrance ceremony fast approached. With a brand-new navy blazer, skirt, and aquamarine badge, everything seemed fresh, and I was keenly conscious that I was embarking on a new life at the Japanese school.

I took public transportation to school for the first time ever on the day of the entrance ceremony. The salaried workers, female office workers, and students on the 20-minute train ride from my local JR Ishikawacho Station looked so shiny and new. I had stepped from the familiar Chinatown, Chinese school, and Chinese restaurant of my childhood out into a whole new life and world.

I watched wide-eyed as a long line of strangers arrived at the auditorium for the entrance ceremony. Tomioka High School had about 500 students and a dozen sections in each grade. Most of the students had come up from middle schools in Yokohama's seafront districts. They knew each other, too.

"Hisashiburi!" [Long time, no see]"

"Which section are you in?"

Former middle school classmates seemed excited to reunite. I was alone. I had nobody to talk to, and nobody came to talk to me. My sense of alienation brought me back to the fast-food joints after volleyball practice, when kids pointed at us and whispered: "Those girls go to Chinese school." I wondered if I would be able to make it at this school. Insecurity enveloped me as teachers gave their entrance ceremony speeches.

"Abe!"
"Here!"
"Ishii!"
"Here!"

The teacher entered the classroom at first bell, then started class by taking attendance. I felt anxious as my turn approached. After a series of Japanese-sounding surnames in the order of the Japanese syllabary, the teacher read out the Japanized variant pronunciation of my Chinese name *Chen*.

"Chin!"

I became flustered.

"He, he…here!"

I was not used to being called *Chin* rather than *Chen* and *Chin Tenji* instead of *Chen Tienshi*. The Japanese rendering of my name embarrassed me, as if I were pretending to be someone I wasn't. This experience encapsulated for me how I had yet to assimilate into Japanese society.

Classes began a few days after enrollment.

My first classes in the Japanese school were given completely in Japanese, and nearly all students were Japanese nationals. The title on the cover of the new textbook lying before me was written in Japanese. The whole atmosphere was different from my Chinese school.

Each section at my Chinese school had just 12 or 13 students, and teachers were far closer to students—literally and figuratively—than in Japanese classrooms. We saw the same cast of characters each year and knew each other well. Before Japanese school, I had never been nervous to speak in class.

I shrank in my seat that first day of high school. Nearly 50 students sat up straight in the classroom. Japanese words darted about the room. Born and raised in Japan, I thought I understood Japanese. But I was unsure of myself when it came to Japanese expressions and the readings of Japanese kanji. I was struck by panic, finding myself in an entirely new environment, with all new rules.

"Ressun wan. Jonī appurushīdo [Lesson one, Johnny Appleseed].… Okay, everybody in a big voice, repeat after me."

"Ressun wan. Jonī appurushīdo."

In my first English-language class, students read from their textbooks, repeating after the teacher. The teacher read out the first page line by line, and we just repeated after him. He seemed to be using a Japanized pronunciation of English, as if the words had been transliterated into the *katakana* syllabary. I couldn't follow along and lost track of the rhythm.

After the students had read aloud in unison, the teacher called on students one by one to stand up and read.

"Okay, then, Yokoyama, please read what we just covered."

Several students went in turn. I prayed not to be called on. After studying at an international school and an overseas Chinese school, I simply would not be able to pronounce English words in this Japanized manner. I had trouble just ordering *hambāgā* [hamburger] at fast food restaurants. Anxiety raced through my brain: *If I pronounce the English words with an English pronunciation, I will from the start be stigmatized as a gaikokujin [foreigner], and doomed to friendless solitude.*

He called on me.

"Chin, next."

"Um, yes…"

I had no choice but to read it.

"Lesson One, Johnny Appleseed…"

After a beat, the class erupted in commotion. After reading my assigned section, I sat in my seat, eyes downcast. I couldn't bear to look at the expressions on the faces of the teachers and students around me.

The bell was about to ring, but, to me, the remaining minutes dragged on for an infernally long time. After class, some students approached my desk.

"Wow, Chin-san! You can speak English?"

"No, not really. It just sounds like I can cuz the pronunciation sounds like Chinese."

"Chin-san, you can speak Chinese, too?"

"It's just I studied at a Chinese school."

"Of course, you can, cuz you *are* Chinese, right?"

They lobbed innocent questions at me, but I couldn't shake the feeling that what they really meant was: *You are different from the other students.*

Similar events came later. In freshman year, Japanese-language studies were split into two subjects—modern Japanese and classical Japanese. I did a poor job in the latter. I had not studied haiku, so I had to learn from scratch the 5-7-5 meter and other rules that everyone else already knew.

Particularly troubling for me as a speaker of Chinese was reading *kanbun* Chinese classics. I had already read the original of Confucius's Selected Sayings in his *Analects* and in grade school had memorized the works of the poets Du Fu and Li Bai (aka Li Bo), which didn't appear in Japanese textbooks until high school. Nevertheless, classics read in the Japanese style were a major hassle for me.

I now admire the scientific methodology with which the Japanese people devised *kaeriten* return markers and other reading aids to help them re-order and understand classical Chinese texts. But at the time, it all looked like gobbledygook to me, and my test scores suffered.

The teacher often had me stand before the class to read Chinese poetry in the original Chinese. The teacher surely had no ill intent, but I felt reluctant and uncomfortable at being singled out in that way.

In high school, I understood I was different from my classmates, but I could not conform or assimilate, at least not completely. Neither did I yet have the confidence or courage to embrace my eccentricity.

Tsureshon, or Peeing Together

It was May, a month after I entered the Japanese high school. My section was known as a *jokura* section, one of two freshman sections among the 12 sections made up exclusively of girls. By this point, cliques had formed based on kids having attended the same middle school, being neighbors, or having a great deal in common. Each clique had four or five students. Cliques were unheard of back at my overseas Chinese school. It had far fewer students, to start, and it seemed we mostly focused on one-to-one interpersonal connections, upon which we based close friendships. Even so, your best friend was free to interact likewise with other friends, and we didn't stick exclusively to an in-group.

In our *jokura* section, students stuck to their own cliques, with little interaction between groups. If a student in one clique made friends with someone in another clique, the members of her original group would grow suspicious of her. That was what it was like in my Japanese school.

There was another custom I found weird, called *tsureshon*.

"Mitchan, let's go together."

Japanese girls often go to the bathroom in pairs or groups. *Tsureshon* means peeing together. For some reason, when one girl sets off for the lavatory, she invites the rest of her clique.

"Wait! I'll go with you!"

If the clique had three, then three would go together; if four, then four. They marched off together, sometimes elbows linked, even though they obviously didn't all have to go pee. The girls' lavatory was like our town square. One girl would be taking care of business in the stall, and the other two brushing their hair in front of the wall mirrors. Banter jumped back and forth over the stall walls.

"Did you watch it last night?"

"Yes, I was blown away."

"I'm thinking of getting a perm. Hmmm."

"Good idea. Maybe I'll get one too."

Perhaps *tsureshon* served as a mechanism to fortify clique unity, which weakens if each girl goes off alone. Perhaps a girl might feel insecure going alone without the others. Feeling ever alone just struggling to assimilate, I was bemused by how the intensity of group behavior extended to the lavatory.

Likewise, with lunchtime. As soon as lunch break started, each clique fashioned an island out of their desks. Each clique displayed their charming little bento box lunches, then enjoyed lunch. In the beginning, I had nowhere to drag my desk and so was left alone in the middle of the classroom surveying those around me. One classmate called over to me.

"Chin-san, come eat with us!"

"Oh, okay."

I moved my desk over to the island by the window.

"Wow! Your bento box has Chinese food!"

"It looks great. Give me some."

Wafting through our classroom was the pungent aroma of my lunch, apparently unique among my classmates, who peered enviously down into my bento box. For my part, I was jealous of their adorably decorated red tomato; yellow-grilled *tamagoyaki* omelet; and green broccoli.

The day in May that I had to register as an alien really drove home my sense of alienation. I left school early that day, as per my father's instructions. Summer break was approaching quickly. Our local ward office had sent a notice to our house that I had to come in before my sixteenth birthday to register as an alien and get issued a Certificate of Alien Registration (now called a *zairyu-kado* residence card).

At the Alien Registration counter in the ward office, I filled in the date and place of my birth, my home address, and other information. An officer directed me behind the counter to get fingerprinted. At that time, I had no qualms about such instructions. I pressed my thumb into the inkpad, then rolled it right to left on the form.

The alien registration card back then was slightly larger than today's residence card. My card indicated that my citizenship was *Stateless*—no country indicated, despite my being registered as a foreign national.

This girl is a non-Japanese foreigner who belongs to no country.

"Weird," I thought.

When the officer issued the card to me, he told me that I must carry the card with me at all times. On our way home, Baba warned me. "You must always carry this certificate on you." It was like somebody had stuck a label on my forehead that read *Stateless Foreigner*; I felt set apart from the Japanese people I encountered walking down the street.

The next day, I surveyed my classmates. All that these high schoolers had for identification was their student IDs. The alien registration card I carried in my wallet symbolized my segregation from everyone else.

I took world history as an elective during my senior year. I was incompetent when it came to ancient history and memorizing the dates required for college entrance exams. But I didn't so much mind studying modern history because I liked listening to the vivid accounts of my parents, auntie and uncle, and their friends. They had lived history. When our class covered World War II, I felt uncomfortable with what was written in our textbooks and with the teacher's lecture that aligned with the text.

He covered the Potsdam Declaration, issued in 1945. In the outskirts of Berlin, leaders from the US, UK, and the USSR hammered out plans for the global geopolitical framework to come after the war and discussed whether victorious allies should break Japan up into pieces or let the Japanese retain sovereignty under a US-led occupation.

I recalled my days at Chinese school learning what each world leader said at Potsdam as well as the roles that China and other allied countries played behind the scenes.

But here, the teacher explained to us that US and UK leaders insisted on US-led governance and later turned that into a reality. He focused on how their positions saved Japan from getting divided up by the allies and made Japan what she is today. No mention was made of what China or the other allies thought. It felt as if the world belonged exclusively to the West.

My textbook at Chinese school had taught us that Chiang Kai-shek uttered the following words on August 15, the day Japan surrendered.

"Yi de bao yuan." [以德報怨: Return good for evil.]

Chiang had waived all claims for reparations from Japan and later laid the groundwork for opposition to allied plans to break up Japan. I raised my hand.

"Sensei, the Chinese leader must have also expressed his opinion about Japan's governance."

Sensei appeared flummoxed.

"Oh, Chin-san, I will look that up and get back to you by next week."

The bell saved us all from further awkwardness. The following week, the teacher confessed to me that his research came up empty.

Until that point, I had merely crammed historical events into my brain right before tests, giving little thought to whether the facts were *in fact* facts. My experience in this class taught me that history can be rewritten and re-interpreted by people and nations in myriad ways depending on their subjective perspectives.

4 Venturing Out into the World

Learning about the World

In Autumn of my senior year, the end of my high school life approached, and I still longed to go to university abroad. That dream grew. I subscribed to a quarterly magazine on opportunities to study abroad, and I read it front to back. My interests leaned more toward global trends than what was happening in Japan. The 1980s wound down, as did the Cold War, and brought the Tiananmen massacre and the fall of the Berlin Wall. The world underwent dramatic change, and I wanted to be right there to see it.

My father still couldn't accept the idea of my going to college overseas, and he urged me to sit for the entrance exam to a Japanese university before deciding what to do. This advice was vintage Baba. He was always warning me not to make decisions hastily and to think carefully before undertaking any endeavor.

In my preparations for study in Australia, I contacted the embassy and attended a *juku* cram school to study for my TOEFL (Test of English as a Foreign Language). I also looked at Japanese universities that offered access to overseas study. Looking into Sophia University, International Christian University, and other colleges gave me a few possible candidates.

As I pushed ahead with study for the college entrance exam, one of my close classmates was already set up with a job, having already taken an exam for the job. Other friends had no plans to go to college and were able to relax while awaiting graduation. Looking enviously at their freedom, my fellow college-bound friends and I kept busy filling out college and vocational school applications and planning for summer school. I took mock exams but couldn't get my college entrance score up. My grades fell far short of what was needed for the universities I aspired to. Around that time, my high school career counselor stopped me in the hall.

"Chin-san, why don't you take a *suisen nyushi* [entrance exam by commendation]?"

"But for what university?"

"The University of Tsukuba. They have a quota for recommendations from schools designated second tier. The pass rate is not as high as for recommendations from first-tier schools, but it's a good opportunity before taking the general entrance exam."

"Hmm."

"Plus, it's a good national university."

"Let me think about it."

"Let me know soon because we will choose our internal recommendees at next week's faculty meeting."

My grades were in the top ranks of my school class, but I was not a true honors student. I studied the bare minimum. To be candid, my high school was ranked as in lower middle of my school district, so my good grades couldn't be compared to college-bound students at top-ranked, college-oriented high schools. Sadly, my mock test scores reflected that.

With my mind focused on overseas universities, I knew nothing about the University of Tsukuba, not even where it was located, what departments it had, or what I could learn there. Entrance exam magazines indicated that admission to the University of Tsukuba required a top-ranking score. I was about to march off to Japan's entrance exam war, having myself only recently entered a Japanese high school and Japanese society itself. Thinking it hopeless, I consulted with my parents.

"Well, take the exam," my father said. "It's a good opportunity."

"But I think it's impossible because the university is better than I thought. I did some research and all my upper-grade schoolmates who tried to get in failed."

"If you fail, you fail. Who cares? You'll still have the general entrance exam waiting for you afterwards."

"Yeah, I guess that's true. Ok, maybe I'll just give it a shot anyway; take the exam just for the hell of it."

I decided to try to get a second-tier school recommendation for the University of Tsukuba and told my teacher to add my name for consideration. I later learned that I had made the quota for the recommendation.

As I prepared my application, I had to decide what department to join. When I explained my feelings during dinner, my elder brother contacted a friend for me. By coincidence, that friend had come from Taiwan to study at University of Tsukuba's graduate school.

"My baby sister is headed to college and wants to know what University of Tsukuba is like. What can you tell me?"

My brother spoke for a while on the phone, telling the friend about me and other universities I wanted to enter. The friend said it was a very international school with many foreign and returnee students. A few years prior, the university had set up a new international relations department. Many students looking for an international institute took the department's courses, which were abundant and varied.

"It's perfect for your little sister, isn't it? It'll be better later if she builds up her language proficiency studying international relations rather than just majoring in English. I bet it'll also help her get out into the international scene. In fact, their international relations department will require much higher English proficiency than just studying English. It requires communication ability rather than grammar or literary skill."

That could help me get out into the international scene.

For me who dreamed of nothing but studying overseas, the friend's last comment sealed the deal. I didn't hesitate.

The entrance exam consisted of an essay section, English, and an interview. I had anticipated that I would need to write an English essay and so I had asked my modern literature teacher from freshman year to tutor me as soon as I reached senior year. He readily agreed and had been correcting one essay for me each week.

The date for the exam for a recommendation spot approached. The only time I had previously traveled within Japan was to visit neighboring Tokyo. I headed off to the testing site, not even knowing which prefecture the University of Tsukuba was in. At that time, the geopolitical situation was undergoing extraordinary change. The paper I had come to read every day splashed over its frontpage the declaration of the end of the Cold War by US President George H.W. Bush and General Secretary Mikhail Gorbachev. On my way to the testing site, I became absorbed with the article.

The students at the testing site were all obviously earnest and talented. Most had likely come from top-caliber schools in their areas. In addition to students wearing uniforms, some wore suits and heels. Running their hands through their long hair, they chatted away in fluent English, while mature-looking, suit-clad boys stood nearby. They were the much gossiped about *kikokusei*, or returnees, who had lived overseas as children. Looking around, I lost my confidence in one fell swoop. No way would I be able to compete with these people.

During the exam break and while waiting for the interview, I didn't speak to anybody. When I entered the interview room, there were five people lined up to interview me. The late Eurasian politics specialist and TV commentator Yutaka Akino was one of my five interrogators. My anxiety jumped to new heights. I couldn't quite articulate what I wanted to say. One question was in English. After the interview, it was as if the wire stretched taut around my heart snapped. I broke down on the stairs. *I had surely screwed it up.*

Gloomy days came one after another for several weeks until the university sent me a notification of the result. *I got in!* I rubbed my eyes. My homeroom teacher was ecstatic for me. Even my principal was happy. My school, which was not really a prep school, took my admission as good news.

My Parents' Home Villages

I started at the University of Tsukuba in April 1990. It was too far to commute from home, so I lived in the university dorm. This was my first time living alone. I was filled with hope but even more with anxiety. I recognized the extraordinary academic level of my University of Tsukuba classmates, who had come from all over Japan after prevailing in the entrance exam war. In autumn, the returnees with their fluent English joined us. I had grown up in Chinatown and gone to a Japanese high school. Even at this point, I felt myself to be neither Japanese nor an international student. I could barely keep up with my course work. The classes were half in English, half in difficult-to-understand Japanese. The courses all seemed hard—international politics, administrative law, economics. I couldn't understand many of the books even after reading them.

I was hounded by a sense that I'd fall behind if I didn't study more.

I was too embarrassed to discuss this with fellow freshmen. I wanted to hear the voices of my family and my close friends back home. The individual dorm rooms had no phone, so in the era before cell phones we had to use the public phone. Come night, and everyone waited in the dark for their turn at the phone. You couldn't talk at your leisure because people were waiting behind you. One of my friends was worried about me and wrote to me to lift my spirits. She had been hospitalized due to complications from a cold just before the college entry exams, and ended up having to take a gap year. Yet still she wrote and encouraged me, saying *gambare* (keep at it). On weekends, I did my best to get home to Yokohama, spend time with my family, and help out at the restaurant.

***

By summer of freshman year, I was starting to get used to my new college life despite my lingering anxieties. My mother took me to her home province of Hunan as my "reward." This was my first opportunity to step foot on the Chinese mainland.

At that time, direct air travel to China from Japan was inconvenient, as there were no frequent flights. Instead, we flew to Hong Kong, and from there took a train over the border to Guangzhou. The atmosphere transformed when we crossed the border. Standing there were men in dark green military uniforms with red stripes. The immigration official spoke Chinese in a kind of scary tone. I was scared and clung close to my mother.

We left Guangzhou station for the city, where we saw people, people, and more people. The sheer number of people and the scale of the town were of a different order. Big. There is no other way to describe it. Crowds of children begged near the station. Seeing my robust mother, four or five of them darted over, stuck out grubby palms, and called out *ayi, ayi* (aunty, aunty). They had grimy cheeks, tattered clothes, and shiny, pleading eyes. One little urchin of six or seven carried a baby piggyback. Mama was kind-hearted and couldn't resist them. They spoke her home dialect. She broke down and pulled money out of her purse. That brought another wave of children who had witnessed the act of charity from afar.

We ran off and headed toward the domestic airport to find a flight from Guangzhou to Hunan. We had to use special foreign exchange notes (*waihuiquan*) and pay an exchange premium well above what citizens paid. We had to use these to buy airplane tickets too.

At that time in China, whether one was boarding a plane or shopping, there was no recognition of the concept of waiting in line. It was whoever got there first. It was a mistake to expect any manner of customer service at restaurants or stores. The customer had to be extremely polite to the clerk to be allowed to look at a product. Coming from Japan where the customer is God, I often felt consumer dissatisfaction while traveling in China.

Mama's hometown was Yiyang, a five- or six-hour drive from Changsha City, Hunan province. The beat-up old clunker clattered and shook over unpaved roads, which made me feel carsick. As we approached her home, there were no longer any roads worthy of the word *road*. Chickens and cows loitered on the roadside. Mama's excitement picked up as we approached her village.

"This is where your mother went to school. Your *wai gong* [grandfather] and your great uncle built it together…. This is the house of your *niang niang* [unrelated grandmotherly figure], who took good care of your mother. *Niang niang* was always so nice to me when your grandparents went off to war and left me all alone. That's why Mama always sent her money, out of appreciation. Lara, you be kind to her too."

My mother had been returning once a year to her home village. After my grandparents died in Taiwan, Mama buried their bones on a village hill visible from the house where they had once lived, as per their wishes. Since then, she returned yearly to visit their graves around June, around the time of their deaths. Distant relatives still lived in the village, farming. They were dirt poor, even by Chinese standards.

The year I went, they still didn't have plumbing. They drew water and carried it in buckets hanging from a bamboo pole slung over the shoulders. It was tough trying to keep the water from sloshing out. Everything about village life fascinated me. I demanded they let me try the water buckets. After staggering about ten meters, the water had been reduced to about a third of the original haul. My mother and relatives enjoyed a great laugh watching me flounder.

"This is your *jiu jiu* [uncle] and your *jiu ma* [aunt]. Over there is your *biao ge* [cousin]."

I greeted each in turn. Even though we had never met, my relatives greeted me warmly, some with tears in their eyes. My aunt and others gave me several *jian mian li*, the gift one gives when meeting for the first time.

"So glad you came. We have nothing compared with Japan, but we are so grateful you are here."

They knew every detail about me and my family in Japan, thanks to letters and photos from my mother. We began by visiting the graves of my grandparents. Mama then took me to the house she had once lived in. After the war, my grandparents' assets had been confiscated, and someone else was now living there.

"Your mother was born in that room."

The room Mama pointed at was covered with dust and was now used for storage. The building stood as it had when she left her village 40 years prior, but no trace remained of her warm home life there. All that remained was the memory in the minds of my mother and other family members.

We went around to each location, full of memories, to meet those who had shown kindness and care for my mother.

Barefoot children and relatives arrived in droves. One small child's trouser pants were split at the back.

"Lara, this is your mother's home village. Take it in with your own eyes."

I began to understand a little more why Mama never wasted anything and saved up her money to send to her relatives back home. The children and relatives in her home village were poor, yet their eyes shined with a simple sparkle that we rich-country dwellers had somehow forgotten. I felt the scene cleanse my heart. The children born in this rural village had access to limited information and usually had no chance to get a higher education. Mama wanted to do any little thing possible to help the villagers and so she sent money for road construction and to set up a scholarship for the school my grandfather and great-uncle had built. She didn't send a fortune, but a few hundred thousand Japanese yen goes a long, long way in China. A little daily effort translates into helping a great many people. Mama's unassuming actions made me want to do something useful for somebody at some time in the future.

The following year, my parents went to visit my father's birthplace in northeastern China. My father had watched my mother go back to China each year with a tinge of envy.

"Maybe I'll go back to the northeast."

He had not been back in over four decades. Even the thought of *going* to China caused his heart to tremble in fear. I was a bit shocked to hear him talk about such a visit.

The People's Republic of China (PRC) had by 1978 embarked on a transition from a closed socialist system symbolized by the slogan *zi li geng sheng* (self-reliance) to an open, reformist economy. Under the banner of a socialist market economy, China began reaching out to other countries, and gradually bringing back Chinese émigrés to visit their home villages.

But the one-China policy dictated that the Republic of China (Taiwan) come out in opposition to the new mainland posture. It also meant that for our family, as holders of ROC-issued passports, China remained a country we could not return to even if we wanted to. This too changed in 1987, the year that the ROC lifted martial law. This allowed Taiwan residents to visit their relatives on the mainland. It also opened cultural, economic, and all other non-political forms of exchange between the mainland and the island. The change in the relationship between mainland China and Taiwan blew in like another fresh breeze, again changing our circumstances. My parents had been unable to visit the mainland for over four decades after leaving their home villages, and now they could. Baba was pushing 70, and day by day the desire swelled in his chest to lay eyes once more on his home village. My father had high expectations for the trip.

He came from Ningan in Mudanjiang City, a vast pastoral area on the banks of the Amur, which flows along the border with Russia. We flew from Narita Airport to Beijing, and transferred there to a domestic flight to Harbin. From there, we rode all night on a shaky sleeper train. In our berth, Baba became uncharacteristically agitated.

My father had moved to Taiwan alongside the Kuomintang government during the civil war that erupted just after the close of World War II. He always worried about his younger sisters that had been left behind. He was finally about to meet the family he thought he would never see again, due solely to the peculiarities of national politics. The situation robbed Baba of his ordinary calm.

Many of Baba's relatives met him at Mudanjiang Station. Stepping off the train, he saw his younger sister's face and bolted toward her. My aunt and father embraced, sobbing audibly. I had never seen my father's tears. My mother standing next to me also looked shocked.

Seeing my father's village for the first time gave me the impression that I had traveled several decades back in time. Walls crumbled but displayed graffiti slogans evidently written during the Cultural Revolution. The world war, the civil war, and the ensuing chaos cast a shadow over the district.

"There used to be a wide, straight road here, but it has been destroyed."

"That was probably the Ma house."

"I used to climb on a huge rock that used to be here."

He visited his former family home, where a new family now lived, and relived childhood memories. At one point, Baba suddenly took off running like a boy.

"This was our land!"

I chased after my fleet-footed father. Cutting through the trees, the horizon opened before us over an expansive field of green. It was the first time I had ever seen such a vast, open land and sky. Even my tall father looked puny before the vastness of the scene. Imitating my father, I spread my arms, straightened my spine, and breathed deeply. I immediately understood organically that this land had raised my father.

Without discussion, we climbed a nearby trail. We forged through a field of corn stalks taller than I was for about 30 minutes before arriving atop a low hill, the location of my grandmother's grave. The modest plot was heaped over with a two-meter circle of dirt. Baba kneeled and bowed his head. In the chaos of war, he had departed without saying farewell to his mother. This was his first time in more than 40 years reuniting with his mother, albeit in a manner nobody could have predicted. Baba stayed for a long spell at the grave, recounting aloud each event that had happened during his absence, first in China, then in Taiwan, then Japan.

After the visit to the grave, we returned to my aunt's home. We talked round the clock as if time was unspeakably precious—about our lives in

Japan, the family, and my grandfather. My grandfather had moved to Taiwan with my father. Grandfather lived there for almost 30 years before coming to live with us in Yokohama just as I entered middle school. He died two years later. Throughout his life, my grandfather had maintained all the customs of his home village while living in Taiwan and Japan, including meals, clothing, and lifestyle. He wore black or navy; in summer white Chinese outfits. He grew his long beard down to his belly.

During my childhood, whenever we had gone off to visit Taiwan, he promised to greet us when we came back to Japan with a feast. One time, he made us boiled gyoza dumplings. We returned home to find gyoza lined up on tables and chairs throughout the house. I plopped down on our wooden sofa, exhausted from the flight, only to discover that I had sat on top of some dumplings. My family laughed when they saw the doughy white powder on my butt. My grandfather patted me on the head, saying "this girl sure is a troublemaker." During meals, he flung his goatee back over his ear.

I loved each of his mischievous mannerisms.

"Lai, ding tou" [Come here. Time for "head sumo"].

My grandfather called me over and pitted our foreheads against each other for a match of *head sumo*. I loved my grandfather's big forehead.

He suffered cognitive impairment in his final years in Japan, perhaps due to loneliness. In his confusion during that period, he often spoke about his home village. He called out the names of fellow villagers and my aunt who was not in Yokohama.

Hey! Xiao feng!

My father told the families left behind in the village that my grandfather had worried about them until the end and longed to meet them again. My aunt cried, letting out a voice that didn't sound like a voice.

After two days, our relatives saw us off at Mudanjiang Station, as we started our journey back to Japan. My aunt gave me a gold bracelet. Despite the harsh life she led, she must have bought this for me thinking she might never see me again. She included with the bracelet a handwritten poem.

My aunt who lived in a foreign land had written a poem for me, her niece, who she was meeting for the first time. I had heard stories about her, but could not really have imagined the kind of person she was. It must have been the same for her. But she listened to others and expressed in a poem how she had imagined me, a niece she had never met. The way she described me in that short poem captured the true me.

My goateed paternal grandfather

They say blood is thicker than water, and I felt then a true sense of what family really means. I never dreamed I would receive such thoughtfulness from an aunt I had never met.

After World War II and the ensuing civil war, the needs of the nation had rent my father's family asunder. Something integral that could not be torn apart swelled within my bosom.

Roadblock to Study Abroad

My longing to study abroad and know more about the world only grew when I reached sophomore year, and so did my desire to improve my language proficiency. I prepared to study abroad. The colleges I aimed for in the US and Australia cost a bundle. Even though they ran a successful Chinese restaurant, my parents had a large family to support. My parents were already sending me money to study at the University of Tsukuba, so it pained me to ask for money to study abroad. I looked into financial aid opportunities. Here, once again, the fact that my nationality was *stateless* stood as a barrier blocking my path.

Nearly every scholarship I could find had a nationality requirement. Those for Japanese students required Japanese citizenship; those for international students required a student visa, which I could not obtain because I was a permanent resident. I couldn't even apply for the scholarships unless I could demonstrate what country I belonged to. I spoke over and over with the university's student services, to no avail. I was stateless—neither Japanese, nor foreigner. I never imagined my state of statelessness would stand between me and my dreams.

The system felt unequal, full of holes and contradictions. Though humiliated, I couldn't give up. I furiously gathered up all the information I could on scholarship programs. Whenever I had time, I stood in front of the university bulletin board taking notes and visited foundations that offered scholarships. I diligently checked eligibility requirements, marking in red the programs available to me, including nationality requirements.

What I found was a summer scholarship program run independently by the study abroad periodical that I had regularly read during high school. The scholarship for a short-term language study program at UCLA (University of California, Los Angeles) covered tuition and lodging. There was an age limit, but thankfully no nationality requirement.

I realized that this program might be my only option. But there were only two available places for students. I had no idea how many students would be applying for it, and imagined that my chances were about the same as winning a magazine sweepstake.

I knew that I was probably grasping at straws, but decided to give it a shot. I filled out the paperwork and wrote the assigned essay on "Why I want to study language abroad." When I stood in front of the red post box to send my application documents in the day before the deadline, I brought my hands together in prayer and said *onegai* (please grant me this).

A few months later a letter arrived, telling me that I had passed the first round. I was asked to come to the program's Tokyo office for an interview. The day before I went, I placed a full-length mirror in the center of the room and practiced every aspect of my interview. I walked through every movement that I imagined might be required of me, including opening the door, bowing, speaking, and introducing myself in English.

The next day, on the train into the city, I was very nervous, and my mind raced as I tried to imagine what they would ask me. The interview turned out to be less rigidly formal than I had anticipated. My previous day's practice opening doors turned out to be of little use. In fact, the bearded lead interviewer opened the door and welcomed me, saying "please come in." The interview was more a chat than a stiff conversation with participants sitting across the table from each other.

After the interview, I took the opportunity to look around at my surroundings. Many students in my age group had visited the office for consultations about studying abroad, including college students, students who had already graduated, and high schoolers with their parents. While they surveyed the overseas study information, I felt a wave of relief after my days of anticipatory nervousness, and instead began to feel real excitement as my desire to study abroad reached new heights.

A few weeks later, the selection results arrived at my dorm. I had been offered the scholarship. Unable to suppress a squeal of delight, I promptly contacted my parents and got them to agree to let me study in the US during summer break.

"We can't very well say no, since you were chosen for the scholarship. Go do your best."

Even Mama, who had been reluctant to let me go to the US, quickly broke down. Her voice sounded delighted even. I had blasted through the barrier of statelessness and attained a chance to study abroad.

Love and Prejudice

I was struggling to improve my English proficiency in preparation for study abroad. I became a member of the English-Speaking Society (ESS), which was meeting to coordinate a drama performance. That's when I met him.

I often spent time in the library after class and before my ESS meetings. Near the entrance on the first floor was the Fishbowl, a glass-enclosed room where CNN played on the TV. ESS members and friends often used this room as a meeting point.

The meeting that day was devoted to discussing what program to run for the spring performance. I was suggesting *West Side Story*, a play that I had loved since I was a child. I was holding the English script and planning to show it to everyone. That's when I heard a baritone voice from across the room.

"The class is on Japan-US trade friction, so ..."

It was a male student explaining the classes being offered at the international relations department I belonged to. The department's students on average boasted high English proficiency. But this student's English stood out even among them as he spoke frankly. I had not seen him much around school. I later found out he was one year behind me and had spent his high school years studying in Australia.

In middle and high school, I was a late bloomer when it came to love. Maybe it was my masculine personality, but I just didn't have it in me to act all cutesy and so had little to speak of in terms of romantic entanglement. My college days consisted of studying at Tsukuba Monday to Friday, then helping with the restaurant in Yokohama on the weekends. Some friends gossiped that "Lara must have an older boyfriend back in Yokohama." All I could do was smile wryly. Because I still felt that I was struggling to keep up in class, I thought that I didn't have the emotional space for love.

I sometimes joked that I hoped to have a boyfriend once in college, but privately, I doubted whether in an environment full of Japanese people any man would want to date someone like me. The campus culture was such that Japanese students tended to date Japanese students; foreign students tended to date foreign students; and returnees tended to date returnees. I was not so easily categorized and found myself looking at all the fun from the outside. I didn't feel particularly lonely. It was just the way things were.

I first saw him in the library, then met him a month later at a welcoming party for new students. He spoke to me for the first time.

"You are Lara Sempai [senior student], right?"

"Yes, ... impressive that you know that."

"Of course, I know. You want some beer?"

"Yeah, thanks."

We took the same class that year. At each break, we kicked up a conversation, paper coffee cup in hand. He would say something like, "Lara-san, can we talk about the Chinese foreign policy the sensei just talked about?" After every Monday class, I rushed off to my Russian tutor

Irena's house to learn Russian. He would say, "I have time until my club activity, so I'll send you off," and we'd dart off on our bicycles. We often studied together. He had his own clear opinions and related them candidly with zero affectation. After a time, he professed his feelings for me. I was glad and hesitant at the same time.

"We can't because I'm a year ahead of you."

"But we're the same age."

"Plus, I'm Chinese and you're Japanese."

"What does that have to do with anything?"

I was still tied down by different prejudices and fixed ideas. I thought he must be some sort of weirdo for going after a foreigner with a different cultural background. I never dreamed he would support me during the most vulnerable period of my life in the following years.

Where Are You From?

My long-dreamed-of study abroad began the summer of my junior year. Landing in the Los Angeles airport, I saw people with so many different skin colors. A flurry of different languages drifted into my ear—some that my ears were used to like English, Chinese, and Japanese; but also, Spanish, Filipino, and Vietnamese. The grand mix of languages sounded like music to my ears. I lived in the UCLA dorm, which also housed many Japanese students on short-term study tours. I kind of cheated and told them I was Chinese.

Pretending I couldn't speak Japanese, I avoided the Japanese students who tended to congregate in groups. Of course, I was anxious to boost my English ability, but I also wanted to forget Japan for a while. But soon it came out that I too had come from Japan.

The short-term study abroad program was divided into separate classes based on levels of language proficiency. I was in the upper intermediate class, able to speak fairly well despite poor grammar. Classes ran from 9:00 in the morning until 3:00 in the afternoon. Tons of homework kept me busy every day. Unlike the classes I had become accustomed to in Japan, in which the teacher teaches, and the students listen, these classes required students to speak up. I felt pressure, since raising my hand to give my opinion took courage. But my life as a student was far more fulfilling than it had been in Japan. I could cool down in the swimming pool when exhausted from study, for instance.

During lunch, I would sit on the grass with my classmates, chomping on a sandwich prepared at the dorm café. The diversity there included Koreans, an ethnic-Chinese Vietnamese student from France, and a slightly older group of Chileans. Back home, I had acquired the habit of speaking to customers and townsfolk who came into our restaurant. I had so much fun talking to people from so many different countries. One friend I met during my study abroad left a particularly intense impression on me. Her name was Asako. I came to know her through my roommate Yumiko. Asako came from Japan's southern island of Kyushu. After studying language at UC Berkeley the previous year, she was now attending a college in the LA suburbs.

Tall and skinny, with long hair, she had grown quite accustomed to life in the US. I aspired to get into UC Berkeley full-time after my short-term study abroad program, but she had already experienced a world unknown to me. She seemed like a big sister.

"I heard you went to UC Berkeley."

"Yeah."

"I would love to study there."

"It's a nice college, with a liberal atmosphere."

I started spending more weekends with Asako and Yumiko. They taught me how American university students had fun. US bars are strict about carding customers, so we had to listen to music, dance, and party in the dorm's lounge. On my 21st birthday, they helped me celebrate my new booze freedom by taking me to a bar.

As the date to return to Japan approached, I told them I wanted to see Berkeley before leaving California. The following weekend, they rented a car and took me there. They were happy to see old friends too and had excitedly been contacting them.

As soon as Friday class finished, I crammed my backpack with my stuff and we took off for Berkeley. We took Route 51 along the west coast, watching the horizon over the ocean and driving through stretches of forest along the way. True to our age, we laughed, squealed, and giggled the entire seven-hour ride. After we all grew tired of talking, I sat in the back watching the scenery move outside my window while Asako and Yumiko in the front took turns driving.

I felt a bit of unease around this time. When meeting people, they often greeted me with the question: Where are you from? The Japanese equivalent would mean nothing more than from what place did you travel to get here. But in English, the expression contains a further nuance of inquiring into the other's origin. It has no deep significance, but I felt that responding "I'm Chinese" would somehow not be telling the whole story. Saying I came from Japan would also be wrong. A proper explanation would take forever. I wondered how to express my identity. This was not a source of unbearable anguish, to be sure, but it gave me pause.

Arriving in Berkeley, we should have been exhausted after the long car trip. But we were in high spirits; we had people and things to see.

UC Berkeley has a special building for foreign students called International House, or I House. Students from different countries gather there in the evenings. We set off first for I House. Many of Asako's and Yumiko's friends were already gathered there as if waiting to welcome them. They were delighted to see their friends again and embraced them cheerfully, saying "long time, no see." I held back and gave a quick nod of greeting, but inside I felt envious. A black man came over to talk to me, as if he had noticed my feelings.

"Hi! Hajimemashite."

I was surprised that he spoke Japanese to me. We stood there speaking for a while. I noticed he wore a watch that had Chinese character numbers on the face.

"Wow, this is cool. Why is it like that?"

In clearly pronounced albeit broken Japanese, he explained he was interested in Asian culture and was studying.

"After Japanese, I plan to study Korean."

I felt ashamed that even though I had been born an Asian, I had not appreciated Eastern culture as much as he did. I introduced myself as a Chinese person. Even though I had an Asian face, he came to realize that I didn't know much about China or Asia. It happened so many times. I would say "I am Chinese" only to then be asked "Where in China do you live?" or "What kind of music is popular in China these days?" It made me squirm. I knew what music was popular in Japan but nothing about China. When people asked me about Asia in general, I could make only trite, boring conversation.

My attention had all gone to the outside world, and I knew little about myself.

The next day, my new friend Eliot showed me around the campus of the university where I most wanted to study. The weather was good. We spoke about our lives at college while walking near the department I was looking to get into, and also visited the library and Cal's famous clock tower. He introduced friends who passed by. When lunchtime came, people showed up at the university's central square to play string instruments and perform. We bought sandwiches and sat on the grass with the live performance as background music. The campus filled me with a pleasant sense of liberation. We discussed many things, immersed in that environment. As he got to know me, he told me about his own upbringing.

"I look black, right? But my mother was German. My black father studied abroad in Germany. He fell in love with my mother there and I was born. I spent my early years in Germany. So, I live in a very German way."

I began to feel good about him as he little by little unraveled his story to me in a way that was easy to understand. How others see us does not always match our self-identity. And our self-identity need not be one-dimensional. Hearing his story altered how I explained my own situation.

"I'm Chinese but born in Japan."

At a party that night, when he introduced me to a friend, I felt relief to find myself describing my background in that way, as if it was completely natural. Asako had come with me and had a dramatic reaction to the new way in which I introduced myself.

The party was at the home of a friend who lived near the school. The table was covered with pizza, chips, and an array of drinks. Guests danced and tried to speak above the pop music rhythmically reverberating from the stereo. Not knowing most people at the party, I felt a bit nervous. But people came up to talk to me, with no discomfort. I introduced myself. Asako was chatting away next to me, then suddenly turned to stare at me with an intense look on her face. Checking that Yumiko was not nearby, she said,

"I envy you!"

She had always spoken to me in Japanese, yet she said this in English and with a grave expression on her face.

"What? What's wrong with you?"

"Lara, I'm so jealous of you. I have feelings I cannot say to anyone, feelings I cannot even say to my best friend Yumiko."

Asako said the reason she had wanted to study in the United States was to find herself and to be able to live with her head held high. She was in fact a Japan-born Korean. Until she was in high school her parents had hidden from her the fact that they were Korean. But one day when she needed to get her alien registration issued, they informed her of her heritage. That revelation and the yawning gap between the Japanese surname she had always used and the Korean family name she suddenly learned about shocked her, and the very next day at school she was overwhelmed with a strong sense of being different from everyone else. She could not shake the feeling and found herself feeling constantly guilty, as if her life had been a lie, lived wearing a mask.

She decided to go to the US with the hope that if she were to be in the racial melting pot that is the US, she surely would be able to live proudly and openly as a Korean.

But the reality was different. If she answered the inescapable "Where are you from?" with "I am Korean," it would be no better than lying. She had never been to Korea, knew nothing of the culture, and could barely even say the place names. Worse, what if she met Korean students who had been born and grew up in Korea? Her Japanese-ness and her Korean-ness were both fraudulent. Coming to the States only exacerbated her dejected state. She ended up with a life no different from the one she left behind in Japan.

"I am Asako from Japan."

It was easier to introduce herself that way. She couldn't even tell her best friend Yumiko. Filled with this complex of emotions, she was startled to hear me introduce myself: "I'm Chinese but born in Japan." That's why she envied me, she said.

"Asako, I can't explain it so simply either."

I didn't know what to say to her. Should I have said: "Someone suffering the same pain is right here," or "Other people in Japan feel alienated for the same kinds of reasons"?

All I had thought about was escaping Japan and going overseas, but this was the first time I understood that Japan has others who feel like I do. This moment made me sense that perhaps a more profound problem lurked. I realized during my short-term study abroad program that other people suffered like I did, and their stories stayed in my mind even after I returned to Japan.

International Issues Made Personal

Before going to the States, I had begun a course called "Cross-Cultural Education." While studying politics and economics in the international relations department, I had looked at the world one nation at a time from a macro perspective. The books tended towards the theoretical and were often dry and academic. I thought it was cool to use arcane, technical language to debate and comment on international affairs. I admired the larger-than-life international politics experts on TV who analyzed current affairs and described the world as if it belonged to them. That was my dream in college, and my eyes were always focused on the world *out there*.

The Cross-Cultural Education class was offered by a different department than my home department, and I had enrolled because I assumed it would enable me to learn about other cultures and better come to know the outside world. But, in fact, I learned to focus on education, culture, and people and to see the world in a more intimate way. This course, for example, explored how a teacher at a foreign elementary school should educate students of myriad cultural backgrounds. We were assigned to write a report over summer break about our thoughts on cross-cultural education. I was used to writing dry, academic, carefully reasoned papers on politics, economics, and other areas of international relations. But would I be able to discuss these things from cultural and educational perspectives? I started worrying even before summer break.

During summer break, I went off to the States, and by the time I got back to the university, my worry had evaporated. For my report, I spelled out what I noticed and thought about while I was in the US. I contrasted white and black communities in the US that I had come to know a little about through the friends I had made at Berkeley, then explored the meaning of skin color. I wrote about the complex emotions of Koreans living in Japan, as I had come to understand through conversations with Asako. I went to the university library and binge-read books on minorities. I realized for the first time that in fact Japan is home to many ethnicities and that multiple cultures coexist.

Despite my very own existence providing evidence that it was not, I had once thought that Japan was a homogenous society. I look back at my thinking then and want to crawl into a hole from embarrassment. Without questioning the schema of a nation made up of a single ethnicity, I had believed that minorities stuck out as unimportant people who could never play central roles in the nation. I negated my own existence, seeing myself as an outside minority who had no voice, and was able to change nothing.

Reading further, I expanded my vocabulary, adding the word *identity* to *minority*. Identity is the pillar of our consciousness, indicating being the same as something and a sense of belonging to a certain group. It means "I am a ...," but I had thought that ellipsis naturally called for the name of a nation state. I recalled how even though I had always lived in Japan and self-identified as Chinese, that self-identification wavered during my stay in the US. I remembered how my simple statement that "I am Chinese but born in Japan" impacted Asako. Looking back at my time in the US, I had an odd sense that I was maybe seeing myself objectively for the first time. Through my experience in the States, I had discovered that identity does not simply consist of the name of one country affiliation. I suppose the scales fell from my eyes.

In my report, I discussed the identity conflicts particularly suffered by minority groups and suggested that conflict creates roles that minority groups may be able to play in the nation. The Spike Lee film *Malcolm X*, about the black American leader, was playing in US theaters at the time. It provided me with additional insight.

I was able to take a positive look at the existence of minorities, who for some reason could not assimilate into society (as I couldn't) or who were not accepted into society. Did they have no useful role to play, or did they have a special role to play precisely because they are minorities?

In class, my professor said he wanted to read my report aloud to the entire group. I was then called to the front of the class and asked to speak more about the friends I had discussed in the report and about being a Chinese person born in Japan. This was quite unusual for a large lecture class, and I was nervous.

The professor commended me for using my experiences to reevaluate the world. I welcomed the praise, naturally, but it was also a surprise. I had become so accustomed to analyzing the world in a logical manner from a macro perspective that incorporated the entire world. I was not used to looking at things from the perspective of individual human beings. I had half expected to be ridiculed for using my private experience to write childish drivel bereft of objectivity, more befitting a middle school book report than a university paper.

I felt I had discovered something else. I could find international issues near at hand, without venturing off to the outside world. Without leaving Japan, I had many opportunities to learn about the world. Asako taught me that knowing myself is as important as knowing the world.

After this, I began reading books about foreigners living in Japan. But while bookstores and libraries had racks full of works on Korean residents of Japan (from both the north and south halves of the peninsula), there was nothing published on Chinese living in Japan. That made me want to learn about it more.

Interviews in Chinatown

At the end of my junior year, I chose cross-strait relations and the *huaqiao* (overseas Chinese) community as my research topic. At this time, in the early 1990s, against the post-Cold War global trend toward peaceful talks, the mood in East Asia was tense due to a clash of ideologies on the Korean Peninsula and in China. In particular, the PRC and ROC (Taiwan) were deadlocked, both sides flying the banner of unification.

The Kuomintang had clung to power in Taiwan through one-party rule. The election of Lee Teng-hui, however, saw the advance of democratization, leading to the meteoric rise of the Democratic Progressive Party, which advocated for the independence of Taiwan from Chinese rule. It was a period of a shift in power in Taiwan, and the growing push for independence deepened tensions between the mainland and the island.

The growing militancy of the two-China conflict, into which the China of my roots had bifurcated, irritated me. It was surely not just me who thought: We are all the same Chinese! But what could a lowly college student like myself do about it, particularly from Japan? Nevertheless, as a *huaqiao* resident, I increasingly felt that maybe I could do something.

That is when I took a new look at the neighborhood where I was born and raised—Chinatown in Yokohama—the Chinatown that raised and nurtured me. Some in Chinatown were tossed around by the fickle changes in the domestic and international political situation. Even Chinese schools and organizations had split due to the PRC-ROC dispute. There were also those who clung to their ideologies and dreamed of a united fatherland. I came to feel that there must be something I could do for the Chinese community.

Even the Chinese community living in Yokohama's Chinatown was diverse. Some residents had migrated from Guangdong, Fujian, Shanghai, and other places in China before World War II; others came over after the war via Hong Kong, Taiwan, or other places. Still others came over from the mainland after China's 1978 opening and reforms. The lived histories and the resulting ideologies varied from person to person. What they had in common was that as Chinese people they continued to be affected by the decisions made and actions taken in mainland China and Taiwan. They were, at times, caught up in the transitions of power. These *huaqiao* had left their country and now were subject to the winds of history even in their small Chinatown community. But I sensed from my father and the adults around him that some in the community felt a strong obligation to do something for the fatherland.

I decided to interview Chinatown Chinese residents to find out what they felt about cross-strait ties. There were a number of different perspectives. Some, like my father, had migrated to Taiwan along with the Kuomintang government. They saw the growing movement in Taiwan for independence from China as pushing further away their dream of a united China. They were *huaqiao* and believed they needed to do whatever they could in a cool-headed manner to stem the push for independence, while at the same time persuading others not to resort to military pressure or threats against the mainland to force unification.

There were of course those who thought differently. Some were pro-ROC, others pro-PRC. The latter sympathized with the Communist Party government and condemned the pro-independence movement in Taiwan. They believed that Taiwan was an integral part of China.

The power struggle between the Kuomintang and the Chinese Communist Party didn't end immediately after the founding of the PRC in 1949. Even in Chinatown in Yokohama, Chinese residents split over issues, such as ownership and control of shared resources, and which Chinese government each school should support. Those who supported the new China launched a new system of Chinese education, including brand new pro-China historical education and Chinese-language education, using the new, simplified characters. Chinese education in Yokohama's Chinatown community henceforth split into parallel pro-ROC Chinese schools and pro-PRC Chinese schools. What it meant to be Chinese now depended on which school you attended, the ideology that either the ROC or PRC reflected in the education there. This impacted personal relationships.

Although the China-Taiwan relationship was a power struggle on a governmental level, for me who grew up in Chinatown, it was also a personal problem that affected my daily life. Parades took place in Chinatown both on October 1 to celebrate the 1949 founding of the People's Republic of China and on October 10 to celebrate the 1911 founding of the Republic of China. Students were rounded up by the respective factions to join the parades, and perform dragon dances, lion dances, and traditional folk dances. Each event created camaraderie *and* rivalries.

Identity, patriotism, and camaraderie became imprinted on the minds of individuals without their awareness. This should trouble us. It shows how the will of national governments reaches out even to those living outside the country. This impacted those overseas sometimes more than those in the country.

Truth be told, I was terrified to interview residents of my childhood neighborhood on the topic of cross-strait ties and the *huaqiao* community. It felt too close to home, like a problem preferably avoided. But I believed that I had to start there if I was to deepen my understanding of China and Chinese migrants and my own history. The many feelings that arose during my time in the States led me to face my mixed emotions and explore the topic more deeply.

I interviewed not only pro-Taiwan residents, but also the chair of the pro-China Yokohama Overseas Chinese Association, school principals, and other community leaders with strong political awareness and opinions.

I knew nothing about the pro-China leaders who had long been my neighbors. I had little but a vague impression that they were pro-China, but now I would visit them as interview subjects. I knew their faces, but they seemed distant to me. Approaching and talking about cross-strait relations with them took courage for me, particularly since they all knew that their interviewer was the daughter of Chen Fu Poo, who belonged to the rival faction. I felt a little uncomfortable interviewing one person in particular.

"Welcome!"

We discussed many aspects of China and Taiwan. At the end of our conversation, he said:

"We haven't had much chance until now, but as fellow Chinese, we should maintain good ties."

His tone suggested that he was open to dialogue with a person who held a different opinion. I appreciated that, but also recognized that in another sense we both shared the experience of being victims of manipulation by our respective national governments.

Huaqiao of different positions still struggled under the one dream of a unified fatherland. What I saw in my home village of Chinatown through countless interviews was *huaqiao* Chinese migrants being buffeted about by a historical tempest created by the nation state. This was a Chinese community driven to the point of rupture by competing ideological banners raised by the respective governments. My paper, entitled *Cross-Strait Relations and the Role of Huaqiao*, delineated my expectations for the *huaqiao* to play a special role, precisely because they lived overseas. It also expressed, I think, the sense of powerlessness vis-à-vis the nation state felt by the community, as they were tossed about by the political storm winds.

Study is Your Real Fortune

During my senior year, unlike my classmates who were focused on job hunting, I was engrossed in writing my bachelor's thesis and preparing to go to graduate school. Perhaps I wanted to repress my insecurities about job hunting and my future.

I had given up looking for a job before even beginning. I had recently learned from research on foreign residents of Japan that discrimination in hiring occurred based on nationality. This disgusted me. On top of that, Japan was a man's society. I was a stateless woman. I knew that I would face inevitable discrimination. I preferred spending my time studying and improving myself rather than wasting time and trouble encountering discrimination and still not finding a job. People in my position needed to learn specialist skills and knowledge that nobody else has. I told myself I had to work twice as hard to avoid discrimination.

Looking back, I think I should have gone out on the job market. It can be a university student's rite of passage, a rite I could only have experienced at that time. I now sort of regret not finding out directly how I would be treated. But I pretended to be strong back in those days, even though I was twice as scared of getting hurt as others. So, I came up with excuses not to search for work.

I did indeed have a desire then to start working. I had a nebulous idea of getting into mass media, flying around the world, and doing a job that enabled me to extend a helping hand to families and children in war zones and other tragic circumstances. My boyfriend—I was now dating the student I had first met that day in the campus library—provided emotional support, and I always spoke to him about my desire to "work someday on the world stage." He was studying for the diplomatic service exam. We studied international relations and were both attracted to the idea of a job that would have us flying around from one country to another. We innocently spoke of our dreams for both of us to get that kind of job and live overseas.

It didn't turn out that way. Whenever I was alone, my insecurity grew. My stateless status had almost completely blocked me from studying abroad. Even the Chinatown of my childhood was caught up in a political vortex. I became more convinced than ever that nobody would accept me. Thus, the idea of job hunting filled me with terror.

Looking back, I see that the cause of that terror was close at hand. My brother, 15 years my senior, had a bad experience looking for work. I was in middle school at the time. My brother had come back to Japan after graduating from National Taiwan University but could find no work even though Japan was heading toward a bubble economy and expanding its industrial strength, centered around big construction companies. He wanted to get a job where he could make use of the civil engineering knowledge he had attained. Back in Japan, he applied for jobs at each major construction company but was pretty much turned away at the gate. They didn't even tell him whether it was because he was not Japanese, or because he was stateless, or because he had not graduated from a Japanese university.

In the end, he got a job at a major construction company through the good offices of a friend. But the job was not in Japan. Instead, he was hired on a short-term contract to be sent to the Middle East. He hesitated, but recognized that a door to Japanese society had opened slightly. I was in middle school but intuited the difficulty of finding work and making a living in this country for those of us who were neither "Japanese" nor "foreign."

My boyfriend's phone call came late at night. I often talked to him about the future.

"Lara, you should do what only you can do. You know well the pain of Chinese living in Japan, don't you? You don't have to get hung up on job hunting. Anybody can look for work."

He embraced my desire to escape. After hanging up the phone, I broke down in tears.

That autumn, the notice of my acceptance to the University of Tsukuba's graduate school arrived at my parents' home. I was happy but anxious too because, unlike all my friends who had now started working and had become independent members of society, I was going to continue my life as a student with no income, and continue to live off my parents and burden them with tuition and living expenses. That was intolerable to me. I couldn't even talk about this to my friends, with their lined-up jobs and twinkling eyes. After agonizing over it for a few days, I went home and opened up to my father.

"I am thinking of looking for work rather than going on to graduate school."

"Why do you say something like that this late in the game?"

"I am thinking of working a few years and then going back to graduate school. I am too ashamed to be always relying on family and never growing up."

"You don't have to worry about stuff like that. Different people lead different lives. You don't have to go out in the world at the same time or for the same reason as those around you. Don't hesitate; just do your best."

"But the tuition!"

"Don't worry about it. We aren't rich, but we'll manage your tuition."

We discussed it for about an hour. My father encouraged me by telling me not to worry, giving me permission not to give up on my dream to pursue the issues I wanted to pursue in graduate school. I remembered what my mother told me as a small child while we bathed together in the tub.

"Study a lot, because that will be your true fortune. You may lose your money or get conned out of it, but knowledge never diminishes. It gives you true wealth."

My parents had lost everything in the chaos of war, started over penniless, came to study in Japan and were overwhelmed with the duties of raising children. As much as possible, they gave us children the educations that were out of reach for them. It was partly in that spirit, I believe, that my father pushed me to go straight into graduate school. With that realization, I determined to repay their love by doing my best.

5 Off to Hong Kong, Off to America

Studying in Hong Kong

Graduate school presented me with my second chance to study abroad. My long-held dream of studying abroad prodded me to research and apply to every single study abroad scholarship program I could get my hands on. I was permitted to study abroad at the Chinese University of Hong Kong as an official international exchange student under the auspices of Japan's education ministry.

I had just entered graduate school and each day struggled with class preparations. I was excited about studying in Hong Kong all the same. I wondered how the trends I saw among the Chinese in Yokohama's Chinatown would manifest in other parts of Asia also experiencing turbulence. What were the leading Chinese businesspeople like in the rapidly expanding economies of the Four Asian Tigers (also known as the Four Dragons)—South Korea, Taiwan, Hong Kong, and Singapore? What were these business leaders doing? It was believed that most Chinese businesspeople in Southeast Asia were based in Hong Kong, but what kind of business were they doing? How did they self-identify? There was so much I wanted to know.

This was the first time I had ever lived in a majority-Chinese community. I had only ever known what it was like to live as a minority. In Hong Kong, I might be treated as belonging to the majority. Yearning for such a new experience, I wondered what it would feel like.

I arrived in Hong Kong in midsummer. I could hear Cantonese buzzing about my ears at the airport. It sounded completely different from the Mandarin that I spoke. I had known of course that the language was different, but I felt culture-shocked to discover that we were sometimes unable to communicate at all, despite our similar Chinese faces. The Cantonese I heard walking down the street sounded like fighting to my Mandarin ears. I was unable to ride a taxi properly.

After a week, I had to go to the airport to meet my parents who happened to be in transit on their way to China. My university friend told me how to get to the airport. "First take a train to Mong Kok Station [a busy commercial district like Times Square]. Then take a cab to the airport." I told the driver my destination in Mandarin:

"*Qingdao jichang.*"

"*Haa?*"

This was prior to the city's repatriation to China, so many taxi drivers did not speak Mandarin. I changed track. If Mandarin didn't work, maybe English.

"Please go to the airport."

"*Aaa?*"

The elderly driver sounded angry. He scolded me in an angry tone. In a panic, I stuck my arms out to the sides and flapped them like wings. Then, I took a wild guess as to what might be the Cantonese version of *jichang* (the Mandarin word for airport):

"*Gaichong, gaichong.*"

"*Haa?*"

His voice got louder, and he glared at me. Just at that moment, an airplane flew overhead. I squealed, "that!" and with all my might pointed up at it. At this new information, the driver yelled,

"It's *geicoeng*, not *gaichong!*"

I wanted him to leave it there, but during the whole ride to the airport the driver scolded me in difficult-to-catch, heavily Cantonese-accent Mandarin.

"Your Cantonese is really hard to understand. Don't speak anymore."

Inside, I thought: *What the …? You couldn't even catch my Mandarin or English!* On the outside, I pouted.

The different languages spoken by fellow Chinese stressed me. The crowds and myriad voices that reached my ear at the airport irritated me. I cut my way through the sea of faces, eventually arriving at an area near the gate. I sat on the floor, and read to calm my nerves while awaiting my parents' arrival.

After a spell, my parents exited the gate, beaming and pushing a cart full of luggage. I hadn't seen them for a long time. They were a bit surprised to see me sitting on the floor with a dejected expression.

"What happened? Why the face?"

I told them of the cab ride, how I couldn't communicate in Cantonese, and how I had been scolded during the trip to the airport. "Hahaha!" Baba let out his classic belly laugh. Mama said the whole thing was ridiculous but added, "It used to be worse."

If you couldn't speak Cantonese in Hong Kong in the past, you would be pretty much ignored at restaurants, they told me, and getting a meal was a regular rigamarole. They told me how my elder sister once brought home a Hong Kong boyfriend she had met at college in Taiwan and that my parents had trouble making conversation.

My father said: "China is a big place. The customs and languages people speak vary by region. So many different people show up to Chinese assemblies in Yokohama—like those from Guangdong and Shanghai—that the common language ends up being Japanese rather than Chinese."

Given that I was born and grew up in Japan, lived there for more than 20 years, and could never really identify myself as someone from that country, I was naïve to expect to be more comfortable in Hong Kong where Chinese were the majority. Entering this Chinese community had already brought me crashing against a rigid linguistic barrier.

A few days later, I returned to my university and met up with a friend during lunch break at the student canteen. I had just begun a weekly language exchange over lunch to learn Cantonese from Hong Kong students while teaching Mandarin and Japanese.

"Were you able to get to the airport?"

"More or less. But the taxi driver yelled at me. Told me not to speak Cantonese."

"What? Why?"

I told my friend about my conversation with the driver. She bopped me on the shoulder, body doubling over in laughter.

"Ahhhh. You said *that*, Lara?"

I had no clue why she was laughing so hard. Then, my friend calmed her breathing and stifled her laughter long enough to teach me the meaning of the word I had used for *airport*. In Cantonese, the sound *gaichong* means *chicken ranch*, and *chicken* can mean prostitute. A series of coincidences—the fact that I was flapping my arms to indicate airport, the fact that the location happened to be the Mong Kok district—had apparently combined to cause the confusion.

"Lara, good thing he didn't take you to a brothel!"

I now understood why the driver had loudly ordered me never to use Cantonese. I felt less humiliated but more mortified at my huge error.

Hong Kong: Getting in Touch with My Inner Japanese

For a time, I dared not say anything in Cantonese lest I commit another atrocious pronunciation faux pas. I usually got by, instead, with English and Mandarin. I couldn't keep up with the conversation of my friends who spoke freely in rhythmical Cantonese.

I used Mandarin during my interviews with Chinese businesspeople. This was obviously no issue with those businesspeople who spoke fluent Mandarin, but with those whose first language was Cantonese, I often used English instead of Mandarin. The sight of Chinese in the Chinese community communicating in English struck me as an objective, albeit amusing, reality. Hong Kongers likely identified me more as *someone from Japan* rather than a Chinese person. But because we couldn't communicate in our native language, they felt I was a foreigner.

Sometimes the businesspeople I interviewed would introduce me to their friends and families as "Ms. Chen from Japan. She speaks Chinese well." A grin and look of fascination would come over their faces. When I insisted on my Chinese identity, noting that I speak well because I am a *huaqiao* (overseas Chinese), they often asked me if there were many *huaqiao* in Japan. I knew that many Asians saw Japan as geographically close but psychologically remote. They generally knew more about Chinese migrants in the US than about those in neighboring Japan.

"Yes, there are a lot. There is a Chinatown and Chinese schools."

"Wow, is that so? But isn't it tough living in Japan?"

"Meh. But you know …"

They showed great interest when I discussed the situation in Japan, the Chinese living there, and what Chinatown is like.

"Still, your Chinese is really good. I'm shocked to hear someone from Japan speak so well."

At the end of the day, I was *someone from Japan*.

It was the same with a friend I made in Hong Kong. I worked on being able to open up to my friends, speaking not only Mandarin but also mastering Cantonese so I could get a little closer to my Hong Kong friends. I practiced the unfamiliar pronunciations and the tones, which differed subtly from Mandarin. My friends spoke to me patiently and slowly despite my terrible Cantonese and playfully corrected my pronunciation. They joked about my strenuous efforts to speak Cantonese:

"Lara's Cantonese is like baby talk. It's charming and adorable though."

I sulked. "Hey, I'm doing my best to speak!"

Some encouraged me. "Well, I think you learn faster than other Japanese people."

Of course, I would learn Cantonese faster than other friends coming from Japan. My Mandarin provided suggestive hints, and I could use Chinese vocabulary. It helped knowing Mandarin, but I flubbed Cantonese pronunciation big time.

Ultimately, my Hong Kong friends saw me as a member of the Japanese group. They often asked me about Japan—what songs are popular, celebrity gossip, manga, Disneyland.

But I wanted them to recognize me as Chinese, because my experience living as a minority in Japanese society made me want to experience living as a member of the majority. I chose to study in Hong Kong mainly out of an intellectual desire to learn about Hong Kong before its repatriation to China and because I figured that the urban network hub of Chinese entrepreneurs would facilitate interviews and broad-ranging research. I anticipated that as a Chinese woman, I would be in the majority.

But it didn't turn out that way. No matter how much I insisted on my Chineseness, regardless of how much I had Chinese consciousness cultivated in my family and behaved according to Chinese social customs, the truth was that the 20-plus years I had lived in Japanese society, with its cultural customs and norms, had enormously impacted the formation of my character.

I bowed when greeting people. I refrained from stating my opinion in class or public. These and other attributes caused my friends to see me as more culturally Japanese than Chinese. This was when I came to recognize aspects of myself that I had not seen while I lived in Japan.

I had always felt resistance toward Japan. I had maintained my identity by asserting my difference from the majority Japanese. I never truly felt at ease in the country where I was born and raised. I had always searched for a place to belong. I thought I would finally find peace in the Chinese community that was Hong Kong.

But it turned out quite the opposite. In Hong Kong, speaking about Japan taught me about myself and spurred conversation with my friends. That often put my heart at ease. I realized my unique identity would be forged by being Chinese but also talking about Japanese culture, customs, and society.

Many aspects of Hong Kong life bewildered and stressed me. At a dim sum restaurant, we grappled with a throng of fellow customers to get a seat. Getting a table and even the food took forever if we didn't assert ourselves. Table servers threw plates and teacups down on the table with a clamorous racket right in front of the customers, then in a poker face asked: "Which tea do you want?" Each time this happened, I wondered if I would be able to survive Chinese society.

Inside, I thought: *This kind of customer service would never happen in Japan.* I had internalized Japanese customer service norms.

For the first fortnight or so in Hong Kong, I was homesick partly due to the rain that continued day after day. But once the semester and classes began, I made new friends and came to enjoy my campus life in Hong Kong. Every day, a letter from my boyfriend arrived by airmail. The Internet was not yet ubiquitous in the mid-1990s, so we corresponded every day by letter and once a week by phone. His kind letters were dated and detailed like a diary. I loved letters in that style. They helped me visualize his far-away life.

In Hong Kong, I wanted to study overseas Chinese entrepreneurial networks, my graduate research topic, so I visited Chang Chak Yan (鄭赤琰), a specialist in ethnic Chinese migrants. I also joined his seminar class. In addition to the college classes, I made the most of the city's geography and found time to go out into the city, and to visit the Hong Kong General Chamber of Commerce and Chinese organizations to interview businesspeople.

While based in Hong Kong, I went to Malaysia, Singapore, Vietnam, and other neighboring countries; walked around each country's Chinese community; and interviewed Chinese businesspeople. The lifestyles of the Chinese migrants varied slightly depending on the country where they had ended up. But they shared a common language, so the various communities at times found ways to provide each other mutual assistance across national borders. I wanted to learn more about these Chinese networks. My study in Hong Kong was so satisfying that my ten-month sojourn ended before I knew it. After returning to graduate school in Japan, I used my research from the Chinese communities and commercial networks in Hong Kong and Southeast Asia in my master's thesis.

Later in my graduate program, I was determined to dig deeper in researching the Chinese migrants I had studied for my master's thesis. I wanted to spend a year in the States to develop my thesis before actually writing it. So, in the summer of 1996, I looked for a way to visit universities around the United States from Berkeley on the West Coast to Columbia University on the East Coast, for short-term research.

On a personal note, my emotional ties to my long-distance boyfriend had deepened by the time I had finished my master's thesis. The long-distance nature of our relationship was such that nobody would have been shocked if we had broken up. But for us, absence had indeed made our hearts grow fonder, but it was beginning to wear on us.

"Lara, don't go far away anymore."

He often said that to me after I got back from Hong Kong. I wanted to be together, of course. Yet I forged ahead with my plans to leave Japan again. He got a job at a major trading house.

"Let's go to the States together!"

"Come on, I just started."

I often said selfish things such as this. I knew that I was partially looking to lands outside of Japan because I was still convinced that I could never be treated equally in Japanese society. As a non-Japanese woman, I believed that I would never be able to do what I wanted to do. I was also driven by a desire to quench the unslakable thirst for knowledge that had seized me during my stay in Hong Kong.

In 1997, a letter arrived via airmail from Harvard University, accepting me as a visiting scholar.

Breaking Up

I had returned from Hong Kong to Japan. But in the summer of 1997, I was pulled irresistibly back to the US to continue my research. My boyfriend reluctantly sent me off, pretending to be calm because it was "for your advancement." I promised to come back in a year. Perhaps it was youthful naiveté, but I believed a year would afford me the time to develop my thesis, achieve something, and get back to Japan. He was busy every day as a young company man at a trading house dreaming of getting an overseas posting.

I became a visiting scholar at Harvard's Fairbank Center for East Asian Research. My goal was to develop a thesis that could explain my doctoral dissertation topic—Chinese entrepreneurial networks and identity. I wanted to model this complex topic as simply as possible. This was also a graduate student requirement to complete the doctoral dissertation. I took classes in politics, economics, anthropology, and other departments that I thought might relate to my topic, in an effort to absorb as much relevant knowledge as possible. I made appointments to discuss my topic with professors individually. I virtually lived in the library.

My days were busy, and only one thing caused me a lot of psychological tension. I had come to America, and once again found myself starting over from scratch, with no family and no old friends nearby. That was fine when I was engrossed in study, but then, out of nowhere, I would feel indescribably lonesome.

My boyfriend never failed to support me emotionally at these times, from far-away Japan. Our long-distance love entailed airmail correspondence and the occasional international phone call. As a student, I couldn't call so often. The 13-hour time difference meant we often missed each other's calls. He sent me many letters. I too sent him letters and picture postcards. His words were gentle and kind. He also wrote that we should be together upon my return to Japan. I was so happy.

I think it was about eight months after arriving in the States. Starkly contrasting the happiness his letters gave me, something was stirring up a tempest in my heart. My research was going nowhere. I needed to distill the essence of Chinese entrepreneurial networks and identity, but I couldn't get it. I couldn't come up with a proper thesis for my research into Chinese businesspeople. When was it that my return letters began to fill with confusion and lack of academic confidence? I also felt his growing stress.

"Lara, as a trading company man, I'm the one who should be running around the world, and you the student should be sitting in front of a desk. We're reversed for some reason. I'm always waiting for you to come back to Japan."

I had just assumed that becoming an academic was my calling. The original plan was to produce results in a year, meaning that I only had a few more months to go. But I felt as though I had accomplished nothing. My long list of tasks to complete was only getting longer. I knew there was no way for me to finish during the few remaining months. What would have been the point of all these years of work if I returned to Japan having achieved nothing?

It'll mean I came just to get away from Japan.
I can't give up now.
I can't go back to Japan like this.

The more kindness he showed in his letters, the more painful it was. After turning it over and over in my mind, I mustered my courage one day to call him.

"Actually, I have something to talk to you about."

"What is it?"

"I want to extend my research in the US for another year."

There was silence on the other end. I didn't realize how much that one statement would hurt him. It created a gulf between us.

"Didn't you promise it would be for one year? You can't extend it. I want you to come back right away."

"I really can't go back now. I haven't done anything. Just wait a bit longer."

"I can't wait any longer."

"I want to be with you too, but I will lose my confidence if I go back to Japan now."

"So what? I'll take care of you."
"So, *you* come here."
"You know I can't do that. I just started working for them."

This man was so important to me. I wanted to be with him if possible. But if I chose a life with him and gave up on my research, I felt that I would hate myself. Would I not regret such a decision? Wouldn't I end up blaming him? I asked myself these questions during the following painful, lonely days.

One day, he called me and spoke in a calm voice, a voice with an uncharacteristically icy tone.

"Lara, you have your own world."

I cried all night. I had thrown myself into what he had counseled me to do, finding "something that only I could do." Had I made a big mistake?

You have your own world.

His words reverberated in my mind for days and days. They well captured the weight of both my sadness at losing someone important who had supported me and of my questioning the meaning of my life up to that point.

My World

In my own way, I had acquired important things from the education I received at the Japanese university, my studies in Hong Kong, and my academic life. I acquired a great deal of knowledge and experience from lectures by celebrated professors, from discussions in classrooms and outside of them, and from interviews with the people I met in my fieldwork. Each interaction was new and stimulating. Over time my hunger for knowledge only grew. I went to every conference and workshop that held interest for me, wherever it was. I also researched what interested me. During free time after class, my place was in the library.

And now, all that devotion had caused the most important person in my life to feel outside of my orbit, to say, *you have your own world*.

It was as if my partner in a three-legged race had suddenly dropped out, and all that remained was emptiness. I endlessly questioned myself.

Was this all worth it?
Am I losing something inside me?
What should I do now?
Is moving forward as an academic the right path?
What is the point of my life?

I got a call from Christoph, a Russian-studies visiting scholar who had an office in the same building as the Fairbank Center. After more than 15 years of experience in Eastern Europe and Russia as a journalist covering popular culture, this Swiss man had come to Harvard to compile a book based on interviews about post-Soviet Russian society.

He often dropped by my first-floor office to ask me to go for a coffee.

We went to cafés, and on nice days bought coffee and relaxed on the campus lawn. He was an expert on Russian issues but also had vast knowledge about international issues in general. We discussed our research with one another.

We routinely went to the pool for a swim in the evenings and sometimes had dinner together. He was 17 years my senior and like an elder brother. He never treated me like a child or flaunted his vast experience. I respected and trusted him. He was the only one I could frankly confide in about the impasse I faced in my career—what I couldn't tell my research colleagues.

"I don't understand my future anymore."

"What do you mean?"

"I don't know what to do. I feel that even if I pursue research, for some reason I can no longer connect to the people around me. I don't even know what I should study. I don't know if I should continue to conduct research."

This phone conversation reminded me of the man in Japan I had just broken up with. Tears began flooding down my cheeks. Christoph spoke even more slowly and gently than usual.

"What are you talking about? The research you are doing is wonderful."

"I love the research too. So many books I want to read; so many lectures I want to attend. But something is wrong. Sometimes I wonder if it's ok to be satisfied with endless debate in the world of words. I no longer know what is really needed or even my own feelings."

I couldn't say anything more, and a long silence ensued. Then, Christoph spoke carefully.

"Lara, maybe what you are missing is the capacity to feel. Some problems can't be resolved just by thinking them through. It's important to see with your own eyes and to feel things organically. I've practiced journalism, but I am most fascinated by what people on the ground are thinking and how they are living. I feel that a nonchalant gesture or quip by flesh and blood people on the ground carries a more important message than any theory. I think academic research is wonderful, but I have a hunch that your doubts will be resolved if you look at the real world."

"You are very sensitive. I think maybe you are using reason to try to control fears that arise. Maybe you are too obsessed with pleasing others— being a good daughter for your parents or a good student for your academic advisor. You have to live true to yourself and for yourself. Likewise, with research—do only what you want to do."

I'm not sure I understood what Christoph was saying at the time, and I may not fully understand now. But I remember feeling that I had been given a hint about what to do about my stuck emotional state.

United Nations: Stateless Need Not Apply

Mulling over what Christoph had said to me, I asked myself what it means to feel with the heart rather than only think with the head. I began to observe myself closely, and found myself more frequently wishing that I could listen to my heart. Later, I thought as well about Christoph's comment about people *on the ground.*

A year after arriving in the US, I felt pressure to begin writing my doctoral dissertation, but also deeply uncomfortable about writing it. I felt an incongruity writing my dissertation before deciding if I even wanted this career path. Days passed without me typing the first word.

Can I rely on composition alone? What is the point of my studies without living there on the ground?

What did I want to do? How did I want to interact with society and people? I thought that finding a way to be useful to society was more important than my life as an academic. It was around this time that I began thinking about working for an NGO, foundation, or other international cultural organization. I began looking for a job online and was drawn to the United Nations.

As I mentioned in the preface, in the summer of 1998, I took a bus for four and a half hours from Boston to the UN Headquarters in Manhattan to try to get a job.

The sun blazed bright from a clear blue sky. The world's national flags fluttered in front of the UN building. I took a moment to gaze up at the lofty heights of the UN building and felt a yearning in every fiber of my body to work for the good of the world. I believed the UN existed to protect peace and the equality of humanity.

Why did I choose the UN? Partly because I could not see myself working for one country or at one organization. I had qualms—as a stateless Chinese born in Japan—about working as a Chinese national for China. I had doubts about working as a Japanese national for the benefit of Japanese society. Having come to the US, my place became even more ambiguous. At some point, a new consciousness emerged in my heart.

There is a job out there for me precisely because *I am stateless. I want to apply my situation to work in the real world.*

I scoured online job ads over the course of several days. UN job ads were updated every day. Areas of expertise, departments, and each job type were divided into detailed categories; with positions such as *human rights case officer* and *program analyst*. Each letter-number code on a long list referred to job information, including if the job was open. I jotted down the long code and job type of one that caught my eye. I held the note with the code written on it tightly in my hand.

I went to the UN personnel office, where many people awaited their turn. This truly diverse group in terms of skin color and spoken language examined files of job information laid out on the tables, as if they were on a treasure hunt. After what seemed like more than an hour, my turn finally came.

"I saw the number X ad. I would like that job."

From a thick file, the manager pulled out the recruitment specifications corresponding to the number I told him.

"For the post about refugee rights and educational assistance, right? Ok, so please show me your CV."

The UN's CV template form had fields for the applicant to fill in basic information—home address, place of birth, nationality, education and job histories, as well as skills, qualifications, and languages spoken. I had obtained and photocopied the form in advance, then practiced filling it in several times until I finally filled it in for real.

One field I left blank, though. I didn't know what to write in the field for nationality. I had never known what to do when I came to the nationality field.

Maybe I was a tad too optimistic. I believed the UN to be an institution whose role was to work for the peace and security of humanity, from a perspective that transcended nationality.

Surely, they would understand my stateless state. Hope mixed with trepidation, and with an anxious face, I handed over the document.

"So, you studied international political economy. You speak Chinese and Japanese."

"Yes."

"Born in Japan and a permanent address also in Japan."

"Yes."

"You left this field blank. So, your nationality is Japanese?"

"No…"

The interviewer took his eyes off the document to cast them at me instead. I enunciated clearly and proudly; it was the United Nations after all.

"I am an overseas Chinese living permanently in Japan. I hold a Republic of China Taiwanese passport. I didn't know what I should write there."

"You don't have Japanese citizenship?"

"No, I am a permanent resident. Sort of like a green card holder in the US."

"Oh. What about People's Republic of China citizenship?"

"No."

"Taiwan. It's not a UN member state."

I gathered that the mood of the conversation was not moving in a positive direction.

"Few can speak Chinese and Japanese both, but the citizenship issue will be an issue. You don't belong to any UN member state."

"Huh?"

I never imagined anyone would say that to me.

"Japan and China would both be fine, but in any event, you have to get citizenship first. Can you get citizenship, then reapply?"

"Citizenship?"

I couldn't believe my ears.

"In your case, Japan might be better. There are more posts available to Japanese nationals. We recruit UN staff through Japan's Ministry of Foreign Affairs, and they send them here. I think applying there would be the best shortcut."

For me, though, that would be rather the most roundabout detour. I felt a chill through my body.

But I'm here!

In my stateless state, I could find no place to belong even at the world's supreme organization aiming for global peace. Unpermitted even to apply for a job at the UN, I felt all alone in the world. I belonged nowhere in the world.

I don't remember what I was thinking during the next few days back in Boston, but I felt distracted.

A few days later, I met a man who had worked at the UN, through a former teacher of mine back at the University of Tsukuba. I told him about why I wanted to work at the UN, my upbringing, and what happened in New York.

"So, it's not ok to be stateless?" I asked.

"Of course! Also, I've never heard of being stateless."

"Doesn't the UN exist for the sake of world peace? Isn't it an institution that works for people's happiness regardless of nationality and national borders?"

"That may be the ideal, but …"

"Huh?"

"The UN is an institution that coordinates each nation's interests. Like arbitrating a conflict between two nations. What you say is indeed the ideal, but the real UN is more pragmatic. I think you are not really suited to the UN. You'd see if you worked there, but it's not a workplace where you can really pursue such ideals. It's not that simple."

I never imagined that you could not realize your desire for peace and equality even at the UN. It underlined for me again that there was no place for me.

Rainbow as Metaphor

I felt distressed for days after the UN incident. Another dream of mine lay shattered. The deep wound in my heart from my breakup had not yet healed, and my sense of isolation grew stronger. I had now been in the US for a year and a half. My goal of finishing the theoretical framework for my doctoral dissertation topic in one year had long ago expired. Just setting that unrealistic goal for myself had led to the loss of my confidence as well as the loss of an important companion.

I felt that I was hitting rock bottom. Often just walking down the streets alone brought tears streaming down my face. I didn't even have it in me to care about what the people passing by me thought. I couldn't get a grip on my own feelings, let alone adopt the theoretical mindset required for research.

I had no confidence in anything. I wondered what would happen to me. I was lost.

In that state of mind, I made a single promise to myself. *I will not go back to Japan until I finish my doctoral dissertation.* To be honest, it was more like, *I'd be too embarrassed to go back.* What excuse could I give to my parents and family who had supported me all this time, having achieved nothing? I'd be too embarrassed to meet my friends who were already out in the world working or to face the many people who had graciously agreed to be interviewed by me for my research.

The doctoral dissertation had to "contribute theoretically to scholarship." To be honest, I didn't really understand what that word *contribute* meant in concrete terms. But I wanted to construct a thesis such that it would well reflect the way of life of ethnic Chinese I had met, a thesis that was easy to understand and that left a deep impression on people.

How did the Chinese migrants I interviewed live? They immigrate overseas and start over penniless. They experience solitude and setbacks in a new land. They spare no effort to toil and struggle toward their goals. Chinese migrants finally build a foundation and gradually put down roots in their new land. While fondly remembering their home villages, they begin to feel affection for their country of residence. Though minorities, they develop a sense of belonging and build various networks precisely because they are minorities, they draw upon networks to get by, and deftly tackle the problems facing them as they overcome adversity.

These migrants construct insular networks upon the foundation of an exclusivist identity as Chinese, and these networks are deemed useful in business. But I learned from my research in different locations that real-life migrants don't always seize upon their Chinese identity. Rather, the stereotype conjured up by others begins to take on a life of its own, creating a gap between how they are seen and how they are. I wanted to capture this gap between how observers see Chinese migrants and how they really exist. Naturally, finding a thesis to describe that was no walk in the park.

I agonized over it day after day, but no good ideas came to mind. I wanted to explore the problem with my heart rather than my head, and so I started my own sort of training. Whenever I got stuck with my dissertation, I made myself take a walk, as a diversion and in order to change my environment. Breathing in fresh air with my whole body refreshed my mood and made me more and more attentive to the flowers, plants, and the animated beauty of nature that my eyes often overlooked.

Boston was still cold in March 1999, and as a temporary escape from thesis pressures, I went for a few days to Florida's Key West, the southernmost spot in the US. It was my first trip ever with no goal. I did nothing but sit on the beach and watch the sky and ocean. This too was for me part of my training.

Birds flew in formation over the clear, blue sky and the sea with its gently crashing waves. I went to the beach each day to gaze quietly at the sky, feeling Florida's warm sunlight and breeze throughout my whole body. One day, I stared at the setting evening sun. The brilliantly shining sun grew redder as it dipped toward the horizon. Moment by moment, the sun shimmered and burned as it quietly sank into the ocean. I sensed a wondrous force and message from that vision of nature.

The myriad objects in the universe take on many forms. The sun's existence is universally known. There is even a fixed mental picture of what it looks like. Yet even that sun and even the color of the light emitting from it change appearance depending on if the sun shines high in the sky at midday or sinks toward the horizon at dusk. I felt even that the Florida sun differed from the Boston sun. Maybe this quality applied likewise to the Chinese migrants. Maybe rather than capturing a rigid, fixed picture of them, I should aim to capture the subtle changes to their aspect.

Returning to Boston after my brief escape, I ruminated on how to unravel the many issues concerning Chinese migrants. My dissertation topic never left my mind, of course when I was at my desk, but also during swims and walks.

Crossing a bridge over the Charles River one day on my way home from my normal swim, I suddenly thought of a rainbow.

Ah, maybe I can use this to explain it.

I felt that maybe I might use the natural phenomenon of a rainbow to capture what I had been pursuing—the essence and salient features of Chinese entrepreneurial networks and identity.

Every day, I went to the library to binge-read an array of books about rainbows. I got many fresh ideas from materials outside my field, such as the natural sciences and literature. I drew out my ideas as they came to mind on a large piece of white paper and devoted myself to investigating in a style different from any previous approach that had depended on old language. I became giddy going about using a rainbow to create my own type of thesis on Chinese entrepreneurs.

As the thesis began to take shape, I began talking about rainbows to those around me. I spoke so much about rainbows that friends began calling me the rainbow lady.

My favorite space was Tealax, a teashop that offered hundreds of different teas. Even when having tea with friends on the weekend there, I spoke of rainbows.

"That's a unique way to conceptualize it."

"Really? You really think so?"

"I had no idea that Chinese people saw dragons in rainbows."

"I didn't know either until I researched it. The Qixi Festival [Jp: Tanabata festival] celebrates the meeting of the cowherd and the weaver girl. The two lovers' rendezvous was juxtaposed with copulating dragons. Villagers pray for rain and bountiful harvests at that time of year. They apparently believed that the rain followed by a rainbow was a blessing from the dragon deity."

"That's amazing."

I spoke of rainbows and Chinese entrepreneurs to other visiting scholars in my office.

"I see. The rainbow comes into being when the light of people's attention strikes the drops of sweat and tears shed by Chinese businesspeople. The rainbow takes the form of a bridge that represents their network, I suppose. It's a rainbow network."

"Yes. But rainbows are usually described in seven colors, right? In the same way, Chinese businesspeople seem all clumped together in a single group, but as individuals they have a broad range of aspects. An individual may sometimes behave as a Malaysian, their country of residence or citizenship, but be seen in Malaysia as ethnically Chinese. They come to cherish their ties to their home province of Guangdong, form an attachment to the UK if they study there, and create a network of university alumni. They form many additional ties too—with specialists, religions, and in-laws. I think this is the true nature of human beings."

"I see. That could work."

"Really? Could that work as a thesis? Maybe it would be weird to turn it into a thesis…"

"Not at all. There is a book out there with a title that is something like *Aesthetics and Politics* or *Metaphor and Politics*. Politics is often explained with formal theories, but that book is a scholarly work that advocates explaining politics using metaphors and beautiful expressions. That is pretty exciting. You might be able to use it, so I'll bring the book next time."

I decided to use the metaphor of rainbows in writing my dissertation. A rainbow is formed when light strikes drops of water. A rainbow is described in seven colors and forms a bridge-like arc. It appears and disappears depending on the angle from which it is viewed. Modeling these natural properties of rainbows enabled me to capture the salient features of Chinese entrepreneurial networks and identity and express their essence. Using the rainbow metaphor to explain the materials I had gathered and the research I had done enabled me to explain the essence of Chinese entrepreneurial networks and identity. What had been a confused jumble seemed to metamorphose into something accessible. I organized the rainbow metaphor portion as best I could, then consulted my academic advisor in Japan and my Harvard professor.

Why don't you give it a try?

Afterwards, I set about writing my thesis. No more hesitating. From the time I opened my eyes in the morning until closing them at night, I did nothing but write. I had my own seat in the Harvard Law School library. With my brutal schedule, I became well-versed in products designed to relieve shoulder tension. On the other hand, I didn't know that the ascetic ordeal of writing a thesis could be so fun.

That autumn, I finished giving an interim thesis report and returned to Japan to receive guidance from my professors. After my academic advisor gave me the go-ahead, I finished my final draft and submitted my doctoral dissertation at the beginning of 2000.

What My Heart Feels

I had submitted my thesis. But until the review, my job prospects and career were in limbo. I was temporarily relieved of the awesome pressure to complete my doctoral dissertation, but anxiety about the future remained.

What path should I take? How should I spend the final six months of my time at Harvard? I couldn't find answers to these questions.

One day, Christoph asked me to go to a movie with him. I, in fact, always felt a twinge of resistance about going to see a film. It might have been my mother's influence. My parents worked around the clock for their children. They had almost no experience with entertainment per se. During Mama's more than four decades in Japan, she never once, as far as I know, went to see a movie at a cinema.

I couldn't bring myself to pay to see a movie during my high school and college years as I would have felt guilty indulging in such an extravagance. That guilt seeped into many areas of my life, including going out with friends, having tea at a café, and even dating a lover. I would always find myself wondering how I would be able to explain to my struggling parents the fun time I was having.

But movies offered a world of wonder that readily transcended such feelings of guilt. The big screen captured people's lives in a way impossible with words—with facial expressions and visual messages. I gradually began to love watching movies. Although I still felt guilty for spending money, movies were one of the few things I simply could not go without. They were perhaps the thing that most comforted me during trying times.

On the way home after the movie, Christoph turned to me and said:

"Lara, some things cannot be described in words. Maybe you should get in touch with that?"

Having completed my thesis, I stood at the starting line of my academic career. Discomfort about just lining up beautiful words to write an abstruse dissertation, combined with the despair I felt after the UN, pushed reality in my face. I simply didn't care anymore.

Was my current path the right one? Could I really do what I wanted? What if I built up my dreams in my mind, only to be let down pursuing them? I would never be satisfied even if I achieved my goals and did what I needed to do to get there.

I had sought a way to come face-to-face with the way real people lived, accurately apprehend their thoughts and feelings, then convey them to others in an accessible way, in a way that touched their hearts. If possible, I wanted to do that kind of work.

Seeing movies more often helped me realize the importance of feeling with the heart rather than thinking with the head. A sense was slowly beginning to emerge that maybe I could reach people more if I express things in film.

I asked Christoph for advice.

"Interviewing Chinese migrants all over the place for my doctoral dissertation made me realize something."

"What?"

"Sometimes I felt so moved hearing their migration experiences and life histories. I feel that maybe it would have been better to show them telling their powerful stories and passions directly to people rather than through words on the page. That would probably reach more people's hearts."

"Maybe you are right."

"I want to make a documentary film. What do you think?"

"That's a good idea," Christoph said, raising his voice in apparent delight. I was unsure.

"But it'll be pretty tough."

"No problem," he said. "It'll work out if you give it a shot."

With all the events of the past year, it was as if I had been wandering around in darkness. The moment I heard Christoph's response, spoken with a smile, I began to see a faint light at the end of the tunnel.

Studying Film

Enchanted with movies, I began to go to them regularly—finding a good place in my studies to break, or after swimming—at the aged Brattle Theatre near Harvard or at the Harvard Film Archive, which preserved historical and academic works. I posted the monthly film schedule on the wall of my apartment and checked to see what film would be shown each day and which director would come to speak.

These cinemas showed different films every day. At the Brattle Theatre, a little art house with about 60 old, wooden seats that creaked and were covered in the *de rigueur* crimson velvet, each day of the week was devoted to selected works on the same theme or by the same director. Works depicting the life of a 1970s Italian artist or China's Cultural Revolution offered a flavor distinct from ordinary Hollywood fare. My friends and I had a set post-movie routine of going to a café where we would discuss the film.

As I further considered the idea of shooting my own documentary, I started to research filmmaking schools and classes. To get information on films and documentaries, I gathered materials and went to workshops where directors talked about film productions and techniques.

One winter day, I found out that there was going to be a workshop run by an NGO that used documentary film to promote human rights. I headed over to the Harvard Kennedy School. The university's department for politics majors drew diplomats and government officials from around the world. It was the perfect place for them to expand their personal connections with people from other countries. Guest lecturers active in the international scene such as government officials and activists were often invited to speak there.

The head of one organization used film to introduce their activities. I listened to her rapid-fire English, careful not to miss a word. The NGO was formed by activists who took and edited footage in a documentary style to report the situation on the ground where they were active.

These films captured the truth about societies we could never know about in our ordinary lives, such as films of people living in dangerous war-ravaged zones, footage taken surreptitiously in East European brothels, and scenes showing negotiations between underground human traffickers. They edited the footage and released them over the Internet. The NGO did all this in order to call for the protection of human rights.

They spoke to us about how they reported stories, what points to be careful about, and what problems they had. They risked their lives to cover events, going under cover with hidden cameras embedded in their clothes, lugging heavy cameras while dodging bullets. Only women could enter some areas, such as the confined spaces where sex workers waited on standby, while a man's strength was required for other kinds of reporting. Failed attempts at reporting were a daily occurrence, yet they risked bodily injury. Many of their reports made me wonder why they would go to such lengths. The head of the NGO said,

"We must start by raising awareness about what is happening. The lack of exposure often makes it impossible to do anything, particularly with human rights issues."

This is it!

The workshop was followed by a Q&A. I asked what kind of members were running the organization and what kinds of abilities were needed to become a member.

The organization was obviously struggling financially. They said they rented a small office. Most members apparently had experience with film reportage. Journalist aspirants had joined as volunteers.

I wanted to shoot a documentary. I was making a radical break away from my academic life towards film production.

I learned that New York University had a great film production department. Thinking I could start by taking a master's course in film after finishing up with my doctoral program, I went to get an information pamphlet. But I immediately ran into a roadblock. The tuition was written on a paper insert in the pamphlet. It stunned me. Annually, it was equivalent to several million yen (tens of thousands of US dollars). To carry on with my studies, I would need living expenses for New York. Pushing 30, I had to think about income, including getting a job. *No way in hell.* Not to mention that my parents who didn't even watch movies would never accept such a career path for me.

Luckily, soon after arriving in the United States, I had received monthly financial aid given to graduate students aiming for an academic career. The assistance, given to me as a special researcher of the Japan Society for the Promotion of Science (JSPS), enabled me to continue my research. Without that aid, I would have had to live off my parents as the US does not permit you to work on the visa given to visiting scholars.

I hesitated a little. Although I had finally written my doctoral dissertation, venturing into yet another educational direction would mean only that my costs would grow. But also, I realized that I had very little time left before I was no longer eligible for scholarships. So, I applied, but understood that if I weren't to get in, I might end up with literally no income and without belonging anywhere.

Working on Site

I wasn't about to give up on the idea of filmmaking, but if I didn't find a professional path, I would not be able to even discuss such dreams. I needed to find a job. I told myself that I couldn't always get to do what I wanted. Better to explore a range of options rather than narrow them by persisting on only one path. There were many ways to realize my aspirations.

I visited and wrote to several organizations, including one that helped immigrants in Italy and a US NGO. I knew that I simply had to get involved in work *on the ground* where I could encounter flesh and blood people struggling with national borders, citizenship, and race, such as work on immigration and refugee issues.

The sad result was that some organizations simply ignored me while others sent letters saying, "unfortunately, we have no openings."

Archbishop (later Cardinal) Stephen Fumio Hamao (d. November 8, 2007) had helped me out back in the day, at a church in Yokohama, and now chaired a council for migrants at the Vatican. I sought advice and decided to visit the archbishop in Italy as well as organizations in several European countries. Europe is not so far from the US, after all.

With my passport, I had to get a Schengen visa to travel to Europe. The Schengen visa permits free travel to all countries that are signatories to the Schengen Agreement. All you need to do is get the visa from the embassy of the first country you plan to enter. It's good for a limited time in all member countries. Crossing borders is a straightforward affair for people from countries with no issues, but for me who always had trouble due to my statelessness, this visa could save me so much trouble. Nearly all EU countries were signed on to the deal, but for others, like the UK, Ireland, and Switzerland, a separate visa was required for stateless people. I inquired about the visa application process, something that I had become familiar with, gathered up the required documents, and prepared to go apply for what was for me, a very stressful affair.

I collected the documents required by the embassy of each country to get a visa. These included plane tickets to each country I would visit, local hotel reservations, invitation letters from friends I would visit, and documents proving my bank account balance.

Fortunately, Italy had a consulate in Boston, but to get visas for Switzerland and the UK, I had to take a bumpy four-and-a-half hour bus ride to New York. It took a few days between handing over my passport and getting the visa issued. Each visit meant a nine-hour roundtrip and a 60-dollar bus fare. The embassies held the passport during the wait, so I couldn't move forward with my visa applications to other countries. After spending time and money to get all these documents together, I again faced the stress particular to my state of statelessness.

I was relieved when the Swiss and UK visas finally arrived. I put my resume in a file and made appointments with organizations that supported local refugees and immigrants.

I first headed to Rome, and to Vatican City, which sat in the center of the capital. This tiny independent city state has an area of just 0.44 square kilometers and runs 1 kilometer east-west and 850 meters north-south. The pope serves as head of state and not only rules the 800 residents of the Vatican, but also wields enormous influence as the central focus for Catholics around the world. It has government agencies in addition to the Holy See, the office of internal affairs, the Department of State, and nine ministries. It has a court, a dozen councils, and a secretariat. Archbishop Hamao chaired a council for migrants. This council supports migrants, refugees, those involved in international transport and travelers. It also cares for sailors, Roma nomads, circus troupes and others who are continuously on the move.

I treaded swiftly over Rome's cobblestone streets, observing a swirl of cadenced spoken voices; a lovely, smiling old lady selling multicolor flowers; and a middle-aged man wearing a shirt unbuttoned down to his chest, who grinned at me teasingly. I found the sign for the council and ducked through a gate. Like that, I had crossed from Italy into a different sovereign state. Archbishop Hamao smiled as he greeted me.

"Oh, glad you could make it. You got here alright."

"Thank you for writing me the invitation letter."

"But it's still so inconvenient."

"Yes, it sure is. It's tough because I needed to get a visa for each place. It's a hassle every time I travel overseas."

"You don't have Japanese citizenship?"

"That's right. I'm stateless. I use my Taiwanese passport whenever I go overseas.

"You're stateless? So, travel must be tough since you need a visa for each destination."

"Yes, doesn't your council help stateless people?"

"Well, I haven't yet heard much about that kind of case. Most people don't even know stateless people exist."

"Yes, I think that's true. So, please do something about the problem of stateless people."

In addition to the archbishop himself going where migrants and immigrants were in order to assist them, he also traveled to attend international conferences in different countries. This council had several departments, and case officers hooked up with organizations and networks to run assistance programs. Archbishop Hamao introduced me to the council's activities and to people working at affiliated organizations.

I visited several organizations. The people there traveled to Africa, South America, and elsewhere. They dazzled and filled me with envy.

The head of one organization aiding refugees told me,

"You have a PhD? So, you can teach at a university. Our work is to go out to the sites, and that takes strength. You might not be suited to it."

"I think research and on-site work are both important. At this stage, I would prefer to experience the work out in the field."

"Hmm, I wonder about that. You might be more suited to editing the magazine that we publish."

"No, I want to go out into the field on site."

"We have no openings right now. Let's think about it if one comes up."

I often got that kind of response; they wouldn't take me on as somebody ready to go. I realized my limitations, and understood that partially due to my citizenship issue, I wouldn't be able to rush out into the field to work on site.

Applying for Japanese Citizenship

I could find no place to call my own, even in the US or at the UN. I carried an ROC passport for *huaqiao* in lieu of a recognized one since I was stateless. This meant that I needed to get a visa to go to any country in the world and assemble an array of documents each time I entered or exited the country. Whether I could even go to a country depended on whether the government agency inspecting my documents let me through and gave me a visa. It limited my ability to rush into the field to help immigrants and migrants on site. And yet, I had become obsessed with film reportage. I had been searching for some different activity, a way to resolve what couldn't be resolved by research and writing alone.

I was considering reformulating my plans even after returning to Japan. Maybe I should go to film school with the goal of shooting a documentary. Or should I get a job? Or embark upon a new research project. Although I had no idea what to do, I was grasping for a vision.

The winter after the UN incident, I used the Christmas and New Year's holidays to go home to Yokohama. It was my first time seeing my family's faces after such a long period of only speaking on the phone. Seeing them in the flesh naturally caused me to weep, tears of relief more than joy.

Having my family nearby calmed my heart, after all. I must have been exhausted from living alone in the US. The warmth of my family's embrace soothed me.

I had a purpose for this trip home.

After I was told that I couldn't get a UN job, I came to understand that my stateless status would limit what I could do working on site for a US or Italian NGO. Although I had grown up in Chinatown as Chinese, I determined to acquire Japanese citizenship. I knew without asking that my parents would not embrace such a move.

Acquiring Japanese citizenship would sweep away the problems I had thus far encountered. Going overseas would become easier. I would be able to apply openly for jobs too. My feelings wavered between discomfort at the thought of becoming Japanese and the convenience of acquiring Japanese citizenship.

For my first family meal in a long time, we sat at our customary seat in the back of my parents' restaurant. That first taste of their home cooking in a year made me forget the winter chill and warmed my body and mind. I broached the subject in a softish voice.

"I am thinking of getting citizenship, as a matter of fact."

My elder brother responded: "Citizenship, Lara? Which country's citizenship?"

"Japan's."

My brother surprised me with: "I'm thinking about it too, as a matter of fact."

My next older brother was eight years older and worked in Yokohama. For a while after graduating from National Taiwan University, he stayed in Taiwan and taught at our brother-in-law's Japanese language school. After that, he returned to Japan and worked at the Chinese Guild Hall Foundation (Zhonghua Huiguan), rather than getting a job at a Japanese company.

My brother too despised the inconvenience of having to apply for visas and visit each country's embassy whenever he traveled overseas. If he got Japanese citizenship, he would avoid all that hassle. He would save time and money, too. Moreover, my brother was naturally interested in Taiwanese politics but also in Japanese politics. He knew or befriended many politicians. He surely wasn't happy that his statelessness put him in a position that prevented him from voting and running in elections.

"Let's go research it together."

"But where should we go?"

I was so ignorant that I didn't even know where to go to apply for naturalization.

"The Legal Affairs Bureau."

"We have to go all the way to Kasumigaseki in Tokyo where all those ministry and agency buildings are?"

"No, there's a government office in Yokohama with a Legal Affairs Bureau, so we can find out stuff there."

"Really? I didn't know that."

A voice interrupted us: "What are you two talking about? What do you mean you are going to get Japanese citizenship?"

My mother wore a stern expression that she had rarely shown her children. She seemed as if she were about to jump up and pound her fist down on the table. Hearing us talk about acquiring Japanese citizenship made my mother's blood boil. We knew it would happen, but seeing her right in front of us raising her voice made me cower in fear.

"Do you have any idea what Mama and Baba went through raising you?"

My brother and I could say nothing in response.

That winter vacation was for me the worst.

I was supposed to come home after being away so long and spend a wonderful time with my family. But now my mother seemed more distant than when I had been in America. It was all my fault. I couldn't even greet her with a casual *ohayo* (good morning). I couldn't meet her eyes. Even under the same roof, the air weighed heavy. The year wound down under those circumstances.

What I felt in the States was perhaps an illusion. Maybe a family gets along better with a bit of distance and freedom from each other. That's the thought that ran through my mind. I couldn't seem to be able to fix what had broken down in my relationship with my mother. My selfish, stubborn character was also a misfortune. It was precisely because they were my family that I had trouble apologizing and conveying my true feelings.

I knew that looking into what I needed to get citizenship irritated my mother, so my brother and I did it stealthily. One day near the end of the year, my brother and I went to ask the Legal Affairs Bureau how to apply for naturalization. My brother told me to go in first while he parked the car.

I got on the elevator alone. In the closed space, I feared others would be able to hear the rapid palpitations of my heart. I arrived on the fifth floor. With my heart beating hard, I entered the office of the citizenship section and stood in a booth. A young staffer sitting at the frontmost table indicated a notebook and spoke in slow, easy-to-understand Japanese.

"You want to discuss naturalization, right? Please write down your name and current citizenship."

"Ok."

I wrote down my name and in the field for citizenship put *stateless*. The staffer said,

"Stateless? Um, put down your current citizenship."

"Yes, I'm stateless."

I had answered self-assuredly. Although it always happened, I hated public offices and government agencies. In such an atmosphere, I got nervous and spoke in a stiff manner. The staffer scratched his head.

"Ok, then, please show me your alien registration card."

I took out my wallet from my purse and looked for my alien registration card. But I couldn't find it. Inside, I panicked.

Immigration Control Law requires all foreigners in Japan to carry their alien registration card, on their person, at all times. On the street, you must present it to police officers if they ask. You can be fined and even jailed for not having it on you. That's why after getting my alien registration card, I always put it in my wallet and kept it close whenever I went out.

But I had grown accustomed to my lifestyle in the US. There is no alien registration card there. I only needed it when going through customs on my way back to Japan. While in the States, it would have been a nightmare to lose it. That's why while I was in the US, unlike in Japan, I kept the bare minimum in my wallet, including cash.

I had started keeping my alien registration card in my passport case along with my passport. At customs, foreigners had to show the card along with the passport. When I got back to Japan a few days earlier, I went through customs then inserted the alien registration card into the pages of my passport, which went into the passport case. I quickly went to get my luggage. I had lacked the mental acuity to think to transfer the card to my wallet.

"I'm sorry. I appear to have forgotten it at home. I just got back from abroad and was keeping it with my passport…"

The friendly staffer changed tone.

"What? You know you must carry it all times, don't you?"

I shrank.

"What is written under citizenship on your alien registration card?"

"Stateless."

"Wait there a moment."

The staffer went into the back and explained the circumstances to his superior. After a bit, an older staffer emerged.

"Are you Chinese?"

"Yes."

"You are a *huaqiao* Chinese migrant, right? Stateless?"

He seemed to understand my circumstances. My brother finally arrived, having parked the car.

"This is my eider brother. We came together for the consultation."

"Elder brother, do you have your *gaito* alien registration card?"

"Yes, I have it."

My brother quickly pulled out the card and showed it to them. The young staffer standing next to him peeked at it. The veteran staffer spoke.

"Yes, stateless. You will both apply?"

My brother promptly responded: "Yes. We came to consult about what we should do for that."

"Ok, so, both of you come into this room over here."

After we entered and sat down, the staffer spoke.

"But you must carry your *gaito* at all times. We'll overlook it this time, but technically, it's illegal."

"Yes, I'm sorry."

"Lara, you didn't have your card?" Then, to the staffer, "We're sorry. My little sister just got back from a long stay in the US."

"Then, I need you to tell me basic information needed for naturalization. Where were you born? What is your job? Where do you live?"

The staffers asked many questions about our background and took notes in a business-like manner.

Changing citizenship was a big deal for me. A giant wall stood in my way to naturalizing to Japanese citizenship, and my own dread added another rough, thick stone to that wall. My big brother being there gave me comfort. In turn, we explained our respective situations. For my brother, that meant business details and our family. For me, it was living in the US as a student of a Japanese graduate school.

"For the older brother, it's possible. But for the younger sister, this won't work. She has been overseas for almost two years. You can't be overseas all the time like this and then try to get Japanese citizenship. You can't apply until you come back to Japan and live here for at least five years. This is a condition for application to naturalize."

He handed me a one-page document listing the prerequisites for applying. The Nationality Act stipulated:

Article 4 (1) A person who is not a Japanese citizen (hereinafter referred to as "foreign national") may acquire Japanese nationality through naturalization.
(2) To undergo naturalization, permission of the Minister of Justice shall be obtained.

Article 5 (1) The Minister of Justice may not permit naturalization for a foreign national who has not met the following conditions:
(i) Having continuously had a domicile in Japan for five years or more;
(ii) Being twenty years of age or more and having the capacity to act according to his/her national law;
(iii) Being a person of good conduct;
(iv) Being able to make a living through his/her own assets or abilities, or through those of a spouse or of another relative through his/her making a living;
(v) Not having a nationality or having to give up his/her nationality due to the acquisition of Japanese nationality; and
(vi) On or after the date of promulgation of the Constitution of Japan, not having planned or advocated the destruction of the Constitution of Japan or the government established thereunder with force, and not having formed or joined a political party or other organization planning or advocating the same.

The staffer said: "Younger sister, you are ineligible due to the first condition."

"I was born and grew up in Yokohama!"

"Maybe so, but now you don't live in Japan. Let me ask you: Why do you want to acquire Japanese citizenship? Don't you think it's strange? If you want to become Japanese, wouldn't you live and work in Japan?"

Here too, a clear distinction was being made between me and Japanese people.

"You are also ineligible because you don't have any income. You said you were a student? You don't meet the conditions unless you get a proper job and income. It would be different if you naturalized as a family, but…"

Anger boiled up in my heart. I wanted to stand right up and leave that place. My brother picked up on my feeling and gave me a knowing look. I think my brother spoke with the staffers for nearly an hour. I had lost my cool and couldn't think about anything.

You can't become Japanese without income? But it's almost impossible for a foreigner even to get a job at a Japanese company. What would happen to our family, which all this time has paid taxes to the Japanese government?

All kinds of anger swirled about in my head. I felt so frustrated and humiliated.

The staffers explained the required documentation while marking this and that with red ink, and the consultation ended.

We thanked them, stood up, and just as we were about to leave, one of them said: "Ah, I'll give you one piece of good news, younger sister. You mustn't marry a foreigner. You should assume you can only get Japanese citizenship if you marry a Japanese man. That would be a good shortcut. That way may not work for your older brother, though."

He probably said it with kindness in his heart. But, for me, what he said was utterly humiliating. This country wanted to take away all my options, even whom I marry? I felt insulted. I couldn't even cry. The anger in my belly seemed to transmit down my legs and concentrate in the arches of my foot, so much so that I thought a hole might open up in the ground.

For much of the trip home, I seethed and couldn't say anything. My brother offered words of comfort.

"I told you it'll be ok."

"At the end of the day, I should never have considered naturalizing. I can't assume they will give me Japanese citizenship. It's all so stupid!"

I had returned to my previous stubborn stance toward Japan.

I regretted going to the Legal Affairs Bureau, particularly since it had caused me to fight with my mother and make her feel miserable. I was ashamed of myself for trying so hard to gain Japanese citizenship that I had abandoned my Chinese identity, which had moored my parents and concentrated their efforts to raise me. Come to think of it, if I hadn't gone overseas and hadn't dreamed of working at an international institution, I never would have even considered naturalization.

Until recently, I had felt the same as my mother about refusing to naturalize. I would hold my head high and live as a Chinese person despite the adversity we experienced as a minority in Japanese society. That enigmatic identity had steeled our family bond. I was so pathetic for having mustered my courage then, only to discard my self-esteem now and end up like this.

"What will we do? It's impossible for me. I would have to return to Japan and stay here for five years! Even then, there's no guarantee my citizenship application will be accepted. If that's the way it is, then maybe it would be easier just to immigrate to a different country. Maybe I should stay in the States."

I had initially felt that maybe I should come back to Japan after staying abroad for so long. That feeling evaporated now that my future was up in the air.

"Quit being dumb. There are all sorts of things we can do depending on how we interpret those conditions and laws."

"Yeah, but…"

"You really are naïve. In that kind of situation, just say yes, shut up, and listen. Getting pissed off at them doesn't help anything. I wondered what would happen with your attitude back there. You're overly earnest at the wrong time. You've got to wise up."

My brother was right on one point. The staffer wasn't being mean to me intentionally, and dealing with government officials in a flexible way was a necessary point of wisdom for surviving as an immigrant or minority. I got a sense of that from my interviews with Chinese migrants that I had done for my doctoral dissertation. Chinese migrants had struggled and endured a great many things in order to survive, to achieve their goals, and to protect their children's futures.

I realized that what my brother was saying fit with the way Chinese migrants lived flexibly while adapting to the environment, circumstances, and those they spoke to.

The 30 to 40 million Chinese émigrés living in countries around the world adapted their citizenship and status to their environment. Yet, they managed to retain their Chineseness. I understood this as an issue for the world's Chinese diaspora but was not yet able to let that inform me about my own problems, particularly as they related to my life in Japan.

For a moment, I felt as if I could objectively see what citizenship meant and how distant it was from my own identity. But it was only for a moment. Soon, that complex mix of hatred and affection I felt for Japan bubbled up again in my heart.

After everything, I decided to give up on acquiring Japanese citizenship. More precisely, I had no choice but to give it up, at least for the time being. To be honest, my outrage was mixed with relief. But I simply could not overlook how the Japanese government dealt with issues related to foreigners and especially to stateless residents. It was a problem I had long avoided because it hit too close to home, but at that point I felt strongly that once finished with my doctoral dissertation, I should research stateless residents in Japan.

6 Learning about Statelessness

Other Stateless People

The issues confronting stateless residents and Japanese citizenship issues for foreigners in Japan were close to home, making me reluctant to choose them as research topics. I felt it would rub salt in my own wounds. Just as I had understood the difficulty of investigating *huaqiao* in Japan, the issue of citizenship in Japan was a sensitive topic for me, and felt impossible to analyze dispassionately.

But my friends urged me to study statelessness, maybe because I spoke about it so openly and sometimes humorously. I always rejected their suggestions.

"Lara, it's definitely interesting. You've got to write a book!"

"You say it's interesting. But, for me, it's really difficult. Everybody says, 'oh, you should write a book' as if it's nothing, but put yourself in my shoes."

When friends introduced me to other friends at cafés and parties, I often related episodes related to my statelessness, like the time I got trapped in the airport. The more I spoke of my stateless experiences, the more I too, slowly but surely, came to have interest in the issues faced by stateless residents and citizenship problems in Japan. I learned how to see it not as my personal problem, but more as an issue of the state and society. I then came up with some odd but fascinating questions.

What is a nation state?
What are national borders?
What does citizenship mean?
What props up our identity?

These profoundly fundamental questions boiled down to inquiring into the relationship between the individual and the nation state. I was unraveling the tangled knot inside me thread by thread.

I began to see the stateless as people who negate the ordinary quotidian existence that most citizens take for granted. It seemed as if stateless people sighed impotently, mocking the nation state's contradictions, and sneering at the meaninglessness of the nation state and its borders.

But much later I realized that stateless people were also the ones who organically understood the awesome power of the nation state, national borders, and citizenship. Perhaps more than anybody, they were the ones who lived in fear and at the mercy of these concepts. I came to understand that stateless people often have a strong sense of nationalism and integrity.

I hardly knew all that at the time. I researched materials out of a new, simple desire to learn about stateless people. When looking for books at the library for my doctoral thesis, I had always searched expressions like *overseas Chinese* or *network*. Now, I began searching terms like *stateless* and *nationality*. Sometimes using the keyword *stateless* produced no results. Even when I got a hit, the book often had nothing to do with stateless people. The topic had remained largely untouched. This fact spurred me on more than ever to find out what kind of stateless people exist and how they ended up stateless.

To start with, my desire to learn about stateless residents of Japan galvanized me to start my research. I hadn't felt like studying or doing anything at that time, feeling pretty disgusted with myself. For several months after finishing my doctoral dissertation, I fell into a funk and my thirst for knowledge receded. The statelessness theme got me back on my feet.

Research on Japan's Stateless Residents

I decided to start my research on stateless residents of Japan and in autumn 1999 I became a visiting scholar at Harvard Law School's East Asian Legal Studies Program. I had researched Chinese and other migrants. But that topic didn't extend to citizenship and other legal issues because I focused on economic and identity themes. I discovered a huge gap between economic globalization and globalization in a legal sense. I wanted to approach migration and identity issues from different angles.

In March 2000 in San Diego, I gave a joint presentation on Citizenship and Japan's Ethnic Chinese with two friends at a conference of the Association for Asian Studies. One researched American war brides, the other, Filipino migrant workers. I touched upon the issue of statelessness for the first time ever.

After that, I spoke about statelessness every time I met anyone. Sometimes, I shared the episode of when I was unable to enter either country, other times I showed my alien registration card upon which was written *stateless*. A professor who had come from Japan as a Harvard visiting scholar gave me some good information.

"I've heard there are people in your position in Okinawa. I think they are called Amerasian."

I immediately began researching Okinawa's stateless residents.

Amerasians are children born from American and Asian parents. In most cases, the American father came to Asia with the military and met a local woman. Amerasians tend to be concentrated in areas near current or former US military bases, such as Okinawa or the Philippines. There are Amerasian schools where teachers try to instill in children an identity not as half-breeds (*hafu*, as they are often described in Japan) but rather as *double breeds* (*daburu*). They want to encourage the children to self-identify in a more positive light (double, rather than half). Before Japan amended its Nationality Act in 1984, many Okinawan Amerasians ended up stateless.

That amendment was a big step for those who were disadvantaged in terms of gaining citizenship. It ended the patrilineal *jus sanguinis* principle of citizenship acquisition in favor of the *jus sanguinis* based on both parents.

In most cases, our citizenship is decided at birth. Of course, we might later lose that citizenship or gain a new one by taking certain procedures. Nationality laws vary from country to country. And there are two main citizenship determining principles: *jus soli* and *jus sanguinis*.

The *jus soli* (right of soil) principle determines the child's citizenship based on the country of their birth. Children born in the US and Australia become American or Australian regardless of their parents' nationality. In addition to countries that practice Anglo-American law, countries that receive large numbers of immigrants also adopt the *jus soli* principle—including Argentina, Brazil, and Chile.

The *jus sanguinis* (right of blood) principle determines the child's citizenship based on that of the parents. If your parents are Japanese citizens, then you automatically become Japanese. This principle is practiced in continental European countries like Germany and Italy, as well as East Asian countries like China, Japan, South and North Korea.

The determining factor for *jus sanguinis* may be the father alone or both parents. Some countries adopt the patrilineal version to avoid dual citizenship when parents have different nationalities.

Some countries that apply the *jus soli* principle adopt *jus sanguinis* in some specific cases, while other *jus sanguinis* countries adopt *jus soli* in exceptional cases. Some countries like Canada and Mexico use both in parallel. It becomes clear that historical contingency and circumstances have determined in large part the national law enacted in each country, resulting in an enormous variety of rules to determine citizenship. Thus, with more and more international marriages and migration in modern society, factors to determine a child's citizenship have become extremely complicated.

A married couple, both with Brazilian citizenship, give birth to a child in Japan. Japan's *jus sanguinis* principle means the child will not get Japanese citizenship and will be registered instead as a Brazilian national. But Brazil uses *jus soli*, meaning the child cannot get Brazilian citizenship, having been born abroad. In this case, the parents can go to their embassy or consulate and send a registration of the child's birth back to Brazil. The child can acquire Brazilian citizenship despite being born abroad. But, if they *don't* send that registration, they will lose the ability to get the child Brazilian citizenship, despite *Brazilian citizen* being written on the child's alien registration card. The child becomes effectively stateless.

What about the reverse case? Two citizens of *jus sanguinis* countries (such as Japan) have a child in *jus soli* Brazil. Despite the parents' Japanese citizenship, the child will become a Brazilian national. The child can also acquire Japanese citizenship because the parents are Japanese. But Japan doesn't recognize dual citizenship, so the child loses Japanese citizenship and keeps only Brazilian citizenship unless the parents submit a notification of intention to retain Japanese nationality to the Japanese embassy or consulate, within three months of the child's birth. The child becomes a dual national but must make a choice when they reach adulthood.

These two citizenship-determining principles produced the many stateless Amerasians living in Okinawa. US military men from the base on Okinawa often date or marry local Japanese women. According to US nationality law based on *jus soli*, for a child born from such a union outside the US, the American parent must prove a minimum period of residence in the US in order to get the child US citizenship. If the American father doesn't fulfill that requirement, the child born in Japan cannot get US citizenship.

Japan determined citizenship using the patrilineal *jus sanguinis* principle until amending the nationality law in 1985. There is a common notion that if the father is American and the mother is Japanese, the child's citizenship becomes that of the father. That means the child becomes stateless, what are called *de jure* stateless children because they are ineligible for any country's citizenship due to the peculiarities of legal regulations.

There are also *de facto* stateless children. In some cases, the American father leaves his wife and children in Japan and either returns to the US or disappears altogether. It's difficult to prove the required period of residence in the US for the purpose of acquiring US citizenship. As a result, the child can no longer obtain a birth certificate from the US government and becomes in effect stateless. According to Kiyoko Kinjo and Yasuhiro Okuda, in Okinawa, the number of *de facto* stateless children outnumbers the number of *de jure* stateless children.

Okinawans

I got back to Japan in the fall of 2000, after completing my research at Harvard. I was applying for a postdoctoral fellowship from the Japan Society for the Promotion of Science (JSPS) on the theme of Borders and Identity for People without Borders. If I got it, I hoped to get up and running with my research on statelessness and, if possible, to be posted overseas to study film at New York University. I had a strong desire to express myself not just through my thesis but also through film, just as I had felt when I finished my doctoral dissertation in the US.

Fortunately, I was accepted as a research fellow at the end of 2000, and the following spring I began my research under a professor in the Department of Cultural Anthropology at the University of Tokyo's Graduate School of Arts and Sciences. My graduate school friends, while finishing up graduate school, were desperately trying to get jobs and part-time teaching positions. My advisors and senior classmates, who had always taken good care of me, were concerned about me upon my return from the US and secured me a job as an adjunct professor. I taught Chinese twice a week at a university in Tokyo. Since I took the adjunct professor post, I wouldn't be able to leave Japan for a while, so I had no choice but to postpone studying film in the States.

Even after returning to Japan, I often went to the movie theater. One day, among the dozens of flyers lined up near the exit of a cinema, I found a flyer for a film school. The location was just above the movie theater, and classes were held just once a week. I thought I could take the class in parallel with my research at the University of Tokyo and my work as a part-time lecturer. The school was attached to a movie theater that showed some of my favorite documentaries. I thought it perfect and started attending in April. Piece by piece, I got a camera, a tripod, and other necessary equipment, then began learning how to use a camera.

During the next summer break, I decided to go to Okinawa to interview stateless residents and, if possible, make a documentary film. I prepared to go to Okinawa for my first field trip to research stateless people. It was my first time ever in Okinawa, and I had no friends or acquaintances there. I was a bit nervous.

At a friend's party, I met a pilot who flew domestic routes. He loved and knew a lot about Okinawa, including many people. He was a godsend. He taught me a lot, and recommended good long-term lodgings and restaurants. When I told him about my research on stateless people, he sent me information on the offices and political parties involved in human rights work in Okinawa.

* * *

The humid, warm air stuck to my skin. My eyes caught flashy patterns of red and yellow as well as the strong sunshine and bright, smiling people. It was my first trip to Okinawa, yet for some reason, I felt as if I had returned to a place from my past.

I visited human rights offices and met people familiar with statelessness issues in Okinawa. I contacted the head of the AmerAsian School in Okinawa.

"There used to be many stateless children, but now not so many, especially since the issue of stateless children between US soldiers and Okinawan women was resolved with the 1984 revision of the Nationality Act," said Masayo Hirata.

Hirata worked as a counselor at the Okinawa Gender Equality Center *Tiruru*. She herself had once been in an international marriage and struggled with the issue of the nationality of her children.

The Nationality Law amendment made it possible for a child born to a Japanese woman to acquire Japanese nationality, so that the child would no longer be stateless. It's a right that was won after much suffering and struggle. Hirata had long called for a revision of Japan's patrilineal *jus sanguinis* principle, which had disadvantaged Japanese mothers and their children. In the *Ryukyu Shimpo* (11 September 1999), Hirata wrote:

> The first nationality law, enacted in 1899, adopted a principle by which women must take the citizenship of their husbands. It stipulated that a Japanese woman would lose her Japanese citizenship if she became the wife of a foreigner, and a foreign woman would acquire Japanese citizenship if she became the wife of a Japanese. For legitimate children (born to legally married couples), the patrilineal preference system meant that they would inherit Japanese citizenship only if the father was a Japanese citizen. When the Nationality Act was enacted under the new Constitution in 1950, the

matrimonial citizenship principle of the old law was abolished. However, the patrilineal preference system was retained in the name of preventing dual citizenship. This later caused the problem of stateless children....

On January 25, 1979, the International Year of the Child, the social welfare corporation International Okinawa Office (Secretary-General: Yasutaka Oshiro) announced International Year of the Child: Proposals from Okinawa, causing a great sensation by advocating for stateless children in Okinawa. To prevent the occurrence of stateless children, he called for the nationality law to be amended so that the child can inherit the citizenship of the Japanese mother. Under the nationality law of the time, the acquisition of Japanese citizenship through birth was stipulated in the following cases:

(1) When the father is a Japanese citizen at the time of birth
(2) When the father who died before birth was a Japanese citizen at the time of his death
(3) When the father is unknown or does not have citizenship, and the mother is a Japanese citizen
(4) If born in Japan, both parents are unknown or have no citizenship

In the case of a legitimate child, the citizenship of the child was determined not by who is the biological father, but by who was married to the mother.

Hirata took out a file and told me about a case she consulted on. A Japanese woman was abandoned by her foreign husband, but was unable to get a divorce without proof that the husband was missing. She then had children with a common-law Japanese husband, and that child was born in Okinawa, stateless. Even the biological child of a Japanese man who was the common-law husband of the child's mother was denied Japanese citizenship because the legal father of the child (and husband of the mother) was a foreign national, despite the fact that the matrimonial father's whereabouts are unknown.

Hirata talked about such cases, noting the fundamental idea in Japan that people don't want to spoil their family register with the blotch of a divorce. This helped me to further understand the contradictions and discrimination inherent in the formalism of the law. Hirata herself was a victim of that law. To help stateless children and their parents, she had studied the law and personally visited the Diet and elsewhere to demand amendment of the law.

I had no knowledge of the problems of other stateless people or the problems of foreigners in Japan beyond what I had personally experienced as a stateless person. So, I thought that by meeting other stateless people in Okinawa and sharing our experiences, we might reach some common understanding and discover something new. I wondered why a stateless person would have to register as an alien. I asked Hirata.

"Alien registration is something that so-called *foreign* nationals must do, right? Stateless people are not Japanese, but I don't think they are foreigners either. I find it hard to accept that authorities include stateless residents in the alien registration category."

"Consider that alien registration cards have bolstered stateless residents' rights. We have worked hard to ensure that stateless people would be included in an alien registration category. At least stateless people can now enjoy the same rights as foreigners. Otherwise, the stateless person would have no certificate and would be placed in an even more inconvenient position."

I didn't know that there was a history of fighting for the rights of stateless people, so I didn't expect such an answer. I couldn't wrap my head around such a surprising response. I learned for the first time that in the past, stateless people had been put in a much harder position than they are in now.

"Until then, stateless residents fell through the cracks between the binary categories of Japanese or foreigners; they were legally invisible," Hirata said. "In most cases, people think that stateless people are less valuable than foreigners. But more people need to know that statelessness can also come about by choice and that it can be considered a kind of nationality. Being stateless in no way makes you less valuable."

In fact, many people who do not agree with a country's changing political regime or political system have chosen to renounce their citizenship and become stateless. White émigrés after the Russian Revolution and Vietnamese during the Vietnam War are good examples.

The Individual and the State

In addition to Hirata, I met people who worked in the office of the Okinawa Social Mass Party, lawyers who specialized in US military base issues and human rights in Okinawa, and human rights activists. I asked them to introduce me to any stateless people they knew. The Okinawans were very accommodating.

They noted that, "The issue of statelessness is tricky. They don't like to talk about it much." I couldn't get a good chance to meet stateless people in person.

"We also have our own identities as Uchinanchu Ryukyuans. We have a different history than the people on the mainland. Okinawa used to be a state called Ryukyu, not Japan. Even after the war, I think it was even in the 1960s, Okinawans who studied at universities on the mainland were considered to be studying abroad and had to carry something akin to a visa and a passport. Now we are all Japanese citizens, but it was quite different back then. So, we have stronger identities as Uchinanchu than we do as Japanese. I would guess that's what nationality is all about."

"I understand that feeling well. But I want to know what the stateless people think."

"One of my friends who came to Japan as a Vietnamese refugee is stateless. He lives in Okinawa now, and I told him that you wanted to see him. But he said, 'I don't have much to say.' He faces a hassle when leaving the country or going to government offices, but he always says he's fine and doesn't want to show his hardship."

I knew how he felt. I had felt the same way. It was hard for me to show my true self. I often thought, *I'm different from them anyway* or *they won't understand me anyway*. I tensed up because it was humiliating to show my weak and struggling side. I imagined he shared such feelings. So, he wouldn't want to meet some stranger just because she came from far away to interview him.

The Okinawa fieldwork made me realize how difficult it is to study stateless people. But just as Hirata and others petitioned the country to change the law on stateless children and just as they made progress on problems facing stateless children born of Japanese mothers, I figured progress was needed on the problem of those who became stateless for other reasons. I felt strongly that stateless residents must raise their voice, or the problem would remain hidden without any hope for progress.

A True Cosmopolitan

The raw voices of the many people I met during my research in Okinawa revealed the impact of government decisions on people's daily lives. There was an unspeakable lament in their voices. US military bases—one cause of child statelessness—exist in accordance with the Treaty of Mutual Cooperation and Security Between the United States and Japan. The two governments have nothing to say about how many people's lives have been upended by the base that exists due to their unilateral decisions.

I learned there was a book about stateless children in Okinawa, by Hideo Honda, entitled *Non-Existent Children* (Chobunsha, 1982). Honda is a writer, playwright, and advocate. I heard about the author's reputation for interviewing stateless children and their mothers living in Okinawa, and I really wanted to read the book. Soon after I returned to Yokohama, I searched for it. But it was nowhere to be found. Although the book was already out of print, with the help of a friend, I finally managed to borrow it from the city library.

The impressive cover of the book shows a large picture of a child's face, drawn with a sky-blue background that seemed to represent Okinawa. The child has a deeply chiseled face, looking like a mix of American and Japanese, with a somewhat worried look. The book lays out the laws and systems regarding stateless children, the mechanism by which stateless children emerge in Okinawa, and the relationship between individuals and the state that develops due to nationality. The book explains in a straightforward, legible way what statelessness means for those involved, what it means to have no nationality, and how being a mixed-race child impacts identity formation. As expected from a book written by a playwright, I was drawn into the story.

I wanted to know why the author focused on stateless children and their mothers in the early 1980s. I sent a letter to the address in the author's introduction which stated my thoughts on the book and expressed my interest in the issue, since I too was stateless. I received a reply from his son. Hideo Honda was close to 90 years old and was physically disabled; he lived in a nursing home. After exchanging several emails with his son, a physician named Toru Honda, I met him. Together we visited Hideo's retirement home in Tokyo.

Hideo Honda came to the parlor in his wheelchair. Despite his advanced age, he had a good complexion and seemed clear-headed. His son told him in a loud but gentle voice that I had read his book on stateless children and that I too was stateless.

"I see. You are stateless too?" the elder Honda said with a nod.

"Yes. My parents are from mainland China. My father is from Mudanjiang in Heilongjiang Province, and my mother..." I told him about my parents and my background.

"Oh, Manchuria.... I used to travel all over China in those days," he said as if reminiscing. Then, looking back on China during the war years, he told us about the *Balu-jun* (Eighth route army) and other episodes far removed from battlefield scenes.

Honda had studied English literature at a university before the war. Once war broke out, young, healthy men and women were sent off to the battlefield whether they wanted to go or not. Honda was sent to China and wandered around the mainland. He was captured and imprisoned by the US military, but his fluency in English came in handy. He was put to work as an interpreter on a US ship. The war ended while he was in China.

"Every day, they gave me all the good food I could eat," he said with a boyish gleam in his eye.

"I thought the Japanese could never win if the other side was enjoying such good meals."

Being forced to interpret for an adversary country made him wonder about the idea of the nation.

"The people put the nation first, and the nation gives them an identity. Everyone believed that they were the Emperor's children."

In fact, many people had given their lives for the nation. But as soon as they lost the war, everything they believed in collapsed. It was the relationship between the individual and the state that he reflected on during the war that led him decades later to research and writing about the issue of stateless children in Okinawa, he said.

"Your father who chose statelessness is extraordinary. These days, people say over and over that Japan must internationalize, but they don't understand what it really means. Stateless people are the real cosmopolitans, aren't they? One has to transcend the nation state."

Honda's words had gravitas and persuasive power. He might have been able to bring his attention to stateless children while living in Japan in the 1980s, at the peak of the bubble economy when people cried out for *internationalization*, precisely thanks to his Manchurian experience during World War II. I think he was calling for true internationalization, to be found from children whose lives in Japan were nearly forgotten.

Toru Honda quietly watched his father as he spoke. In addition to his own work as a physician, Toru also organized and served as president of SHARE (Services for Health in Asian & African Regions), a non-government organization that engaged in international cooperation on healthcare. SHARE dispatches doctors, nurses, and other staff to developing countries and works with local people to protect their health. In Japan, they provide medical assistance to foreign nationals, including *overstays* and those who migrated for work or other reasons. In Japan, *overstays* are those who enter Japan on a tourist visa and stay on even after their status of residence expires.

People who overstay cannot get insurance, so they must pay the full cost of medical care. Many foreigners avoid medical institutions for language, institutional, and financial reasons. But illness and injury are concerns. People working in 3D jobs (dirty, dangerous and demanding) often need hospitalization. Toru Honda introduced us to a clinic in a port town that provides medical assistance to such foreigners.

The doctors provided consultations in a variety of languages, including English, Spanish, Persian, and Filipino. For those unable to come to the clinic, they also traveled to areas with high concentrations of foreign residents to provide free health checkups. He said that Iranian and Thai patients and children often came to the hospital. Some of the patients were born to *overstay* foreigners, and some were stateless children with citizenship issues.

Today, many foreigners come to Japan for work and other purposes. While cross-border migration increases, legal barriers to foreigners in Japan exist on multiple fronts due to the lack of standardized citizenship laws among countries and the fact that Japan fundamentally restricts admittance of unskilled laborers. The issue of children born stateless seems to be caused by something different than the Okinawa case. Parents often do not report the birth of their child for fear of being arrested for overstaying. The cause is different from what it had been during his father's years, but Toru Honda supported tackling the ongoing problem of stateless children.

Madame Hong

One hot, sunny day in the summer of 2001, I visited Madame Hong, who lived in Tokyo, with my friend Teruko Nakajima. Madame Hong showed up wearing a pretty beret and a dress that seemed to light the way around her. She greeted us with a big smile and a cheerful "*Irasshai!*" Looking at her, it was hard to imagine the trouble she had experienced as a stateless person. Madame Hong was born in Taiwan and came to Japan in 1955 at the age of 18 to visit her father, who already lived in Japan.

"It took me eight hours to get from Taiwan to Tokyo by propeller plane, laying over twice en route. I first came here on a visa to visit my relatives, so after staying three months, I went to Ryukyu and applied for another visa so that I could stay in Tokyo with my father as long as possible," she said with a Taiwanese accent, having originally been a Chinese citizen and holding a Chinese passport when she came to Japan.

Her father made a fortune in business, so she lived a prosperous life in Tokyo. She went to beauty school and lived an easy life. Eventually, Madame Hong married a Korean man she met in Tokyo. They had a child and lived happily together. Then, suddenly, her husband's business went bankrupt, and the family was unable to make ends meet. She divorced her husband and started a new life with her son, a Korean national. Fortunately, there was a small amount of property that her husband had left them, so she was able to sustain their life for a while.

In 1972, when Japan and the Republic of China broke off diplomatic relations and the political upheaval led Japan to establish diplomatic relations with the People's Republic of China, Madame Hong too was forced to choose citizenship. She became stateless instead. The foreigner's registration card issued by Japan clearly stated that she was stateless, while she used the passport issued by Taiwan to travel to and from Taiwan.

After her divorce, she opened a Chinese restaurant because she had to raise her child on her own and because she was thinking about her future.

"We faced many obstacles, with everything seeming impossible. I seriously wondered how I was going to make a living."

Her cheerfulness and positive attitude were enough to overcome any hardship, however, and she never gave up. Thanks to her friendly and cheerful nature, the shop has enjoyed a steady stream of regular customers. She showed me photos of celebrity patrons. Business was good.

"But I couldn't get a bank loan at all. A stateless person was apparently considered untrustworthy."

Banks were hesitant to lend to any foreigners in the 1980s, so stateless residents would be simply out of the question. This experience and her son's drafting to military service made Madame Hong decide to get Japanese citizenship. The father of her only son—both born in Japan—was her ex-husband, a *zainichi* Korean resident in Japan. Since both Japan and Korea were patrilineal, their son was a Korean national. He had been separated from his father at an early age and grew up knowing nothing about Korea, so she found it hard to accept her son being drafted and having to go to Korea due to the nationality assigned to him by the government. Her son was surely unhappy, too.

"I applied and was denied so many times."

After many years, she and her son finally obtained Japanese citizenship. Her son barely escaped the draft as well, to Madame Hong's great relief.

Later, seeing the restaurant thrive, an influential local invited her to move the restaurant to a better location and expand the business. She accepted, partly because the new location was near a theater, but the economy went into a downturn, and the town's redevelopment led to the opening of station buildings in other areas, drastically changing the flow of people. Madame Hong, almost 70, still struggled day and night to figure out how to get her restaurant back on its feet. Her perspective and enthusiasm differ from many in her generation who live leisurely as pensioners.

"It's today's challenge rather than tomorrow's security. And I have no pension. I'm still active. If push comes to shove, I'll get a job washing dishes. When one door shuts, another opens, so it's okay!"

With the smile on Madame Hong's face, people likely never realize how much fear and insecurity she overcame, and how she still fights every day.

Starffin and Hemming

Numerous successful and famous people are also stateless. Fedor Dmitrievich Morozoff and Makarov Goncharoff made names for themselves for their chocolate and other Western confections. Victor Starffin made history in Japanese professional baseball as a pitching ace for the Giants, winning more than 300 games.

Morozoff, Goncharoff, and Starffin were all White Russians. Up to 1.5 million White Russians fled their country during the chaos of World War I, wartime imprisonment, the Russian Revolution and the establishment of a socialist regime. Fridtjof Nansen, appointed as the League of Nations' High Commissioner for Refugees, was keen to help refugees.

In 1922, participants at a conference on refugees from Russia decided to issue *certificates of identity* to facilitate the migration of asylum seekers and refugees. It was called the *Nansen Passport* since it was created thanks to his advocacy. Asylum seekers and refugees could use the passport and a visa to enter the visa-issuing country. Japan, which participated in the conference, drew international criticism after initially refusing to allow White Russians to enter the country using the Nansen Passport. By 1925, Japan relented and eased entry restrictions, leading to a great influx of White Russians coming to Japan. A total of 2,356 White Russians lived in Japan around 1925, according to the Nansen International Bureau (Natasha Starffin, *The Ace Came from Russia*, PHP Bunko, 1991).

Once in Japan, they registered as stateless. These stateless White Russians lived in Tokyo, Hyogo, Kanagawa, Hokkaido, and other parts of Japan, making a living peddling bread and *raxa* overcoats on the streets. White Russians not only faced discrimination because they looked different. They also suffered because they had no nationality or passport. Although Starffin remained stateless throughout his life, suffering discrimination and persecution, he devoted his life to baseball and became the Giants' ace. He was one of the most popular players in Japanese professional baseball, winning 300 victories for the first time in history.

Fujiko Hemming was born in Berlin, Germany, to a Swedish architect father and a Japanese pianist mother. She came to Japan with her parents when she was five, but her father did not return to Japan as the mood was shifting toward war. As a result, she lost her Swedish citizenship at the age of 18 and remained stateless until she regained it in her forties. At 30, she studied in Germany to great acclaim, but the sudden loss of her hearing seemed to have ended her piano career.

Nevertheless, she returned to Japan in 1995 and gave a recital in 1998 at the old hall of Tokyo University of the Arts, her alma mater. A documentary about her life aired on NHK, and her debut CD *La Campanella* sold more than one million copies, making her an instantly popular pianist. She donated her profits to help victims of terrorist attacks in the US and concert receipts to the Japanese Red Cross to help refugees in Afghanistan. From her own experience of being treated as stateless and a refugee, she advocates for today's refugees and victims of terrorism.

Eighteen-year-old Nguyen Tran Phuoc An of Toyo University's Himeji High School was selected as an all-Japan high school pitcher in the 2003 Asia AAA Championship. He was a second-generation Vietnamese refugee without citizenship. Some refugees had been politically persecuted in their home countries or had sought asylum because they did not agree with the policies of their home countries. An's family may be one such case. Those granted asylum certified as refugees who decide to settle in Japan are required to register as aliens, but in doing so, they may choose statelessness rather than keep the citizenship of their origin country—in An's case, Vietnam. An was the first stateless athlete ever selected for the all-Japan high school team. His performance likely changed Japanese society's understanding and perception of stateless people. In that sense, his selection was important in raising awareness of statelessness.

Mei Shigenobu, daughter of Japanese Red Army leader Fusako Shigenobu, was also stateless until she acquired Japanese citizenship. In her autobiography, *Secret* (Kodansha, 2001), she says, "My identity as a stateless person fostered my ability to put myself in the same position as those in need and to say *no* to discrimination." She studied international relations and tried to use her experience as a stateless person in a positive way.

There are many others living stateless in Japan, including at least a few of Korean (*Chosen*) descent called *zainichi*.

Zainichi were originally granted status as Japanese "imperial subjects" during Japanese colonialization. But the San Francisco Peace Treaty of 1952 took away Japanese nationality from former colonial subjects and their children. They were required to register as foreign Koreans. These Korean nationals are legally recognized as citizens of the Republic of Korea.

People who are listed as *Chosen* in the nationality field of their alien registration are *de facto* stateless. In Japan, natives of the Korean (Jp: Chosen; Kor: Joseon) peninsula are listed as foreign nationals, but no country on earth is named Joseon. The closest would be the Democratic People's Republic of Korea (DPRK), which uses Joseon in its name, but not all residents of Japan registered as DPRK nationals have DPRK citizenship. Foreigners in Japan unrecognized by either country on the peninsula are stateless.

Many people are stateless, even if their ID doesn't say *stateless* in the citizenship field. In fact, the number of such stateless residents appears to be quite large.

7 Asians and Statelessness

Growing Numbers of Foreigners

Around the turn of the century, some children were born stateless to foreign residents who had overstayed their visas. These cases recently became the main generator of stateless children.

Many residents of Japan would encounter foreigners, particularly Chinese, Filipinos, and other Asians, in their daily lives. It's likely because more economic migrants choose Japan as their country of destination, considering Japan's economic development. The number of registered foreigners rose from 782,910 in 1980; to 1,851,758 by 2002; to 2,078,508 in 2011; and 2,933,137 by 2019.

Although foreigners come to Japan to work, Japan did not accept unskilled workers until 2019. To stay in Japan for longer than a short period, a foreigner had to have proper skills and get a work visa. Before the visa expired, they had to prepare all the required documentation and go to the Immigration Bureau to get their visa (*status of residence*) renewed. This was fine when the economy was strong in the early 1990s, but when the economy turned, job numbers declined, making it sometimes impossible to provide proof of employment, which led to the phenomenon of foreigners overstaying their visa. Others came on a student visa but engaged in unskilled labor. When the student visa expired, they kept working as *overstays*.

The number of stateless children has increased. This includes those born of parents who have overstayed their visas or who go unregistered, as well as children who acquire no citizenship because their parents are missing. More than half of the 2,103 stateless residents registered as "foreigners" in 1999 were children under the age of nine, according to the Japan Immigration Association. Of those 1,063 children, the lion's share (837), were under the age of four. These figures represent only the registered foreigners that the national government can track. One can only imagine how many more are not registered, children in legal limbo.

The common cause of all these stateless cases is the fear that parents have of being caught overstaying their visas.

Perhaps the textbook stateless child case is Andrew Rees. A Shinano Mainichi Shimbun book published in 1995, *I am Japanese; Andrew's 1,500 days*, and a Yuhikaku Publishing Co. book published in 1996, *Family and Citizenship* (Yasuhiro Okuda), deal with the case in detail. TV and mass media also covered the case broadly.

Andrew Rees

Andrew was born January 18, 1991, in a hospital in Nagano Prefecture. His mother was a foreign resident of Japan. Believed to be Filipino, her actual citizenship remains unknown. A few months before Andrew's birth, the mother asked US citizens Reverend William Rees and his wife Roberta to take the child after he was born. The Reeses attended the childbirth, which was uneventful. A few days later, his mother left the baby behind, left the hospital, and disappeared.

Since Andrew's mother wasn't around to register the birth, the reverend and his wife signed and affixed their *hanko* personal seals to the registration.

That registration included the baby's date, place of birth, his mother's name Cecilia Rosette and her date of birth, November 21, 1965. The mother's nationality was not on the registration; nor was any information about the baby's father.

The Reeses submitted the birth registration at their local government office in Miyotamachi, in Nagano Prefecture's Kitasaku County, but it was later sent to Komoro, the city of the hospital where Andrew was born. They could not get the baby citizenship since the registration indicated no information on his father or on his mother's citizenship. With no citizenship, it was impossible to determine if the baby's name should be entered into a Japanese *koseki* family register or registered as an alien.

Komoro City sent a request for guidance to the Legal Affairs Bureau on whether to accept the documentation. The bureau conducted an investigation that included the childbirth's attending physician, hospital officials, the Reeses, and others, endeavoring to garner as much information as possible on Cecilia Rosette's citizenship. Obtaining information that the mother was probably Filipina, the bureau responded to Komoro City, saying that they could probably accept the documents on the assumption that the mother and baby had Philippines citizenship. The city registered the baby as an alien with Philippines citizenship.

The Reeses wanted to take Andrew and their other adopted children to the US, so they went to the Philippines Embassy and applied for his passport. The embassy rejected the application, saying the Filipino government is not bound to recognize his citizenship just because the Japanese government listed him as Filipino on his alien registration card. With neither his mother present, nor a passport, nor other documentary evidence, the Philippines Embassy could not certify Andrew's citizenship. Nor could they issue him a passport.

It makes logical sense since the child's birth certificate didn't list his mother's citizenship. The local investigation that certified Andrew and his mother as Filipino citizens was based on extremely unreliable information, such as asking acquaintances.

The Reeses were concerned that, without a passport for Andrew, not only would they not be able to travel to the US; they would also be restrained in countless other ways going forward. They found out that if they accepted the child as *stateless* for now at least, they could get a re-entry permit from the Japanese government, use that in lieu of a passport, apply for a visa, and go to the States.

The Reeses went to a nearby government office and asked to change Andrew's citizenship. This meant that his citizenship would be re-registered on his alien registration card, changing from the *Philippines* to *stateless*. Andrew received a brown re-entry permit booklet, what the Japanese government issues for stateless residents, refugees and others who do not enjoy the protection of a particular nation state. They were able to get a US entry visa and Japanese re-entry visa stamps, enabling them finally to go to the US.

Andrew had ended up stateless after a bureaucratic runaround, with the Japanese government supposing he had Philippines citizenship and the Philippines government unable to grant him citizenship. His guardians, the Reeses, consulted with Attorney Yumiko Yamada, an expert on international issues.

Because Japan's Nationality Act is founded on the *jus sanguinis* principle, citizenship requires that one parent be a Japanese national at the time of birth. But Article 2, section 3 includes a *jus soli* exception for acquiring citizenship *when both parents are unknown or have no nationality in a case where the child is born in Japan*. Naturally, *jus sanguinis* provides no way to determine citizenship when the identity (and therefore the "blood") of neither parent is known, meaning the child would become stateless. This exception in the law provides Japanese citizenship for having been born in Japan, precisely to avoid statelessness.

Hearing this explanation gave the Reeses hope that Andrew might be Japanese, not stateless, and they embarked on a citizenship confirmation lawsuit in 1992, when the child was one.

The Reeses asserted that Japanese citizenship should be recognized because he was born in Japan, with a father unknown and a mother of uncertain nationality. In February 1993, Tokyo District Court recognized the child's Japanese citizenship, based on Article 2.3 of the Nationality Act. The plaintiffs had won. In January 1994, however, Tokyo High Court overturned the verdict, then on January 27, 1995, the Supreme Court reversed the High Court's verdict, for a final plaintiff victory.

These changing litigant fortunes revolved around: (1) whether the expression *when both parents are unknown* indeed applies to Andrew's case; and (2) which side has the burden of proof for that phrase. Serendipitously, Japan had ratified the Convention on the Rights of the Child in April 1994. This pact required signatory nations, in compliance with domestic laws and treaty obligations, to protect the rights stipulated therein of children to obtain a name and citizenship. In *Minority Children* (1998, edited by Akira Nakagawa, published by Akashi Shoten), Atty. Yamada notes that Japan's ratification of the convention worked in favor of the Reeses' court battle.

Although this textbook stateless child case ended in victory and Japanese citizenship for Andrew Rees, it required a great deal of time, money, and emotional energy spent on litigation. Not everyone has the capacity to overcome such a hurdle. An individual taking on the government in court would endure an inordinate amount of stress.

After the Supreme Court ruling, the Ministry of Justice told the press, "We will take the Supreme Court verdict very seriously, but the issue of citizenship differs from case to case, so we have no intention of taking any particular measures."

Atty. Yamada notes that the time and effort that must be expended in court is due to the "original ambiguous interpretation of the phrase *are unknown* in Article 2.3 of the Nationality Act." She says, "Article 2.3 of the Nationality Act offers too little to prevent statelessness or to account for statelessness arising with a child born in Japan to foreign parents due to legislative discrepancies between their respective home nations" (*Minority Children*). Children would still end up stateless if (1) the father had citizenship in a *jus soli* country like Brazil; (2) the child born in Japan did not meet the citizenship requirements of the father's country; and (3) the mother's country practiced patrilineal *jus sanguinis*.

A total of 882 minors (under age 20) were registered as stateless in Japan as of 1996, the year after Andrew Rees' victory. That figure rose to

1,143 by late 1999. The Andrew Rees' case evidently was an outlier, and the countless stateless child issues that have accumulated over the years remain unresolved. It's impossible even to ascertain how many children go unregistered, for all sorts of reasons.

Those saddled with these problems run up against many obstacles. Without insurance, they face high healthcare bills. Since they receive no school attendance notice in the mail, they sometimes end up missing the start of school. Only a tiny fraction of stateless children have the good fortune to have parents ready to sue the government and win. Most give up. I was one of them. Not all of those who give up are as happy-go-lucky as I was—crying myself to sleep at night, to be sure, but forgetting my troubles the next morning. Many respond to the daily pressure and stress by turning to delinquent behavior or end up suffering from mental illness.

Nationality of Illegitimate Children

In 2000, cases resembling Andrew Rees' revolved around the question of citizenship for so-called *illegitimate* children, those born to a Japanese father and foreign mother who are not legally married. Article 2.1 of Japan's Nationality Act entitles children to citizenship if the *"father or mother is a Japanese citizen at the time of birth."* The *father* here means the legally-recognized father. The law does not recognize paternity if the biological father is not married to the mother and refuses to acknowledge paternity. To establish legal paternity, the man must go with the expectant mother to the local city office and declare paternity of the fetus before birth, acknowledging that, "the child in this womb is mine." (As of 2008, the Supreme Court recognized post-partum paternal recognition.)

Few knew about this regulation. Most people found out when they went to register the birth of the child. Even when they did, it was quite an ordeal for the expectant mother to go down to the city office for the declaration. The city office could refuse to accept the declaration if the paperwork was lacking in any way. It's not a good idea for expectant mothers to suffer stress preparing documents as they may already be stressed out trying to ensure a safe birth.

The mother has no need to acknowledge maternity, which is well established at the moment of childbirth. Out of wedlock, however, it's difficult to demonstrate paternity. If the mother is a foreign national, Japan's *san sanguinis* principle means a child born in Japan will take the mother's citizenship. Acquiring citizenship is difficult even when the biological father is Japanese. If the mother has a long-term residency visa or other strong visa, the problem does not become too troublesome. But if the mother is on a short-term entertainment visa or has overstayed her visa, that situation affects the child's visa. The child ends up permitted to reside neither in the country of birth nor the father's country.

The most famous illegitimate child court case is that of Daisuke, born in September 1991 to a Filipino mother and Japanese father. Florida Apelin Plares had entered Japan in 1988 on a forged passport, then soon met and fell in love with Yoshio (pseudonym). In late 1990, she became pregnant with his child. Yoshio already had a wife and children so could not marry Florida. But he decided to take responsibility and care for the child.

A friend familiar with the situation told him about the need to acknowledge the unborn child to enable that child to acquire Japanese citizenship. Yoshio prepared to get the required documents sent from the Philippines, including Florida's birth certificate. But even with the delivery date approaching, the documents failed to arrive from the Philippines. Yoshio went to the local city office and explained. When he tried to submit a form to recognize the unborn child along with the mother's consent form, the official said the mother's birth certificate is required.

The mother was undocumented; a broker had confiscated her passport. Trying to work through the problem, they tried to get ID sent from the Philippines, but postal system issues caused delays. The documents eventually arrived but only after Daisuke was born. The city office registered the paternity acknowledgement *post-* rather than *pre-*partum, precluding Daisuke from Japanese citizenship.

Since Daisuke had no visa, he could not remain in Japan. It was discovered that Florida had entered the country with a bogus passport, thereby violating Immigration Control Law. In March 1993, mother and child were ordered to leave the country. Deportation would tear the family apart, with only Yoshio remaining in Japan. Yoshio had tried unsuccessfully to acknowledge paternity before Daisuke's birth, but the law only recognized his post-partum paternity.

They went to court to confirm the child's citizenship, asserting that the city office should have accepted the notice of paternal acknowledgement of the unborn child even if mother and child failed to get all the documents in order. On November 18, 1996, the state and the family settled, with the government recognizing pre-partum paternal acknowledgement and Daisuke's Japanese citizenship (*Minority Children*).

Japanese-Filipino Children

In the early 1980s, the number of Filipina and Thai women coming to work in Japan skyrocketed. They came on entertainment visas as dancers and singers, but their real work was nearly always as club girls and bargirls (known as *hostesses* in Japan). "Filipino Pub" graced countless signs hanging outside the establishments. More than 50,000 Filipinas came to work in Japan each year. It's no surprise that male Japanese patrons and foreign women working there sometimes became intimate, leading to pregnancy and childbirth.

The Philippines is known as a country of emigration. Many Filipinos go overseas to work. The messages at the Manila airport departure gate encouraging emigrant workers illustrates how important the Filipino government considers the money remitted by these workers. Most go off to the US, the Middle East, Hong Kong and other countries around the world, but one thing stands out among those coming to Japan.

Eighty per cent are women, and nearly 40 per cent of those Filipinas enter the country on entertainment visas. Filipino men go to work in construction or at hotels in other countries, and Filipinas often work in other countries as maids. In the late 1980s, the number of marriages between Japanese men and Filipino women soared. The offspring of such couples, believed to number up to 100,000, are called Japanese-Filipino children, or JFC.

Couples consisting of a Japanese man and a foreign woman came to be a common sight in neighborhoods and churches. Having become so sensitive about citizenship and issues involving foreigners, I began to wonder about the citizenship of their children, as if it were personal to me. Of course, many JFCs live happy lives with no citizenship issues. I have a few friends with families like that. But some have trouble with their children's citizenship because they were born out of wedlock, and some women are exploited by irresponsible men who bed them then leave.

Maybe some of them have children struggling with problems related to statelessness.

This is the thought that crossed my mind each time I saw such people in town.

I wonder how JFCs feel. Since I have experienced statelessness myself, maybe we have something to share with each other.

Reinvigorated, a keen interest in stateless children stirred in me, and I started visiting relevant organizations and gathering information.

In early 2003, I decided to join a Philippines study tour run by the Development Action for Women Network (DAWN), an NGO that provides not only moral support, but also job training and other humanitarian aid to women who come to work as entertainers, to help them make an independent living in Japan. DAWN also helps their JFC children find their fathers and to get Japanese citizenship. The NGO organizes annual study tours to the Philippines and coordinates a theater production in Japan performed by JFCs and their mothers living in the Philippines.

Before departing on the study tour, we held a briefing in Tokyo with DAWN Japan volunteer staffers and tour participants. A young graduate student researching Filipina migration coordinated the tour for us. The small list of participants included a graduate student interested in the Philippines and preparing to study abroad; a man in his eighties researching Japanese soldiers who fought in the Philippines during World War II; and several others like me who were interested in the issue of stateless children. We were few but represented a broad span of ages and interests. It seemed like it would be a fun and educational trip in many ways.

I want to meet JFCs. Some of these children may be stateless like I was. What concerns them? What do they want? I want to help them any little way I can.

This is how I felt. A week later, I left for Manila with this feeling.

The Filipino Condition

"She's Ana-chan. She came back to the Philippines when she was two."

"Hi, how old are you?"

"Seven."

She had an accent influenced by the Filipino language. Ana-chan greeted me in proper Japanese. She grinned, but something behind her big, brown eyes radiated a sort of loneliness.

"And he is Hiroshi. The one in the red t-shirt is Masa."

Before I could even greet them, they scampered off giggling, one chasing the other in an apparent game of tag. The children always look forward to spending time with their JFC friends again. They cherished meeting and playing with friends living under similar circumstances. They didn't have time to sit down and talk with an adult like me.

The day we arrived in Manila, DAWN held a party organized by staffers to celebrate the organization's founding, with nearly 30 children and their mothers. Even those of us participating for the first time came to feel like we were with old friends and began singing and dancing together before we knew it.

The children began singing a gentle melody, with choreography. I realized that scattered throughout the Japanese lyrics were references to a longing to meet their beloved fathers in Japan. Even Hiroshi, a mischievous boy running around the room, moved his body to the melody he was singing and looked like a little bird perched on a tree branch. Ana's big black eyes seemed to stare off in the distance, thinking about her father in Japan.

The JFCs I met in the Philippines all lived separate from their fathers. Some knew their fathers; others had never met them before. DAWN helped some children in their desperate search to find their fathers, even if just to meet them once. The children became overjoyed each time any shred of information about one of their fathers arrived. The *DAWN Theater Akebono* stage production was held each year in locations around Japan, but for the JFC kids, it was a trip to find their fathers. Their dream that their fathers might come see the show drove them on during rehearsals.

Many JFCs are born out of wedlock to a Japanese father and Filipino mother. In many cases, the mother had overstayed her visa, making it impossible to make the marriage official. The child is born outside of a legal marriage; then the child and mother are later deported back to the Philippines. Or the child was born to a Filipino mother who had already been married in the Philippines and so could not marry the Japanese father. In other cases, parents return to the Philippines and get married unofficially but cannot register their marriage in Japan because the father secretly already has a wife and children back in Japan. Some children find out that their parents are unmarried, so they have no citizenship or right of abode and must return with their mothers to the Philippines. Some children's parents are married, but the marriage is so full of discord and violence that the mother becomes emotionally disabled, divorces her husband and returns to the Philippines.

The JFCs I met in Manila had many reasons to leave their place of birth to return to the Philippines. Few children were born to Japanese fathers and had acquired Japanese citizenship. Nearly all acquired the Filipino citizenship of their mothers, and the citizenship of some was undetermined. They were unable to live together as a family due to a plethora of problems. The victims were the innocent JFC kids.

I stayed at Anna Paz's home, where she lived with her aunt, mother, maternal uncle, and two male cousins. (Paz is a pseudonym.) Anna's aunt, the mother of her cousins, was off working in Japan. Every day, Anna's mother nursed her bedridden grandmother. The rowdy cousins were always messing with and annoying the taciturn Anna. I often heard Anna's uncle in the next room yelling at the children for monkeying around. With one hand always holding a bottle, the uncle looked like an alcoholic to me. Perhaps the drink helped him forget his wife in Japan. Anna's home was a typical one in the Philippines; many families send one member overseas to work because they cannot find work domestically.

Anna's mother had gone to work in Japan when she was young. She worked as an entertainer, having entered the country on that visa. Anna's seriously ill grandmother, her toddler uncles, and other family members stayed in the Philippines and depended on the money sent from Japan by Anna's mother. Her mother stayed in Japan after her visa expired and kept sending money back as much as possible. She became the mistress of a Japanese man who had a wife and children, then became pregnant with Anna.

After Anna's birth, her mother stayed a while in Japan, but support from the man was limited, and with Anna now in tow, her mother could no longer work or send money back to her family. She had overstayed her visa, was involved with a man with a family, had a small child with citizenship and visa issues, a family back home dealing with illness, and other troubles in a foreign land. Anna's mother fell into depression. Five years before I visited, Anna's mother had given up on life in Japan and returned to the Philippines.

She joined DAWN, got counseling and job training. Anna's mother was on her way to emotional recovery. But at night, Anna sat in the corner of the room and watched her mother turn to alcohol.

The night I stayed over, Anna's mother cooked a feast for me, including honey-glazed pork and a tasty-looking roasted chicken. During dinner, she stepped out and came back with drinks.

Kampai.

I began to drink beer with her. She was a good cook. While the adults were enjoying the delicious dinner, Anna finished up her meal, grabbed toys from shelves situated in the middle of the living room, and began to play.

As I finished my dinner, Anna showed me various things her father had sent her from Japan, including juggling beanbags, origami paper, and a kaleidoscope. Each object was a treasure to Anna. Anna's mother came over with a smile on her face to show me a photo displayed in the living room, showing her shoulder to shoulder with a stout, grey-haired middle-aged man.

"This is Anna's father. He's a kind, good man," she told me.

Anna remained quiet, wearing a complicated expression on her face, as if to say *I love him but can't be with him. I am close to and far from my kind father.* When I asked her about her father, her face looked innocent as she said,

"I love my father."

I felt as if my heart would break when I thought of how they wanted to be with him but simply couldn't.

Why Japan?

The short study tour to the Philippines brought me into direct contact with JFCs and their mothers. I felt that I had come a little closer to understanding their lives and feelings. I saw with my own eyes and heard with my own ears the structural reasons Filipino women are sent to Japan.

The Philippines was one of the Asian countries that developed the most just after World War II. Some people from surrounding countries went to the Philippines to study. But it was clear that half a century on, it was no longer one of the most prosperous countries in Asia. Just walking around the streets, you saw not only street children but entire street families. They don't even have enough space in the streets to sleep, and families must take turns lying down on a bed-like area made of boxes.

I also went to farm villages. The soil had been overcropped; the rice paddies were desolated. The land was probably non-arable. When people heard we had come from Japan, it was not uncommon to hear people say: "My daughter is over there." Even in these villages, I saw families depending on money sent from abroad.

I went to a strip club at night. Of course, it was my first time in such a place, and as a woman it felt weird to be there. I felt restless and uncomfortable. The club was dimly lit except for the stage, where women appeared one after another in various outfits to dance. I was able to call over women still waiting their turn to dance and others who had finished their set.

We went to this club to find out why Filipino women work as entertainers. The woman at our table was obviously still a child.

"How old are you?"

She didn't catch my English question, so one of our members who had spent a year studying in the Philippines translated it into Filipino.

"Sixteen."

"Why do you do this job?"

She answered quickly: "I want to go to school but don't have the money."

"I want to go to Japan too. But I can't speak the language."

She spoke broken English.

"I want to save up money fast, learn the language and earn more working for overseas customers."

Somehow, I couldn't bring myself to see that as a better career path. Ironically, she was in an environment in which she could only think of such a path for herself. I felt lost on the ride back to Anna's place. A man approached trying to stop our car. We opened the window a crack, and he said,

"What do you think? We got a babe for you."

The man evidently sex-trafficked minors and was propositioning us, pointing to a small group of slender, long-haired girls standing behind him. During our stay, we didn't manage direct contact with sex-trafficked women. But we did visit a few NGOs that support female sex workers. They counseled women who suffered mental illness and trained them to find new work. Several of these women had their own children.

"How did you come to be doing this kind of work?"

"My friend's uncle told me he would introduce me to waitress work in Manila. I grew up poor and always dreamed of going to the capital. But I worked as a waitress only for a week."

She had been in her early teens when she first arrived in Manila. She didn't even have enough money to flee back to her hometown. A 16-year-old girl next to her held a small baby.

"I had to make money after my child was born. That's why."

She didn't know who the child's father was. She had nobody to depend on and so had to go all in using her skinny body to make a living. Visiting farming villages and NGOs enabled me to catch a glimpse of the horrific conditions that made these girls want to work overseas.

Japan has an entertainment visa. I visited an organization that trains entertainers and sends them to Japan on this visa. It was like a vocational school, teaching young female students dance, sing, and other skills as well as providing classroom instruction in the Japanese language. They cannot get a visa to go to Japan unless they pass an entertainer exam. So, they attend this type of school and take bootcamp-type lessons. The girls apparently get a loan for their tuition, to be paid back from what they earn in Japan.

I saw lessons they took in preparation for their entertainer exam.

Dance came first. The dance room was mirrored on one wall, and women in black leotards learned steps to music. It was probably beginner level, and they were a far cry from what could be called dancers, even in flattery.

Voice lessons were taking place up on the second floor. In a large room, they worked on releasing their voices, while women practiced singing in a small, adjacent room. I peeked in on the students taking a lesson in the small room. About 15 students crammed into a room the size of about five tatami mats watched a TV screen. One held a mic and was singing a song in English. It was like a karaoke box.

The classroom in the adjacent building was teaching Japanese. The teacher had herself once lived in Japan. When we peaked in, we were welcomed into the classroom with a *dozo* and a quick nod of the head in the Japanese fashion. The women sitting at the desks too all greeted us with a *Konnichi wa*. They were being taught simple Japanese.

Gohan tabemasu ka? [Do you want to eat something?]
Kōhī-wo nomimasu ka? [Do you want some coffee?]
Anata-wa tabako-wo suimasu ka? [Do you smoke?]

Everyone practiced pronunciation by repeating after the teacher. They were apparently studying verbs and interrogative pronouns.

"Ok? In Japan, if a customer pulls out a cigarette, it's good manners to light the cigarette for them. That's good manners. Please keep this important point in mind."

This took me aback. The teacher was not just teaching the language, but also the manners and communication skills required in Japan's *mizu shobai* night-time entertainment industry. It was like a prep-school teacher teaching key points not included in the official textbooks.

The students listened attentively to the teacher, with an expression as if to say *ah, indeed*. The teacher smiled in our direction, apparently pleased with herself. The experience kind of freaked us out. These women were struggling to master Japanese quickly to be able to live in Japan and learning each of these Japanese customs and culture. That was what they were studying.

While watching these women learn Japanese, I thought to myself that maybe they too will go to Japan as entertainers, and, some day, some among them may give birth to JFC kids.

On the day of my return flight to Japan, after the study tour was over, I stood in a long line at the ticket counter at the airport in Manila. I saw people with great volumes of luggage for their departure to work overseas as well as frequent travelers who probably stopped home for a visit and were now on their way back to their overseas workplaces. As I checked in my luggage and headed toward the departure gate, I saw a great banner hanging from overhead, written in Filipino:

Maligayang Paglalakbay.

I approached a pleasant, friendly looking guard and asked him what it meant.

"In English, it would be *happy trip*. It is a message to encourage people going overseas to work hard. Our country's economy is supported by our people going overseas to work. We must cherish them."

On my trip back from the Philippines, I thought about these migrant workers who cross national borders to find work. The country depends on them in some ways. The country receiving them has the demand for it. But I got a sense that the national governments tried to control the flow of people. Each international migrant had various expectations and limitations. I knew their move overseas would entangle them in a growing list of problems related to law and citizenship. Statelessness too could not be separated from the migrant worker issue. With the growing frequency of migration in an increasingly borderless world, I felt we had to revisit this issue.

Passport control at an airport

Unconstitutionality of Nationality Act

Ten children born to unwed Japanese fathers and Filipino women sued the national government for Japanese citizenship. The Grand Bench of the Supreme Court on June 4, 2008, recognized citizenship for all ten plaintiffs and ruled that the Nationality Act's rejection of citizenship when the father acknowledges paternity after birth violates the principle of equality before the law as stipulated in Article 14 of the Constitution. The ruling opened up a path for JFCs to acquire Japanese citizenship, but it still depended on the father acknowledging paternity.

8 Applying for Naturalization

Making a Documentary Film

In 2001, I attended film school while working as a research associate at the University of Tokyo. I often grabbed my camcorder and went out. I wanted to point my lens at everything—birds in the air, the hustle and bustle of the streets, people on the trains.

As my first year studying film was winding down, talk turned to our graduation project. We each had to make an individual film to graduate. The work would be screened publicly. I had been at the film school for a year, but I was a bad student. I had bought a camera and filmed a great deal of material, but did I ever get even one decent shot? It seemed that I had just wasted a lot of videotape. Naturally, I had no confidence that I could complete my graduate film.

I told my friends I didn't think I could make it. They encouraged me, saying, "Well, let's just give it a shot." After agonizing, I decided to go for it, prepared for inevitable embarrassment. I still lacked confidence, but I wanted to express in film what stewed inside me. I wanted to depict a sort of world that could put national borders, citizenship, and the notion of the nation state itself in perspective.

Red shoes straddle the white line drawn on the asphalt. People of many skin tones walk down the road.

Wanting to capture the unvarnished reality of globalization's advance, I went to the airport and peered through my viewfinder at the posted flight schedule and the immigrants entering and leaving. I also interviewed passersby on a busy city street.

"What is your nationality?"

"I'm Japanese."

"What is your nationality?"

"Canadian."

I narrated it: "I'm Chin Tenji and I'm stateless. What do you think about statelessness?"

Living just like any other Japanese person. Yakitori skewers, salad, Japanese sake, wine at a favorite Japanese-style pub. Jazz playing; boots and geta clogs lined up at the entrance.

Interaction at a party with friends from different countries. Languages mix—Chinese, English, Turkish, Japanese.

Me going off on overseas travel.

I explained my papers showing my stateless situation. I recorded the process I had to go through to get the required visas whenever going overseas.

"I must take many documents each time I go overseas. These are my Chinese traveling papers. I had to get many visas sealed or stamped on my Taiwanese passport. Without the seals, stamps, and visas, I might be refused entry to the country."

Me on the streets of Hong Kong, entering a building and getting on the elevator. Those doors open onto a street filled with neon lights in Tokyo's Shinjuku district. I wanted to convey how small the world is. Birds flying in the air. Waves undulating on the ocean.

"Why do national borders exist? What is the purpose of citizenship?"

Looking down on red shoes (representing a song about a Yokohama girl who went abroad with a foreign man) that had straddled the white line on the asphalt. The shoes begin walking; eventually the white line disappears.

"The empty canvas of my national identity caused insecurity and loneliness, but maybe the silver lining is that I can paint on it whatever I like."

By inquiring into daily lives and various familiar matters from various angles, all centered on the keyword *stateless*, I wanted to question why citizenship exists in the first place and revisit the meaning of national borders.

This was hard to express via the media of film. I was groping blindly to try to make my first ever film. Editing took longer than shooting. My parents worried about me because I worked all night every night. When I told my friends how much trouble I was having, some of them helped despite being busy themselves. I have no idea how much time I spent on it. I hadn't realized how tough it was to make a film. I dared to dream of making a documentary film, but making one really took it out of me.

Still, I ended up with my maiden documentary: a 20-minute graduate film, entitled *Mukokuseki—Stateless*.

For three decades, I had carried papers which said *Stateless* in the field for citizenship. Just as most people rely on their nationality as a key part of their identity, I had without realizing it, established statelessness as my very identity. I keenly felt the impact something as simple as an identification card can have on a person's identity. Citizenship/nationality binds the individual to the state. It is bestowed at birth and exists as the most natural of notions, like the air itself. Since the state confers to each individual citizenship at the time of birth, in accordance with the *jus sanguinis* or *jus soli* principle, the state also simultaneously confers upon the individual an identity.

Yet, citizenship can change during one's lifetime. The individual might be forced to change citizenship through marriage or moving to another country. The individual might choose to change citizenship due to migration or in order to naturalize.

The relationship between the individual and the nation state was such that the state bestows citizenship upon the passive individual. This has begun to change, as individuals take a more active role in deciding what country to live in and choosing their citizenship. In that sense, the relationship between the individual and the state has become more diversified. The individual's identity also seems to have begun to take on more dimensions than just one inextricable link to the nation state.

It was that thinking that led me, for my graduation film, to want to ask ordinary people who do have a state about their sense of the word *nationality* or *citizenship*.

What does it feel like to have a nationality or citizenship? How is it different to live with and without a state? What process would be required to acquire citizenship? What emotional impact would attaining it have? And, how would one's identity change? I took an interest in these questions.

Statelessness Prevents Me from Meeting Fellow Stateless Persons

I began researching Chinese migrants and immigrants living in Borneo, having joined a project with a professor to whom I owed a great deal. Borneo, also known as Kalimantan, is an island close to the Philippines and shared by three countries—Indonesia, Malaysia, and Brunei. Part of its charm is the people of many different nationalities and ethnicities. It's known also for its lush, abundant natural wealth, including many rare wild animals and tropical rainforests covering 70 per cent of the island. The professor had a project in Borneo and asked me to study the Chinese community there. I began going off to do fieldwork each year beginning in 2001.

When going overseas with other researchers, I often caused worry to professors and others around me due to my visa issues. When we coordinated our schedules, I did my best to consider the number of days needed to get my visas and what route to take, in order to minimize trouble for them. I couldn't engage in fieldwork that involved crossing back and forth over national borders, such as an island like Borneo that encompasses three nations, as I was usually issued single-use visas. So it would be impossible for me, for example, to enter Malaysia, drive or boat to Brunei for a few days, then come back. Once I left Malaysia, my used visa was invalid, and I would have to apply for another visa.

Having experienced a lot of visa troubles, I was an old hand at handling it. I prepared quickly, dotted all the i's, and crossed all the t's. No matter how I tried to avoid causing trouble to my colleagues, I often needed their help with my visa applications. Running around town, I managed on my own to get together the documents required for my visa review, including proof of bank balance and my alien registration certificate. But a travel agency would have to provide our itinerary and ticket reservation voucher, while my fellow researchers would have to help me prepare items such as recommendation letters and invitations.

When I visited ethnic Chinese Malaysians in the state of Sabah the previous year, I mentioned that I was a stateless *huaqiao* living in Japan. They told me that many stateless ethnic Chinese lived in the neighboring country of Brunei, a one-hour flight or a quick boat ride away. Brunei is a separate, independent country, so even though people go back and forth as if it were a neighboring town, they are in fact crossing an international border. I naturally couldn't do so without a visa.

I wanted to know the background of the stateless Chinese in Brunei, so that year I included the country on my itinerary. As per usual, I made inquiries to apply for a visa to Brunei. They told me that with my passport, even a tourist visa would take a long time. With less than a month before departure, they advised me to give up on Brunei. Since I couldn't go to Brunei, I decided to go instead to Labuan Island, a Malaysian free-trade port close to Brunei.

I finally finalized my itinerary, got all my visas for Taiwan, Malaysia, and Hong Kong, and went off for a month of fieldwork. I was supposed to meet up with the other researchers after finishing up about five days of research in Taiwan. I got up at 5:30 a.m. and headed off to the Taipei airport, so I could join the others as promised in the Malaysian city of

Kota Kinabalu. When I tried to board that day, an agent at the Malaysian Airlines counter said to me,

"You cannot go to Malaysia."

"Why? I have a visa."

The agent leafed through my passport, studying each page.

"No, your visa has already expired."

What the…

"That can't be right. I was issued a visa based on my flight itinerary, which takes me to Malaysia today."

From a file in my bag, I took out a copy of the flight itinerary I had sent to the Malaysian Embassy. I showed him.

"Yes, but your visa issuance has nothing to do with our airline, so …"

Why would the embassy issue me a visa that expires before the date of my flight? I stared at the visa in disbelief. The stamp ink was smudged and hard to read. Two stamps overlapped.

"I think this says the 17th. If it were the 19th, it'd still be valid."

Now that he pointed it out, I saw that the number did look like a 17. That day happened to be the 19th. The English under the visa said that the visa was good for a month but that if I didn't enter the country by the deadline, it would become invalid. My thorough preparations had backfired. In any event, I seethed that the embassy would issue me a visa that would expire on the day they knew I planned to enter the country.

"You should maybe get that reissued where you first got it issued."

"I got it issued by the Malaysian Embassy in Japan."

"In that case, your only choice is to get it reissued in Taipei."

"I am going for work. Isn't there anything you can do?"

"No, there isn't. You have to get a new visa issued."

"If I get it by midday, can I leave on the evening flight?"

"Unfortunately, the next flight to Kota Kinabalu, the city where you are going, will be the morning of the day after tomorrow."

Well, that wouldn't work.

"So, please let me board this flight, for now. Once I get there, I will work it out."

"We can't do that. If it were Kuala Lumpur, you could get a visa in the airport, but in Kota Kinabalu, you can't. So, I cannot let you board."

"Can't you …?"

"No, because we are not permitted to board someone without a visa."

I was at my wit's end. I suppressed the anger welling up in my heart, grabbed all my luggage, and called the home of my professor who was about to leave Japan for Kota Kinabalu.

"Sensei, we promised to meet today at the airport, but it turns out I can't go."

"What happened?"

"I have a visa issue again."

Fortunately, the professor was still at his Tokyo home—just about to leave for the airport. I explained the situation and we agreed I would call the hotel in Kota Kinabalu once my new plans were in place. For the time being, at least I wouldn't stand Sensei up. But our fieldwork schedule would have to change. I had ended up causing trouble again.

I didn't mind so much taking a taxi from the airport back to Taipei to apply for the new Malaysian visa, but the office wasn't open at 8 in the morning. I called my elder brother's home, where I had stayed the night before, but he had already gone off to work. The taxi driver commiserated with my predicament of having nowhere to go. I had the driver stop at a bank so I could withdraw the fare and tried to kill time. My second call went to my brother-in-law.

"Eh? Weren't you off to Malaysia this morning?"

"Yes. But they told me my visa is invalid, so I have to apply for a new one."

"Nothing is open this early. Come to my place for now."

He told me the street address, and I went there to stay for a while. I couldn't drag my suitcases all over town.

"Thank you so much. I'm so glad you were still home."

"Good timing because I have time this morning. That's really tough. How can you do a job that requires you to fly all around if visa issues hinder you every time?"

"Yup. This time, at least I was able to contact Sensei and change today and tomorrow's schedule."

"For businesspeople like me, that could ruin multimillion-dollar projects."

"Yeah. I can't just apologize when it comes to work. I have to think of something."

Stateless Servants of the State

In the summer of 2002, soon after I returned from fieldwork in Hong Kong and Malaysia, a professor who had helped me back in college suggested I answer a posting for an open position related to global phenomena at the National Museum of Ethnology (Minpaku). The museum was incorporated as a business in 2004, but in 2002 it was state-run, as the name suggests. Its staff were all national government employees. Hiring requirements included research on global phenomena as well as a PhD or equivalent. No mention of citizenship.

I had studied the Chinese diaspora scattered around the world and was always interested in global phenomena. The identity of these migrants astride the world was multilayered like a rainbow. They harbored great potential as global citizens, I thought. Recently, I had become interested in globalization, national borders, and particularly statelessness. I organized my thoughts and what I wanted to tackle into a research project and applied for the job.

I also began thinking about my own nationality. A professor who had helped me advised me about the job I wanted. "You know, I think you might be better off getting Japanese citizenship, including for getting a job." Many things made me think so, too.

No matter how much I want to continue to study the statelessness and migration that accompanies globalization, my own statelessness interfered with my ability to move across borders, making it impossible for me to meet stateless people out in the field. I also couldn't just keep causing colleagues trouble.

I decided to overcome my own resistance and try again to get Japanese citizenship.

I would record each step of my own process to acquire Japanese citizenship. What documents are required to attain citizenship? How does gaining citizenship change a person's identity? How does it change their daily life? I wanted to know proper answers to all these questions. I had my friend help me video record it all. I thought it might be fashioned into a sequel to my documentary film.

I brought Teruko Nakajima to my consultation on applying for naturalization. Teru-chan had helped me make my documentary film and had accompanied me on my interviews, including Hideo Honda and Madame Hong. On my citizenship application, too, her enthusiasm drove my irresolute self forward, with comments like,

Just do it, before you overthink it.

Lara-san, let's give it a go!

In the July heat, I headed down to the international section of the Legal Affairs Bureau in Yokohama's Naka Ward. I already had the one bad memory of when I went with my older brother after getting home from the States. This time, I made sure to carry my alien registration card, and the consultation went without a hitch. The case officer was kind and friendly.

"Ok, *Chin-san*, you're ok with Japanese, right?"

"*Hai.*"

"Where are you from?"

"Yokohama."

"Do you have a driver's license?"

"*Hai.*"

"Have you ever broken the law?"

"*I-ie.*"

We spoke for about an hour and I gave him my date and place of birth, and information about my parents and family and about the current work I did. I showed the officer my alien registration card and passport.

"I'm a bit concerned that you went overseas too much. Only two years have passed since you came back from the US. That may be tricky, but shall we go for it?"

"*Hai.* The nature of my work is such that I often have to go overseas for academic conferences and research."

"I understand. But during your application, refrain from going overseas as much as possible. Once you get citizenship, you can travel freely as much as you like."

"*Ha… hai.*"

"Ok, so now for nationality-related documents, bring me whatever you have at home in terms of passport—in your case, your Taiwanese passport; your travel papers for the People's Republic of China; if you have a re-entry permit, that; then, your birth registration and your parents' marriage certificate. You are already stateless, so if you can get me your expatriation certification…"

"Ok, I'll ask my parents."

"Make two photocopies of each document. Remember to bring the original."

"*Hai.*"

"When you have all the documentation, contact us again."

The case officer handed me a 37-page, sky-blue pamphlet called "Applying for Citizenship," which explained the documents that had to be submitted, listed the kanji Chinese characters authorized for use with personal names, and included a chart for converting between the Gregorian calendar and Japanese imperial years. It also carefully explained points such as the application prerequisites, procedures, and the dos and don'ts when writing the application.

"Read this and use it as a reference."

"Yes. Thank you very much."

I decided to start by getting ahold of the documents he marked in red. As soon as I got home, I asked my parents where their marriage certificate and our expatriation certificates were. My mother asked the inevitable.

"What are you going to use them for?"

"To apply for Japanese citizenship. Teru-chan and I are going to shoot a documentary about citizenship. Right, Teru-chan?"

Teru-chan answered with her usual grinning cheerfulness. "Yes, ma'am."

"The marriage certificate and the expatriation certification are on the sixth floor, I think," my father said. By sixth floor, he meant a nearby apartment that he had previously used as an office before converting it into storage for our home. "Just be careful. They are important."

Baba had always squirreled away every newspaper, document, and paper he got his hands on. He made a habit of placing every document into an envelope, marking the date in red, and filing it away. Mama saw the mountains of paper around the house and complained that, "We are cohabiting with garbage." Sometimes, I had to make an official announcement before throwing away some old newspaper or magazine.

But thanks to my father's hoarding, I readily found documents that would normally be hard to get ahold of, including my expatriation certificate and my parents' marriage certificate.

Their marriage certificate was embroidered cloth with the Chinese words *kang li zheng shu* (伉儷證書; matrimony certificate) written in gold letters on a red cover. Inside, butterflies, flowers, and other images graced a pink background, along with my parents' birthplace, date of birth, wedding time and venue, the signature of the common friend who had introduced them to each other, both sets of parents, the wedding witness, the bride and groom's signatures and seals. They had married in Taiwan, so they went to court (as a notary public) to get the official stamps and seals affixed. Come to think of it, this was the first time I had ever laid eyes on their marriage certificate.

Then, there was the Interior Ministry Citizenship Authorization Certificate, issued by the ROC, equivalent to an expatriation certificate. I had lost my citizenship on September 28, 1972, Year 61 of the Republic of China. It listed my age as *one*, and the photo showed baby me swaddled in a cotton blanket. Documents for my parents and elder siblings were filed alongside mine.

The certificate had a photo of my then 50-year-old father and 40-year-old mother. It stripped citizenship from them and their six children, making us all stateless.

I used both hands to spread open the B4 (250mm x 353mm) certificate, then examined it.

What did my parents feel at that time?

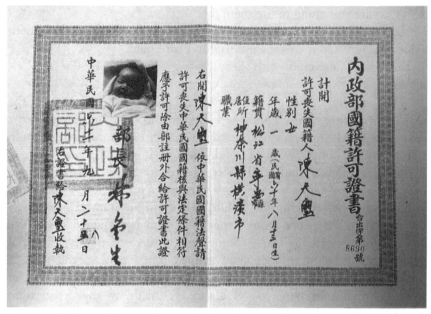

Interior Ministry Citizenship Authorization Certificate issued by the ROC on September 28, 1972

A few years after my birth, my father had apparently prepared documents to apply for naturalization. He had gotten the family's documents together, including the Reason for Applying for Naturalization document he wrote in his shaky Japanese, and had put them all in an envelope.

I remember that my family seriously discussed getting Japanese citizenship when I was in elementary school, but I opposed it. My father had gotten the required paperwork, but, in the end, didn't apply. This was back in the 1980s, when attaining Japanese citizenship was seen to be a feat as difficult to accomplish as climbing to heaven. My parents clearly anguished over our future. That is what I remembered while examining the documents.

I went to the local city office to get proof of my birth. Previously, visiting city hall meant going to the alien registration counter, but not today.

"Can I get a birth certificate here?"

"Whose?"

"My own."

"What are you going to use it for?"

"Naturalization."

Hearing the staff member's questions made me realize that birth certificates aren't used so often. It made sense that the staffer would look at me strangely for asking for mine. She handed me a copy of my birth registration, with an attached birth certificate that had the name of my birth hospital and the attending obstetrician. This was the first time I had ever seen my birth registration.

Seeing my father's handwriting assured me that I was indeed my parents' child. My parents had me at a pretty advanced age, and among my siblings, I was chronologically far removed from the rest. As a kid my siblings used to tease me:

"We found Lara under a bridge when we were playing."

Even though I knew they were teasing, I couldn't help sometimes thinking *what if that's really....* These were my thoughts as I looked at my birth registration. There was a field for *honseki*, or registered domicile. Inside parenthesis were the words: ("If you are a foreigner, please write your nationality.") My father had written *Republic of China*, but that had been crossed out and replaced with the word *China* placed to the side. My father had registered my birth on August 26, 1971, but I don't know when his nationality had been overwritten.

About a fortnight had passed since my last consultation at the Legal Affairs Bureau. I had gathered all my papers together as instructed and so returned to the citizenship section.

"Did you find your parents' marriage certificate and expatriation certificate?"

"Yes."

"Great. This will get much easier now. Often, it's a real struggle to get the registered domicile, marriage certificate, and other documents back in the home country. Sometimes applicants' parents don't even know where these certificates are. They really have a tough time. You should really appreciate your parents who kept them safe."

"Yes."

That was indeed true. Among the growing ranks of stateless children, many cannot get citizenship due to a missing document. After saying that, the inspector laid out the original and the copy next to each other and checked each line with a pencil.

"Ok, next time bring me your parents' alien registration card, your naturalized elder sister's *koseki* family register certificate, your tax payment certificate, the diplomas and transcripts from all the schools you have attended."

"Ok. Yes."

I had already procured many of these materials. Ordinary folks would get sick of getting documents together and writing paragraph upon paragraph for the application, but for a budding scholar like me, it was not so bad. It was troublesome, to be sure, but research was my forte. This process related directly to nationality issues, my own field of interest, so I even managed to have fun getting it all together. I discovered many things.

The inspector had broken down the document preparation process into two or three steps, which helped to prevent confusion.

In the end, I amassed over 20 documents, including my birth certificate, my passport, visa, and other citizenship-related papers, expatriation certificate, parents' marriage certificate, papers for five sisters and brothers, my tax payment certificate, withholding tax certificate, proof of payment for local city and prefectural taxes, my diplomas for every school I ever attended including in the US, and my driver's license.

Using the forms given to me, I had to write the application itself; give an outline of my family and relatives; explain my motive for naturalization; provide every address, school, and job on my bio; and note every country I had visited over the past year, including the dates I was away from home, the objective of each trip, and my travel companions. Finally, I had to write down any skills, awards, and any fines, penalties or criminal convictions.

How much income did I make? How much did I spend each month on food, housing, education, utilities, and healthcare? How much did I have in savings and on deposit? I had to write down all my assets—real estate, stocks, cars. Fortunately, I didn't have any stocks or real estate, so I didn't have to append any documents for those. I had to submit proof of employment, payroll slips; to draw a rough map of the neighborhood of my workplace; and to write the name of my superiors, coworkers, clients, and whether each of these people knew about my citizenship situation. I had to create the same report for my last three workplaces. I also needed the address and a rough map of the neighborhood of my last three places of residence; and the names, addresses, and phone numbers of neighbors I was close to.

I couldn't count them all, but I likely compiled or wrote over 30 documents. I submitted two snapshots of me with my family. I felt laid bare and exposed as I submitted such extremely private information.

It took me almost two months from the time of my first consultation until I had all the required documents ready. Yet, my case went relatively smoothly, I think. On my last visit to the citizenship section of the Legal Affairs Bureau, the staffer inspected my documents. For post-naturalization name, I wrote the three characters of my name as: 陳天璽 (pronounced *Chen Tienshi* in Chinese; *Chin Tenji* in Japanese). I was worried that the officials might ask me to change it. My friend who had just gone in to consult on the procedures for naturalization told me that the inspector advised her in a very suggestive manner about her post-naturalization name:

"If possible, I think a Japanese-sounding name would be better for you later on. It's not compulsory, but…"

My inspector was looking up something while saying,

"You are Chin Tenji-san? Um, just one moment."

"Is that no good?"

"They're in there. They're in there."

Fortunately, the three characters were in the list of kanji designated for use with personal names that was attached to the manual. So, I was able to use them for my name.

"The final document."

The inspector handed me a written pledge, on which was written,

I swear to uphold the law and be a good citizen.

I wrote the date August 29, 2002, signed and sealed it.

"All right, then."

The inspector handed me a green piece of paper after affixing several stamps to it. On it were written the receipt date, assigned number, and the case officer's number. If I had any questions, I had to use the case officer's number rather than his name, which I never learned.

"If anything like your address, contact information, or job changes, promptly call the phone number written here. When the decision is made, we will contact you."

I had officially submitted the application for citizenship and now had only to wait for the Ministry of Justice to authorize my naturalization.

"If you leave the country, be sure to inform us beforehand. And take extra care not to commit any traffic infractions."

I felt a complicated mix of hope and doubt, excitement and anxiety about what would become of this application, especially as I was using myself as a research case study. Teru-chan and I captured on video all the documents I submitted and my complex emotions.

A few months later, someone contacted my parents' home. I thought it was the Legal Affairs Bureau, but it was Minpaku (National Museum of Ethnology). After examining my resume, plans, and other documents, they wanted me to come in for an interview. The interview that took place two weeks later in Osaka went smoothly.

The week after the interview, I got a call from the professor in charge.

"Your research project idea on statelessness is fascinating. We would love for you to conduct your research with our institution. But since you yourself are stateless, hiring you as a national civil servant is tricky. Our institution has proactively hired foreigners, and we can hire foreigners or national civil servants for research posts under the jurisdiction of the Ministry of Education, Culture, Sports, Science and Technology. But this would be our first case of a potential hire who is stateless. Early next week, I will go to various ministries and agencies to ask about hiring you. For that, please send me the reason for your statelessness, the cause, and any other supporting information, right away."

The professor's comments confirmed a dread I had held in the back of my mind.

"But Chin-san. This too will fit into your research project. Let's give it a try."

That one comment emboldened me. I quickly wrote and sent the professor a composition expounding on the background and details of my and my family's state of statelessness. Research posts at institutes and universities under the jurisdiction of the Ministry of Education, Culture, Sports, Science and Technology are for national government employees, but foreign nationals too can be hired with certain restrictions, such as a limited number of years under contract. Foreigners with permanent residence, as I had, were eligible to become civil servants. Even stateless, I had no problem on that score, thanks to the successful fight of Masayo Hirata, whom I had met in Okinawa, to get the national government to include stateless as a category of foreign national.

In April 2003, I became a national government employee despite being myself stateless. I would research globalization and statelessness as an assistant professor at the National Museum of Ethnology.

Saying Goodbye to My Stateless Alien Card

When I began my work at the museum, it was my first time working as a member of an organization. Of course, I no longer had the freedom I had in graduate school or as an independent researcher when I could decide my own research schedule. But I was lucky working at the Minpaku in the sense that I could research whatever I wanted to research.

I immediately waded into research on statelessness, my top area of interest. Until then, the most well-known domestic cases of statelessness were the many Amerasians in Okinawa in the 1980s; and, more recently, the illegitimate children born from foreign women who overstayed their visas and Japanese men, and also those who became stateless after falling through the cracks of the Nationality Act. But I got the sense there were many varieties of stateless people, including my own case. Research made me realize I was right.

Although I moved from Yokohama in the eastern Kanto region of Japan to Osaka in the Kansai western region to work at the Minpaku, I made many trips back to Kanto. I ended up shuttling back and forth between Itami and Haneda Airports.

It was probably early June. I was busy running around for work, when I got a phone call from the Legal Affairs Bureau. I had been authorized for Japanese citizenship, so they wanted me to come in within a few days.

"Yeah, yes. I'll come in early next week."

After hanging up the phone, I felt weird inside. *The decision already?* People who had gone through the naturalization process had told me that it usually took over a year between submission and the result. Some said it took them two or three years. For me, only about nine months had passed since my official submission in late August, so I felt it was unexpectedly soon.

The next week, I dragged my sister to the international section of Yokohama's Legal Affairs Bureau.

"I have receipt number 199. Can I speak to No. 5, please?"

"Yes, Chin-san, right?"

His was a new face, not the staffer who had helped me in the previous visits.

"I am No. 5 case officer, who took over your case file. *Konnichi wa.*"

"Thank you."

"Yes, Chin-san, your naturalization application was accepted. Congratulations."

"Thank you very much."

He grinned in a very friendly manner.

"Yes, this is the document."

He laid the naturalization authorization notice, my naturalized person ID, and other documents out on the table.

My naturalized person ID proved I had been naturalized by notice from the Ministry of Justice and indicated what should be written on my *koseki* family register, naturalization items, and other details.

"Take this and go right away to the local ward office to report your naturalization and do any other required procedures. Also, return your alien registration card and change your license and other certificates soon. As it says here, you can be fined if you don't surrender your alien registration card within 14 days or don't submit your naturalization report within a month."

"Um, when can I get a passport?"

"Passports are a different office. That's under the Ministry of Foreign Affairs. It's pretty complicated. You can get it at the passport center, so go there. For Yokohama, the center is near Yamashita Park."

"Oh, ok."

"But you will need a transcript of your *koseki* family register and a *juminhyo* residence certificate, so the first thing you do is take today's documents, go to your ward office, and file the naturalization report. Until you get the *koseki* family register and *juminhyo* residence certificate, you can't get a passport. If you have plans to travel overseas, then that is even more reason to get this done quickly. I suggest you go there on your way home from here."

"Ok. I will do that."

I left the office. The case officer was so kind he came out after me into the hall to see my sister and me out, saying. "Congratulations. Really!"

On our way home, we stopped by the Naka Ward office, which happened to be located down the road from the Legal Affairs Bureau. I went to the *koseki* section, showed them the naturalized person ID I had just received, filled out and submitted a naturalization report.

My old and new names were the same 陳天璽 (*Chin Tenji* in Japanese). I also wrote my birth date, address, parents' names, and nationality. For citizenship prior to naturalization, I wrote *stateless*; for my *honseki* official address, I checked *I will create a new koseki family register*; and for head of household, I put the three characters of my name, 陳天璽.

After the name, there were parentheses in which to put the kana reading of the Chinese characters of my name. I was about to write the kana for *chin* but hesitated. The ward office staffer saw me and said,

"You can put anything you want. It's just the reading for the sake of convenience. The reading won't go into the *koseki* family register."

"Oh, really? So, can I use the Chinese reading?"

"Yes, sure."

"Then, let's do that."

For my name 陳天璽, I adapted the Chinese reading, *Che-n Ti-en shi*. I wanted to avoid trouble caused by having a different name depending on where I went. When I went to the States, people had started spelling my name using Latin script, so I thought it would be better to achieve some semblance of consistency with the correct pronunciation of my name. I thought it was totally natural that news media changed how they pronounced then-President Kim Dae-jung (金大中, 김대중) in Japanese, from *Kin Dai-chu* to *Kimu De-jun*. I thought my naturalization provided me a good chance to do likewise, so I wrote my name with that pronunciation.

By reporting my naturalization, I had created a brand new *koseki* family register.

"Ok, so go to that alien registration counter over there and go through the procedures to surrender your alien registration card."

The staffer had already spoken to his colleague at the other counter.

"Yes, now, write down the required items on this document."

I was handed a document entitled Alien Registration Card Surrender Report. I filled in my alien card number, my original (lack of) nationality, my address, my post-naturalization name, my date of birth, and other information. Below that was written:

(1) I was authorized for naturalization to Japanese citizenship by force of Justice Ministry notice No. ____, dated ____. I therefore hereby surrender my alien registration card.
(2) I have acquired Japanese citizenship through notification of Article ____, Section ____, of the Nationality Act (or its supplementary provisions) on the date of ____. I therefore hereby surrender my alien registration card.

I wrote the number corresponding to the field for (1), affixed my signature and seal. This document was the last bureaucratic thread tying me to statelessness.

"Now, surrender your alien registration card."

I took my little alien registration card out of the place in my wallet I always kept it.

"Here."

I stood there for a moment.

"Is that all?"

"Yes, that's it."

With my sister, I left and descended the stairs. That little card that I had kept with me at all times to prove who I was no longer belonged to me. I loathed that fact. I felt as if someone was somehow pulling my hair from behind. So, I ran back up the stairs and back to the counter.

"Excuse me. I would like to keep that alien registration card as a souvenir."

"You can't do that."

"You can punch a hole in it or cut off the corner or something. It's really important to me."

"No, you can't. We shred them all."

It felt like a merciless response. People nearby looked at me as I begged, as if I was saying something bizarre. It was clear my persistence would not be rewarded. I understood that the city office cannot make an exception due to concern over fraudulent use of the card. But to me, it represented an important part of my personal history.

"It will go into the shredder?"

I whimpered to my sister that it was somehow sad.

"We shouldn't have gone through with it today."

"What are you talking about? The papers said you have to do it within two weeks."

"Yeah, but still."

Most of my life, I had carried around that card at all times. Its designation *stateless* carried the word that helped to shape my identity. I was not yet psychologically prepared to say goodbye to it.

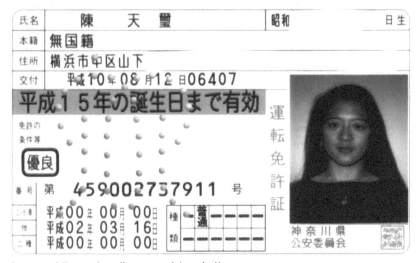

The word "stateless" on my driver's license

Passport Application and Name

As soon as I had my Japanese citizenship, I made plans to go to Brunei. I had heard that there were many stateless residents there, but it was one country I had just about given up on visiting because of the forementioned visa challenges. Now I had my *koseki* family register and *juminhyo* residency certificate, so in early July, I went back to Yokohama to apply for my first ever passport since naturalizing.

First, I went to the ward office to get my *koseki* certificate and *juminhyo* residency certificate.

I had always been a resident of Japan but had not had a residency certificate—even though I paid residence and income tax. My parents even paid real estate tax. But foreigners can neither vote nor run for office. The *juminhyo* residency certificate is created based on your *koseki* family register, so foreigners who have no *koseki* didn't get a *juminhyo* at this time. Even Tama-chan the Seal had a *juminhyo*, but I, a resident of Japan, didn't.

It had always puzzled me that the program for my health insurance card had been National Health Insurance, which in Japanese begins with the word *kokumin*, meaning citizen, even though I wasn't a citizen. I realize that I have touched upon this before, but I could never understand why my alien card said I was *stateless*. Was it just something to call my nationality? Still, there were many strange things like that.

I went to the ward office to get a document different from ever before. I felt keenly how different what I held was and saw as a foreigner and as a Japanese national. Even when circumstances remain the same, the world sure seems to change when your social position is different. This new document was unfamiliar to me, so I had to be careful filling it in.

On a piece of green paper entitled Request for Copies of Juminhyo Residence Certificate, I filled in the usual address, name, and date of birth. I wrote in the number of *juminhyo* and *koseki* family register copies I needed, then submitted the form at the counter.

"Uh, I think you might have indicated the wrong documents."

"Eh?"

"Are you the requestor?"

"Yes."

"Are you Japanese?"

"I think so. Please check. I should have a *koseki* family register."

It was the first time for me getting a document like a *koseki* family register or *juminhyo* residency certificate, so I was a tad nervous. But I thought it must be there, so I answered confidently. After a while, he returned.

"Sorry to keep you waiting. Yes, it was there. Boy, what an unusual name. I tell you…"

This middle-aged man at the counter had assumed I was a so-called foreigner. On top of judging a person's nationality or origin based on skin color like in Western countries, in Japan you are also judged based on your name. Many children end up bullied, and many people end up suffering discrimination as a result. Thus, many people take on Japanese-sounding names even if they don't naturalize.

I had grown used to being different from others from the time I was little. Perhaps it was due to my personality. Perhaps because I kept using my real name. Perhaps it was my environment. It caused me a great deal of hassle, because I repeatedly had to correct people and explain myself. I believe these hassles led to positive developments, such as discoveries and improved communication. I managed to find amusement in being different from others.

Even now that I was a Japanese national, I recognized the impression and impact my "foreign-sounding" name had on others.

I got together the required documents and rushed off to the passport center. I wrote up and submitted the application as per the guidance at the passport application information counter at the entrance to the passport center.

"We can't use this Latin alphabet spelling for your name."

"Huh? That's not gonna work."

"We use Hepburn romanization to transliterate names, so we cannot do *Chen Tien-shi*."

"But it's my name."

Changing the romanization of my name meant disjointing my future self from every certificate thus far received in the US and other Western countries and every dissertation submitted. I wanted to avoid this.

"But the Hepburn system has no *che* or *tie*."

"You say that, but doesn't Japanese have the sound *che*? I don't know what the Hepburn system is, but this is my name."

I had no intention of yielding. The middle-aged woman who was handling my application was stumped and went to the back to speak with her boss. Scratching his head, the superior eventually said,

"The name on your *koseki* family register is 陳天璽. What furigana syllables are used there?"

Without skipping a beat, I showed a copy of my naturalization report, upon which was written *ch-e-n t(e)-i-e-n shi*, the furigana syllables I wrote when creating my *koseki* family register; just as on my passport application.

"You have naturalized, I see. If so, then please show me the passport you used before naturalizing."

"The Legal Affairs Bureau said they would keep my passport, so I don't have it."

"Then, please go get a copy of it. We will apply to the Ministry of Foreign Affairs to see if we can make a passport transliterating the name using a non-Hepburn system."

I contacted the Legal Affairs Bureau where I had applied for naturalization, explained the situation, and had them send me a copy of my old passport. When I naturalized, I was relieved not to have to change my name, thinking I was done with the name issue. I never imagined the issue would hound me like this.

My anger didn't subside even after I got home.

"What's the matter, Lara? Did something happen again at the city office?"

"They told me I can't spell my name in Roman letters the way I do. They told me to use the Hepburn system. I think they want me to spell my name using the Japanese reading *Chin Tenji*."

"Oh, geez. Well, who cares how it's spelled in English? Your kanji characters will stay the same, right?" My sister was so happy-go-lucky about the whole thing.

"You say that, but what am I supposed to do about my certificates written in English? There's gonna be a discrepancy. Your problem is you just let people walk all over you. If you don't change contradictions in the rules and laws, then society won't get any better!"

"There you go again…" My sister was fed up with me.

Ironically, James Curtis Hepburn was known as an exemplary and compassionate physician and founder of Meiji Gakuin University. Ironically, he would have been my neighbor, as he had lived in a hilly section of the city less than ten minutes from Chinatown.

When I first heard that they used the Hepburn system of romanization, I didn't know what it meant. After researching, I came to feel sympathy for the good doctor, since unlike Audrey Hepburn, who is romanized as *Ōdorī Heppubān*, James Curtis Hepburn is transliterated in a non-Hepburn manner of romanization as Hebon.

I had returned to Osaka, but after a copy of my old passport arrived in the post, I went back to the passport center. My August trip to Brunei was fast approaching, so I had no time to dawdle.

"You're here about the romanization of your name, right? Were you able to get a copy of your passport?"

"Yes. I brought it with me."

We negotiated for about an hour. Even if my citizenship and the color of my passport changed, I simply did not want to change my name. For me, my name was the first thing I present to people which expresses who I am.

After a few weeks, I returned to Yokohama to pick up my passport. The day arrived and I was anxious about how my name would be romanized.

"What is your name and date of birth?"

"Chen Tienshi. August 13, 1971."

"Which prefecture is your *honseki* official residence in?"

"My *honseki*? Um…, Kanagawa Prefecture."

This was the first time I was ever asked for my *honseki*, as only Japanese citizens get this official residence. So, I panicked a bit. As soon as I got my hands on the passport, I opened it up to the name page.

Chen Tien-shi.

They had recognized a non-Hepburn romanization of my name, which would not need to change. My brand-new passport with a red cover had my photo and my name as a citizen of Japan. There was a note that read:

> The Minister for Foreign Affairs of Japan requests all those whom it may concern to allow the bearer, a Japanese national, to pass freely and without hindrance and, in case of need, to afford him or her every possible aid and protection.

It felt strange to the touch.

I had lived for so long as a stateless person that I tended to gravitate toward stateless people. I felt the contradictions and limitations of national interest, war, and other things based on the nation state, so I didn't want to immerse myself in that. But my way of life and identity remained the same. I retained a strong desire to approach everybody as if I were still a stateless person, just like before. I told myself it would be possible because even though I was no longer stateless on paper, the psychological aspect remained.

Returning home from the passport center, my number two sister asked to see my passport. I handed my Japanese passport to my sister and said,

"I didn't change my name."

My sister examined my Japanese passport carefully and said "*Omedetoh*." I just couldn't let her comment go. Is *congratulations* a word you say to someone for getting a passport? Because I didn't have to change my name?

"What do you mean, *Omedetoh*?"

I had unintentionally used a defiant tone with my older sister. Being a kind sister, she let it slide. But at that moment, the most on edge of any of us was surely my mother, sitting at the nearby table. Mama had resisted my getting Japanese citizenship to the end. She didn't want to join our passport conversation.

"I don't want to see it."

Mama said this to my sisters near her. My mother and I avoided each other that day and even averted our eyes.

I couldn't sleep that night. I couldn't stop thinking about my mother to whom I hadn't spoken a word all day. No matter how much I closed my eyes, I kept seeing my beloved mother's face.

It wasn't that I didn't understand how she felt. My mother placed her identity in one place. As with many people, my mother believed she should feel a sense of belonging to the nation state. I too felt that way when I was little. So, I understood her insistence on her nationality. But I had anguished over my identity, worked through it, and came to feel that, in truth, identity is not tied to your nationality or citizenship.

People come to have a feeling of attachment to various locales because they move around and migrate. That's a natural way to be, and there is no need to stick to one country or repudiate other countries in order to protect something. I thought there was no problem thinking that way. Thus, there was no need for me to place my sense of belonging in one particular country only. Some people don't even have that luxury.

People like me might be accused of disloyalty. But those caught between countries in that way have a feeling of attachment to many places, so they want peace for every country to which they feel attached. They would have trouble otherwise. They don't want those countries to go to war. They simply cannot choose one country over the other. What they long for is coexistence and coprosperity.

I believe that these people—precisely because of who they are—can serve as a bridge between countries. This thinking reminded me of the rainbow metaphor which I used in my doctoral dissertation for the Chinese diaspora.

The ties that bind human beings go beyond nationality to include many factors, including where they are born and the languages they speak. I believe that judging people only by their nationality and passport is incomplete, like looking at but one of the seven colors of a rainbow. Interaction must take place between hearts and minds. Such ties are crucial and enable us to transcend borders in a true sense. Experiencing statelessness enabled me to come to that realization.

9 Statelessness in Other Countries

Stateless family near the Thailand-Myanmar border

Refugees and Stateless People

In July 2003, I got a call from the United Nations High Commissioner for Refugees (UNHCR). The caller had read an article about my statelessness in the *International Herald Tribune/Asahi Shimbun* and wanted to meet me. I went to the UNHCR office in the United Nations University Building in Tokyo's Shibuya district. I was asked to help with a project about stateless people in Japan.

I had just begun my research on stateless people, and I made clear that I wanted to meet real stateless people and find out directly what kinds of issues they faced.

The commissioner told me about a stateless person named Wuyi Kroengyu and faxed me a three-page-long letter that Wuyi had written about how he ended up in Japan, what had caused him to become stateless, and how he had trouble getting by.

I met up with Wuyi right away and arranged to speak with him about his issues with statelessness.

Wuyi was 31 years old. He was stuck in Japan during 14 years of statelessness. While Vietnam and France engaged in fierce fighting at Diên Biên Phu, Wuyi's parents were driven out of their native Vietnam, fleeing to northeastern Thailand. Wuyi was born and grew up in Thailand, then came to Japan at the age of 17. He entered Japan illegally on a fake passport, given to him by a broker, and was thus detained by the Immigration Bureau in 1992. The Japanese government tried to deport him, but the Thai government refused to accept him because they didn't recognize him as a Thai. The Vietnamese government also refused to accept him because he had no evidence that he was a Vietnamese citizen. He was therefore stateless, and no country would take him in after his deportation from Japan. With no country to return to, he stayed in detention for three years. In 1996, he was granted *kari homen* (provisional release).

"I want to go back home to Thailand. My family and everyone are there. I was called to interviews at the Thai embassy dozens of times. Each time, I asked them please to issue me a Thai passport, but they said they can't because I don't have citizenship. The Japanese immigration agent told me to try it with Vietnam, but that didn't work either."

Wuyi showed me documents with many different seals imprinted on them. During his provisional release, he had to show up at the Immigration Bureau each month and be questioned about his living circumstances. He was not free to leave his prefecture without applying and getting permission beforehand.

He was thinking about getting married to a volunteer Japanese instructor named Etsuko Kosuge, a year his senior.

"Earlier is better, after all. We're only getting older. We want children, too. But we are in no position to get married."

Etsuko nodded quietly next to him.

"Let's figure it out. Don't give up hope. Those who have everything like citizenship and wealth may suffer more than you because they have no goals or dreams. Hang on to your hope and let's show them. We'll find a way."

Wuyi told me of the myriad troubles he had due to being stateless. Having been stateless myself, these stories outraged me. Love has no borders. The nation's laws try to obstruct the love between two people and build a wall between them. I wonder if the people who make these laws and systems have any idea how much these issues cause suffering or that these things even happen.

Statelessness in Brunei

After getting my Japanese passport, I went ahead with my plans for fieldwork, including visits to Brunei and Malaysia. I no longer had any anxiety about needing to run around busily to get visas and re-entry permits, like I had to do when I was stateless. My travel agent said,

"Chin-san, things are a lot easier for you now."

I had caused my travel agent a lot of headache when I was stateless. She had helped me with visas when I went overseas, told me where each embassy was located, written up my travel itinerary, flight reservation confirmation and other documents needed for my visa applications. I felt keenly how much many different people had supported me.

The day of my departure for Brunei approached. My objective was to learn about the lives of ethnic Chinese people who were stateless. I was fascinated by how they self-identified. I felt empathy for them too. For my research, I wanted to compare their cases with my own case of becoming stateless because of a government policy change. If possible, I wanted to shoot a documentary, so I brought my camera. An NHK announcer who wanted to cover these cases with me accompanied me with his camera. A fieldwork friend of mine who thought my plan to do research in Brunei sounded interesting also tagged along.

Brunei is a tropical country in the northern part of Borneo. Malays make up 70 per cent of the population. Oil and natural gas account for 90 per cent of its exports and 60 per cent of its GDP. The sultanate is centered around Malays and Muslims. The people maintain a high standard of living thanks to abundant natural resources. The government pays for healthcare and school from elementary to college.

We headed for Labi, a town in central Brunei. Oil drilling had begun early in the outskirts of Labi, so many ethnic Chinese workers had migrated here. There were reportedly about 350 of them, in 70 households. Many of the ethnic Chinese residents of Brunei are stateless. Unlike Brunei citizens, they must pay for part of their healthcare and the education of their children. Inheritance is also restricted.

An acquaintance living in Brunei arranged a visit to the home of 65-year-old Wang Laifu (pseudonym), who managed an orange grove.

He greeted us topless, apparently waking up from a nap. Wang was tan, rugged, and muscular for a 65 year old. While throwing on a shirt, he introduced his live-in daughter and her Filipina friend.

"Can we use our camera?"

"No problem."

He was as tough as he looked. With most stateless people, I did all I could do to get them to agree to an interview; most refused filming.

I could see Wang's home through my viewfinder. On the wall of the waiting room hung photos of the sultan and queen, as well as several of Wang's family.

Wang was born in Borneo which is now East Malaysia. Soon after birth, he and his family moved to Bruneian territory. Both Malaya and Brunei were under British rule at the time, not independent countries. During the chaos after World War II, he was in no position to gain citizenship. His parents had moved to Brunei, seeking work in the oil industry, and had remained stateless since that time.

During our hour-long conversation, I told him I was researching statelessness. Wang showed me his permanent resident travel document issued by the Bruneian government.

"It used to say *stateless person*, but now it says *permanent resident*. It's great not to be called *stateless*, but I'm not a real citizen."

"Do you still have the passport that says *stateless*?"

I just wanted to look at it. But Wang slowly shook his head.

"Of course, I have it. But I can't show it to you. They treat me like a permanent resident now. I don't want people to think I'm dredging up the past."

In a flash, his unexpected words opened my eyes to the ongoing crisis in their stateless lives—exactly what I had been seeking to understand. It's easy to listen to everything casually. Wang continued in a quietly suppressed voice.

"It's because the government and we ethnic Chinese think differently. If you are born Chinese here, you have no option but to persevere. It's better not to say too much."

Upon hearing how disconsolate he felt, I did all I could do to stop from bursting out in tears. It was perhaps a feeling Wang and I shared, having lived as a stateless person. We both wanted to love our country of residence. That was why we continued to live there. But would the country love us? Would we have to live in this land without ever being loved? Wang quietly placed his arm around my shoulder as tears made it so that I could barely get the questions out.

That night in my hotel room, I spent some time in a daze. On an ordinary night after an interview, I would write up a report of what happened. But I sat facing the PC having no idea what to write. The gravity of each word Wang spoke weighed heavy on me. The pain stateless residents of Brunei felt was more than I had imagined.

Up until then, I had thought maybe I might find some way to help stateless people by learning more about their issues and by raising awareness in different formats, including making a documentary film. Instead, I risked making them suffer and maybe even endangering their livelihoods.

Many people were willing to be interviewed but feared showing their face to the camera. I was embarrassed by my own naiveté. I completely lost confidence. With all this, they could easily refuse to speak to others, yet Wang spoke to me in front of the camera. He surely cooperated because he thought a stateless person like me could understand him. The truth is that deep in their hearts, everybody wonders if there might not be some way to rectify the situation. What could be done to take a step toward resolving the issue? I felt only impatience.

The next day, we visited an academy run autonomously by the Chinese community. Stateless Chinese students in their twenties, thirties, forties and fifties learned Malay in this school with the aim of acquiring Bruneian citizenship.

Around midday, I spoke to the director of the academy, who let me film, with several conditions, including: "You don't show the sign and don't make it possible to identify individuals or the organization running the academy." I had finally gotten someone to let me film them.

Every year, Brunei holds exams for stateless residents to acquire citizenship. To become a Bruneian citizen, you must learn many facets of Malay culture, including the language. Although about 300 people get citizenship each year, the standards for passing are not publicized, so many examinees reportedly have trouble trying to figure out how to prepare. Chinese residents may be able to speak Malay, but they don't understand fine grammar points. On the day I visited, the teacher was going over rudimentary grammar.

One Chinese student in his fifties managed a shipping company. He had been born in and grown up in Brunei. When he was small, he did custodial work in the day and worked as a cook in the evening. He worked day and night to build and grow his company. He paid taxes. But he could not get citizenship. He had taken the exam twice and failed twice. They would not tell him why he had failed. He continued his studies and had not given up.

"What the hell are you doing?"

During the interview, we heard a commotion outside the windows of the door. In Chinese, we heard,

Why is there a camera in there?

Who gave permission to do interviews?

I ran out of the classroom to talk to them.

About five or six academy personnel stood there, apparently outraged. They surrounded us.

Who are you?

If you interview people here, they might not be able to study.

Are you accusing us of something?

I didn't know how to respond. The NHK director stood in front of me and explained that we got permission from the person in charge and we were filming in such a way as to ensure the location could not be identified. I trembled, hiding behind the director.

Their anger did not subside. Their tone became more aggressive. They insisted we stop filming and get the hell out.

My heart filled with melancholy. We were all stateless Chinese. We were all away from our home country, seeking a place overseas for us to make a life. We only wanted to live like the citizens of the countries where we were born and had lived, yet we were rejected. They simply wanted to do whatever they could to protect this school. I understood their feeling so much it hurt. But if something wasn't done, then nothing would change. It's not just you; we cannot just leave this problem to our children.

I shouted at them.

"Please listen! Me too, I've experienced living stateless, in Japan. Our pain and suffering may not be the same, but I want to find some way to change things. I can just walk forward with my eyes closed. I can pretend I haven't seen anything. But even if it is rough and painful, I'm going to open my eyes, look at what is going on, and communicate it to other people. By telling many people about this, can't we find some way—*some way*—to come one step closer to a society of happiness and equality? I just want to help with that…"

At this point, maybe I was more crying and shrieking than speaking coherently. I desperately tried to continue with gestures. I just broke down. My voice became hoarse, and I simply couldn't speak any further.

Nobody ventured to break the ensuing silence. A man came to stand next to me. Those who had gathered around me at a distance now approached, reducing the gap between us. The scariest-looking man came over and hugged me tightly. The others crowded in and enveloped me, some with tears on their cheeks.

What would I really be able to do for these people? But I knew I had to try to do something. Within their circle, I felt extraordinary pain.

They had really persevered. They struggled desperately for their beloved families.

Why do people have to suffer because of nationality and national borders? I traveled to the border between Brunei and Malaysia to watch people come in and out of the country for a while. You can't get alcohol in Brunei, so I saw people crossing into Malaysia, wallet in hand, to buy beer. They went back and forth nonchalantly. But for some people, like me the previous year, the border stood like a big, thick wall. A different little passport in my hand enabled me to stand where I stood. An indescribable wistfulness welled up inside me.

The sun sank in the border area. Birds flew gracefully across the reddening sky. The birds freely flapped their wings in the dusk sky, with no concern for national borders.

The birds looked freer and happier.

Paris Charles de Gaulle Airport

One case of statelessness outside Japan drew great attention. Both the Steven Spielberg film *The Terminal*, starring Tom Hanks and released in December 2004, and the 1993 French film *Tombés du ciel* (Lost in Transit) told the story of Alfred Mehran, who made Paris Charles de Gaulle Airport his home for 18 years. All his daily supplies were in his luggage. He took a "shower" each morning and evening in the airport lavatory and ate in the airport café. He sat on a bench in Terminal 1 and watched people leave Paris for other countries.

He was born circa 1945, with the name Mehran Karimi Nasseri (Persian: مهران کریمی ناصری) in a southern Iranian town, to an Iranian father and a British mother. Upon his father's death in 1967, he went to his mother's home country, the UK. During the 1970s, he studied at the University of Bradford and took part in a protest demonstration against the Shah of Iran. He returned to Iran in 1976, where he was detained for participating in the demonstration. His citizenship was expunged under the pretext that he had died in prison, and he was ordered to leave the country. He fled right back to the UK as a political refugee, but was refused entry. He drifted from place to place around Europe, ending up detained for illegal entry.

In 1988, he arrived in Charles de Gaulle Airport. This arrival changed his life, as the airport became his home and place of residence. An international airport exists in the space between nation states, as we see from products sold duty free; it is located, in a sense, on the national border. In a sense, it is a zone liberated from the nation state. It was perhaps the most comfortable place for a stateless person like Mehran.

The airport was stocked with many things, including an airport medical center akin to a hospital. Mehran even had his own attending physician. He didn't cause any trouble to airport workers. He never inconvenienced other travelers. So, nobody ever tried to drive him out of the airport.

In 1999, France offered him refugee status. But the inspector had written his Iranian name on the form, instead of *Alfred* as he insisted to be called. So, he refused to sign the form and remained in the Paris airport until 2006, for a total of 18 years.

Many people came to see him after the release of the movies based on his experience. He got fan mail addressed to Alfred at Terminal 1.

In 2005, I got a research grant from the Ministry of Education, Culture, Sports, Science and Technology and began frequent visits to the United Nations High Commissioner for Refugees (UNHCR), the International Organization for Migration, and other international institutions, as well as to the Vatican's council for migrants.

I studied the efforts of each institution and countries of the world for stateless persons. Many people live stateless in Europe, including itinerant Romani. During my research of stateless Europeans, I finally got a chance to visit Alfred at the Paris airport.

I asked people at the airport counter and cleaners to direct me to Alfred. After walking around the large airport, I finally found him. Benches that could sit six to eight people were amassed in a corner that received sunlight filtering in through a large window. That collection of benches had become Alfred's abode. Next to a cart with his luggage sat Alfred himself. His suitcases, bags, and other belongings were propped up on the cart. Several suits hung from the cart's front push handle. The small upper section had been transformed into an ad hoc bookshelf carrying several books. On the bench he sat on were old newspapers, magazines, coffee, and food bought at a fast food airport kiosk. Alfred was dressed normally, with groomed hair and beard.

"Hi, Alfred! I came from Japan to meet you. I'm Lara."

"…"

Alfred remained expressionless.

"I was stateless for more than 30 years."

"…"

Alfred sat with a blank expression, as if he had lost all interest for anything in the world. I might have detected a slight reaction when he heard I had been stateless. But he made no sound.

Looking at his cart, transformed into a bookshelf and dresser, I said,

"You read many books. What do you think about statelessness, nationality, and national borders? I would love to hear about your experience living in the airport."

"..."

Alfred told me nothing. Silence persisted. I felt awkward just standing there, and bad for him.

"I will come see you the next time I'm in Paris. Stay well!"

After saying this, I departed his home, Terminal 1 of de Gaulle Airport. I never got a chance to hear his voice.

It seemed as if Alfred had great pain in his heart, or perhaps he had simply lost interest in people. I promised myself that the next time I came to Paris, I would come see him.

Six years later, in June 2011, the UNHCR and non-governmental organizations (NGOs) held a conference in Geneva to mark 60 years since the adoption of the 1951 Refugee Convention; 50 years since the 1961 Convention on the Reduction of Statelessness; and 150 years since the birth of Fridtjof Wedel-Jarlsberg Nansen, known for introducing the *Nansen Passport* for stateless persons. The NGO Stateless Network, the first ever in Japan to tackle stateless issues, was invited to the conference. I visited Geneva and Paris for this conference.

I took a red-eye from Haneda Airport to Paris, where I transited at Paris Charles de Gaulle Airport, then on to Geneva. I went through immigration control in Paris during my transit and had five hours to kill before my flight to Geneva. I headed to Terminal 1 to keep my promise to Alfred.

But neither he nor his bookshelf or dresser were there. Alfred (Mehran Karimi Nasseri) died November 12, 2022.

Alfred became famous after the release of the Hollywood film *The Terminal*, loosely based on his story. I heard a rumor that not only did he make money from the film, but the US also granted him residence and he left his Paris airport home for the States. I felt sad to think that my list of friends in Paris had become one name shorter. But in my heart, I hoped he was happy and healthy in his new home.

That year marked a turning point in my life. I had gained a lot through my research while living in Europe, but it was also a year of personal fortune—the year that my partner and I made our vows during a lightning wedding in Rome.

Anne Frank's Dream Deferred

Anne Frank is the globally celebrated author of what was published as *Anne Frank: The Diary of a Young Girl*. It's less well known that she was stateless. When she wrote the diary and when she left this world in 1945, Anne Frank was stateless. The diary, written by a teenager, stands as a historical testament to those who suffered persecution and were killed during World War II. She never lost hope and lived with relentless enthusiasm, even under the Nazi occupation of her country. The way she lived her life gives hope, courage, and the strength to go on, to countless people throughout the world even today.

Recently, more than 75 years after her death, an incident happened that brought to the fore the fact that she was stateless. In the Netherlands in October 2004, a debate raged in newspapers, media, and in the parliament over whether to grant Anne Frank citizenship posthumously.

Dutch TV network KRO used newspaper and other media to ask its viewers their opinions, to create a program on who was the *Greatest Dutch Person*. The poll resulted in Anne Frank among the top ten, a list that included the painter Rembrandt. The diary was written in a secret attic in her Amsterdam home. The Anne Frank House is now a museum that memorializes the Holocaust and displays Anne and her family's personal effects in order to appeal for the peace and equality of humanity. Visitors to the Netherlands always make sure to visit the house. The country is proud of Anne Frank.

Born in Germany in 1929, she and her family fled Nazi persecution to Holland, as many Jews did in the mid-1930s. In 1941, the Nazis stripped Jews living outside the country of German citizenship, rendering Anne Frank stateless.

Although stateless, her ties to Holland were profound. In her diary, she wrote, "I want to become Dutch." KRO viewers in the Netherlands naturally cited her as an example of a great and revered Dutch person.

KRO TV producers and many Dutch citizens learned that Anne Frank didn't have Dutch citizenship and petitioned the Ministry of Justice to grant her posthumous citizenship. It developed into a political issue, including a movement in the States General of the Netherlands parliament to amend the law to clear her path to citizenship.

The Ministry of Justice looked for some sort of loophole in existing law that would permit it, but the country's nationality law did not permit posthumous naturalization. Anne Frank remained stateless.

The network's efforts to produce a program using Anne Frank's memory as a vehicle to overcome the barrier of the nation state fascinated me. The feedback from the citizens driven on by the posthumous citizenship campaign and the parliamentary support were encouraging signs. Unfortunately, the government was unable to translate the people's wishes into legislation.

As is clear from this case, what determines people's nationality and legal position is always the national government. In other words, the affiliation and legal status that serve as an important foundation for the formation of a person's character are often controlled or manipulated by the national government. But how credible is the notion of confining each individual within a framework of nationality and the nation state? Why did Dutch citizens think now to accept her as one of their own? Over 75 years ago, when she wanted to become Dutch, why didn't they accept her in that way?

In the end, the efforts of the Dutch people to extend citizenship to Anne Frank went unrewarded.

In an October 7, 2004 interview with the newspaper *Trouw*, Justice Minister Jan Pieter Hendrik Donner was quoted as saying,

> Anne cannot be naturalized because making exception just for her would not be fair for all the others who cannot become Dutch, and who were in the concentration camps as well. She is not ours; she is of the world [Anne Frank is niet van ons; zij is can de wereld]. It is utterly impossible.

Stateless Anne Frank does not belong to one nation; she belongs to the world.

Anne Frank, who lived as a stateless person, challenges us to explore the meaning of nationality, over 75 years after her death. Looking at the world through a stateless person's eyes might give us crucial insight into how to build a world at peace. Let's hope that the diary of Anne Frank represents that dream.

Marrying a Stateless Person

I was exhausted after returning from Brunei. Every day, the words of the people I had met in Brunei swirled around in my head. I lost four or five kilograms. I just wanted to be of some use to stateless people. That's all I thought about. About two weeks after getting back, I went with Wuyi Kroengyu and Etsuko Kosuge to a volunteer group that helped foreign workers in Yokohama. I had learned that the *Kalabaw-no Kai* (Association in Kotobuki for Solidarity with Migrant Workers) provided consultations on countless issues facing migrant workers.

"In his case, his parents migrated from Vietnam to Thailand during the war before he was born in Thailand. His issue is that he can't marry Etsuko officially because he doesn't have a visa."

I spoke with the *Kalabaw-no Kai* staff on how to enable Wuyi to get a special visa to have a happy married life with Etsuko. It was then that Wuyi began confiding in us that he could not get married.

"When I can get my visa on my own, then I can say 'marry me' to her. It would be useless as it is now."

"You both want to get married, right? Whether city hall recognizes it or not, you should get married."

After the volunteer said that, the two remained silent. I said,

"I myself was stateless. I understand how Wuyi feels. It's natural that he feels the proper order is to get visa or citizenship first. A marriage proposal in particular brings with it responsibility. More than that or anything else, the issue is how you feel. You don't want to get married just because you don't have a *zaitoku* special stay permit granted to those who have overstayed their visas. If you are deported, you need to be ready to take her with you, even if you have to carry her piggyback."

Wuyi became quiet. In effect, he had just been told that the goal was not to get a *zaitoku* special stay permit; but rather to maintain an unshakeable resolve to marry. Etsuko's eyes gazed downward. I painfully understood how Wuyi felt. As the volunteer had said, forget marriage registration and other legal procedures—a common law marriage might increase his chance of getting a *zaitoku* special stay permit that would enable him to live legally in Japan. This was truly an ironic reordering of steps.

You don't need to self-deprecate because you are stateless. I wanted to liberate Wuyi from the anxiety he lived with. I wanted him to gain confidence to live as a stateless person while holding his head high.

About a year later, Wuyi's circumstances were largely unchanged. I heard from Etsuko that someone at the Immigration Bureau had also recommended marriage and childbirth. They told Wuyi to get his birth certificate, proof that there was no impediment to marriage, and other documents from the Thai or Vietnamese embassies.

Both Wuyi and Etsuko were terrified to go to the embassies. They believed that they would be ignored if they went alone, so I offered to go with them. We went in the morning to the Embassy of Thailand. I happened to have acquaintances there, so I contacted them. They told me that with no certification, the embassy would be unable to issue any documents. They advised us to have Wuyi contact his family in Thailand and ask them to go to a local office to get his birth certificate and proof that no impediment to marriage had been issued. Then apply for citizenship. If that didn't work, get the Vietnamese embassy to issue the certificates. If that didn't work either, then they'd have to rely on the Immigration Bureau.

We decided to contact Wuyi's family in Thailand and go to the Embassy of Vietnam in Japan. We arrived at midday. Embassy staff took a long lunch break and wouldn't hear our inquiry until after 2 p.m.

We decided to have lunch and dropped in at a restaurant in Tokyo's Shibuya district. We hadn't met in a while, so we began catching up.

The previous day's call from Wuyi and Etsuko had unnerved me a bit.

The two had some sort of difference of opinion regarding the embassy visit. The quarrel had culminated in Etsuko storming out of the house and Wuyi going out to search for her.

As we ate, Wuyi talked nonstop about a recent dispute he had become embroiled in—a fight with a Japanese neighbor. Wuyi said that he had long been enduring the neighbor's mockery, and that the neighbor had instigated the recent fight. I wanted them to assimilate to Japan without incident, so none of these stories pleased me. I ended up lecturing Wuyi, telling him to continue to endure the challenges and to consider Etsuko's feelings.

As I spoke, I noticed his fork and knife barely moved. He looked down and said very little, then mumbled,

"I just don't care anymore. I really just don't care anymore. I'm so glad that you are doing this with me, but I just think it's not going to work no matter what I do. It just makes me want to go off by myself somewhere far away."

He was getting desperate. Etsuko was confused.

Having experienced statelessness, I thoroughly understood how he felt. I too had felt that way countless times. I felt that way when I was barred from entering Taiwan, when the UN rejected me, when I was told applying for Japanese citizenship was impossible.

When the country where you live tells you *no*; your country of birth tells you *no*; your parents' country tells you *no*; and when everyone tells you *we do not recognize you*, you lose even your ability to face life's challenges in a calm, cool, and collected manner.

A wall stands before you. Other walls stand beside you, above, and below you. You begin to question why you are alive at all. The reality of statelessness includes a sense of utter emptiness.

After lunch, we tried to calm Wuyi, who said he didn't want to go to the embassy. We began driving, saying, "Let's just check out the location of the Vietnamese embassy."

The Embassy of the Socialist Republic of Vietnam in Japan was located in a high-end residential area near Shinjuku. Vietnamese were lined up at the counter. Wuyi's face was inscrutable as we waited our turn. He expressed no more qualms about doing the procedures and negotiating. He kept his head down, and his eyes suggested he was trying not to feel anything. Etsuko and I asked the agent at the embassy counter,

"His Japanese papers say he has Vietnamese citizenship, but could you check to see if he is Vietnamese or not?"

"Please show me some of his documentation."

"This is a document created by Japan's Immigration Bureau."

"Not that, something issued by the Vietnamese government."

"He doesn't have anything like that."

"Then, it's impossible."

His tone was one of outright rejection.

"You say it's impossible, but you have cases in which there is no documentation, right? What if the documents are stolen or destroyed in a fire?"

"Even in those cases, you'd still have to go to where the documents were issued and get them reissued. Without documentation, we have no obligation to check to see if he is Vietnamese or not."

"Even if he *is* Vietnamese?"

The government agent replied with a hostile tone and gesture.

"What are you talking about? You came here with no documents!"

They would recognize no document that was not issued by the Vietnamese government. There was nothing that could be done with neither a passport nor a certificate issued by the hospital where he was born. I asked the agent a question.

"What is someone like him with no documentation supposed to do?"

"There's nothing that can be done, right?"

The agent said this so casually. Fed up, I just laughed bitterly. I felt so bad for Wuyi, who stood next to me, probably feeling hurt yet again. We had gone beyond feeling indignant at the agent's attitude, and were just fed up. Returning to the car, we felt determined to do whatever we had to.

"Etsuko, if this is the way it's going to be, let's go to Thailand."

"What? Really?"

"Why don't Etsuko and I just go to Thailand and get the documents from the hospital where Wuyi was born and from his parents?"

Of course, we knew that Wuyi couldn't very well go to Thailand since he was on provisional release. But a lust for battle was growing in my heart—for us to leave no stone unturned.

"Let's take off at the end of the year and go! Ok?"

Etsuko and I were pumped. Wuyi had stayed pretty quiet next to us. Now he smiled shyly.

Buttress for the Lives and Minds of Stateless Persons

In the summer of 2004, I left for Malaysia and Brunei to join an international workshop organized by a research project on the movement of people and goods across the border in Sabah. I gave a presentation on migration and nationality, using the case of stateless Chinese in Borneo at the meeting in Sabah.

I had another important objective in addition to the meeting—to visit the people who had agreed to be interviewed the previous year. I wanted to thank those who had trusted me to share their painful experiences, had put themselves in danger to do the interview, and had helped me make the documentary. During my field trip the previous year, I was shocked to learn about the painful situation stateless people were in. I anguished over what I could do to protect them and to improve the situation, losing five kilograms in the process. I lost confidence that I could continue my research.

But the one thing I could not do was to run away. What did they feel? How did they live their lives? I felt that I must continue to look carefully at those questions.

I contacted Wang of the orange grove.

"How are you doing?"

"Not good."

"What happened?"

"A lot happened. Can you come see me?"

"Of course. That's why I am in Brunei."

I rented a car and promptly headed to Labi, where Wang lived. I got there in about four hours. When I parked the car, a crowd of about 20 emerged. What looked like Wang's grandchildren and children gathered.

But Wang was nowhere to be found. I had expected to see his usually shirtless figure welcoming me. There was a very old man sitting alone in a chair in the back. The pajama-clad, white-haired man looked small. His pajamas were buttoned wrong, making them crooked. His eyes were downcast, but then he looked up at me. Barely raising his hand, he was clearly waving at me.

Oh, my ...

I couldn't hide my shock. I ran over to him. This once muscular Wang had lost about half his bulk, and his black hair had gone completely white. His burly appearance had disappeared without a trace, as if he had aged two decades over the past year. It was painful to look at. The skin on his skinny hands was covered in wrinkles. His hands were cold.

"I got cancer."

"..."

I was speechless. All I could do was slowly rub his thin hands.

"..."

"Wow, you came to see me."

The previous year I had met his daughter, who lived with him. She now came out from the back and saved us from an awkward silence. This formerly quiet, mild-mannered presence had transformed into a robust and vivacious woman. She spoke enthusiastically about various topics, including the previous year. She seemed frantic somehow. Wang looked down, hands rested on his belly, and said in a low voice.

"Thank you for sending the DVD you took last year."

"You watched it?"

"No, actually, I only have VHS, so I haven't seen it yet. I lent it to a friend of mine, who hasn't given it back yet. But I heard it's really well done. I heard that my friend showed it to people."

"I'll send you another one. We have only burned a DVD, but I can convert it to videotape and send it to you once I get back to Japan."

Wang's son spoke up, "Hey, old man, I got a DVD player."

The father said happily, "Well, then, send me the DVD. I'll see it really soon."

"Ok, I will. Then, I'll copy it as soon as I get back to the hotel today and bring it tomorrow."

A full year had passed. It seemed like the blink of an eye, but so many things had changed during that time. We meet new people and say goodbye to others. Our lives are filled with laughter and tears. A year had passed since I first visited Wang, and I was able to visit this country again. Their lives had changed dramatically. Next time I left Brunei I would have no way of knowing when I would ever be able to return. Even if I did return, I had no way of knowing whether I would be able to meet the people I wanted to meet.

"Thank you for coming. I'm glad I was able to see you."

"I am so happy too. I'll be back next year, too, so let's meet then."

"..."

Wang gazed downward, bereft of his usual confidence.

"Promise me you will. I can't wait."

I smiled as I left Wang's farm. His eyes as he saw me off seemed dimmer, somehow alone. Inside, I had no confidence that he would be able to keep the promise to meet again that I had just forced upon him.

On my way home, I visited my close friend Liu Xiaoshen (pseudonym), who had introduced me to Wang. Liu was director of an overseas Chinese organization, had agreed the previous year to be interviewed, and had introduced me to many people. Liu looked cool but characteristic creases appeared in his face when he laughed. The director I worked with had fallen in love with those wrinkles of Liu's and had asked me the previous year to put Liu's story in our documentary.

But Liu had rejected the suggestion outright.

"No way. I have too many things I must protect. My children are still minors, and any impact on our organization would cause trouble to a lot of people. I'm sorry but drop it."

Other than that, Liu had helped us in so many ways. When I called him this time, he immediately suggested that we meet.

"Did you see Wang?"

"I just came from there."

"Oh? Pretty shocking, eh?"

"Yes."

"He doesn't have much time left."

"Oh, I see...."

"There's nothing we can do about it because he is stateless."

"What do you mean by that?"

"If domestic treatment is no good, you can go overseas to get treatment, like in Singapore, and the [Bruneian] government will even pay all the costs, even the costs to your family to look after you. But only if you are a citizen. If you are stateless, you have to pay for everything yourself."

The unreasonableness of the idea that whether you have or do not have citizenship could affect whether you lived or died was horrifying. This point was driven home to me when I returned to Japan. I realized that foreigners who have overstayed their visas and stateless children unable to enroll in insurance for many reasons suffer the same situation. In Japan, too, citizenship and legal position impact people's lives in many ways.

Still unable to get a special *zaitoku* visa that would enable him to live and work legally in Japan, Wuyi Kroengyu remained on a provisional release program. He could still not propose to his beloved Etsuko.

With uncertain legal status, Wuyi's plans didn't go as he had hoped, and his work remained precarious. The psychological pressure he continued to face led to more fighting, which impacted his and Etsuko's relationship. Etsuko's generally understanding parents became concerned about the future of their beloved daughter and advised her to live separately for a while.

Etsuko and Wuyi agonized over what to do. They were in the midst of this when I spoke to Wuyi.

"If I really end up breaking up with [Etsuko], I don't need a *zaitoku* anymore. There would be no more reason to be in Japan, so I would just save my money, get a fake passport or whatever, and go back to my family in Thailand."

Wuyi had lived in legal limbo in Japan for 14 years. He had no home country to return to. He couldn't lead a stable life in Japan either. He was hemmed in on all sides. Etsuko represented for him his one place of refuge.

Etsuko called me. She wanted to meet with me.

"Lara, this is so painful for me. All I feel is anxiety. I really just don't know what to do."

"This might be rude to Wuyi, but I'm sure there are plenty of potential husbands for you in a better situation that he is, like someone at work or one of your friends."

"…"

"If all you want is to lead a stable married life, then it might be better to break up with him and choose someone else."

"But …"

"Does it have to be him?"

"…"

Sobbing, she nodded.

What provides refuge for people? What provides emotional support? It's neither the nation state, nor a happy married life. Etsuko's irreplaceable refuge was Wuyi, stateless and all.

Hit or Miss When It Comes to Local Bureaucrats

Legal technicalities impeding the love between two human beings illustrate deranged priorities. With that in mind, I accompanied Wuyi and Etsuko to their local ward office to help them register their marriage. They had come to this office for consultation many times before. We figured that with me with them, the ward office would be a bit more cooperative.

"Ah, the case you were here about before! Did you get proof of being single?"

"Actually, I am their acquaintance. This is me." I handed the case officer my name card. "After hearing their story, I went with them to the Thai and Vietnamese embassies, but they were unable to get a marriage competency certificate. They really want to get married. Isn't there anything you can do?"

"Well, um, I see…" She scratched her head. "Just a minute. Let me talk to my supervisor."

She went into the back of the office, returning after a time.

"Please write a statement. Include why you are in this situation, that you went to the embassies but couldn't get the certificate of marriage competency, and how you feel. Attach that, and let's see if we can get the marriage registration accepted."

"Yeah, yes! Understood." Our voices sprang to life as we felt a ray of light had broken through.

"But, please don't expect too much. It's not certain that it will be accepted."

"Ok. Understood. Thank you very much!"

We left the ward office.

A few days later, Etsuko and Wuyi went to the ward office to submit the statement Wuyi had written to the case officer. Written in the hiragana syllabary and simple kanji characters Wuyi had learned in Japanese class, the simple statement of a few lines stated when he had come to Japan, what kind of life he was living now, that he had never been married, and wanted to marry Etsuko and live in Japan.

"Ok, so I will try to submit the registration with this statement attached. Understand that your date of marriage registration will not be today."

"Yes. Understood. Thank you."

We prayed it would be accepted without any problems. A while later, Etsuko contacted me.

"Lara-san! Thanks to you, they accepted our marriage certificate!"

After years of perseverance, twists, and turns, the two had finally become legally recognized husband and wife. Etsuko sounded giddy.

Afterwards, Wuyi got a visa and gained status as a legal resident of Japan. While he had been on provisional release from detention as an illegal alien, he had needed to apply to immigration officials simply to visit a friend living in a different prefecture. Now, it was like an invisible wall had come crumbling down the moment he got his visa. He was also able to get insurance and finally live a stable life.

For a while, the couple felt blessed with a brand-new life. The birth of an adorable little boy brought laughter to Wuyi, whose face had rarely even smiled. Now a father, he devoted himself more than ever to work, and the three lived a happy, modest life.

In the summer of 2012, I went with a group of researchers and attorneys to Thailand to meet fellow academics researching statelessness and cooperative organizations. While there, I visited Wuyi's family. Wuyi regularly sends money he earns in Japan to his family in Thailand. Apparently, he was hoping that some of the money he sent would fund a business he was starting up there with his brother. He had dreamt of returning to Thailand to work in business. The family said, "We can't see Wuyi, but we are happy that he is healthy and working hard."

Wuyi had gotten his visa and now lived a stable life, but he remained stateless. He could not get a passport from Thailand. The re-entry permit that Japan's Legal Affairs Bureau issues to visa-holding foreigners unable to get a passport becomes a substitute for a passport. He would need to get a Thai visa on that re-entry permit. But in order to enter Thailand, the Thai government requires proof of employment in Japan and more than six months remaining on the Japan visa. It won't issue a visa to enter Thailand without all that paperwork. To visit his home country and his family home was difficult for Wuyi. He wanted his parents to hold their grandchild in their arms, but it wasn't so simple.

I got a call in 2018. The normally reticent Wuyi spoke in a heated manner.

"Lara-san, my family called me. My father has cancer."

"What?"

"He doesn't have much time left. I want to go back and see him. But I can't get a visa in time."

"You can get a visa and a ticket? Can you get time off work?"

"My father is about to be moved from the hospital to a temple-like hospice. He's gotten so thin."

Wuyi phoned me again a few days later. Holding back tears, he said, "My father died."

When you are stateless, it is simply impossible to rush out and buy a plane ticket to go overseas. Stateless persons are usually unable to respond to emergency situations like this. They cannot be with their families even in their last moments.

10 Launching the Stateless Network NGO

Raising Awareness of Issues of Statelessness

In 2003, publisher KK Shinchosha invited me to write a book about statelessness, based on my first-hand experience. I had mixed feelings about the prospect of doing so. One the one hand, I really wanted more people to learn about the issue of statelessness. I looked forward to the prospect of reaching many people, and potentially deepening their understanding and recognition of the problems engendered by a world centered on the nation state. I hoped that increased awareness might make society more understanding of people who belong to no nation.

On the other hand, it felt strange to write a first-person autobiographical essay, as requested. I had always thought of an autobiography as something that an illustrious figure with a wealth of experience wrote. I was an extraordinarily *ordinary* woman, barely 30. Certainly not illustrious, I felt in no position to pen an autobiography.

I decided to give the project a try. I almost gave up many times, torn between a great sense of responsibility and a nagging reluctance. But editor Masatoshi Imaizumi helped me get it done. The reaction to publication was beyond what I could have imagined. Many readers were shocked to learn of the existence of stateless people. Most had never had any doubts about the nature of nationality. Many people saw nationality as a natural feature of society. How was it possible that someone would not have a nationality?

After the book's publication in Japan, inquiries and work offers related to statelessness poured in. I got inquiries from attorneys, as well as stateless persons themselves, their families, friends, and aid groups. One stateless person told me excitedly,

"Until now, nobody ever understood me, no matter where I went."

I met with them directly when possible, or, if separated geographically, spoke to them by phone. I spent time learning about their backgrounds, issues, and feelings. Sometimes, I got worked up after listening to their stories for two or three hours. I spent even more time researching the information they needed. Most of the stateless people I spoke with faced difficult and intractable legal problems that required expert assistance to resolve. Many cases involved not just Japan's legal system, but those of other countries as well.

Increasingly, I had to connect with specialists in the local languages, laws, and customs that came into play, to ask them to share some of their wisdom. If I was going to improve the situation for stateless people, I needed more people to become aware of the issue. I felt a keen need for help from people in many different fields.

After publication, I went beyond just consulting and began giving lectures on statelessness in places around the country. I always started my lecture with a question:

What does the word stateless bring to mind when you hear it?

A surprising number answered—in all seriousness—that what comes to mind is: *fusion cuisine* or *fusion bars*, because the *fusion* of these terms is rendered into Japanese as *mukokuseki*. Like stateless persons, fusion cuisine belongs to no particular nationality. I often went further and asked attendees their thoughts about stateless people—what image did they have of them? Nearly all held negative views, associating the stateless with terms like: *defectors, illegal aliens, invisible* or *pitiable people*. Few thought of potential positive traits, like *cosmopolitan* or *global citizens*.

Before my book came out, I could count on one hand the number of people who raised their hand when asked if they knew of the existence of stateless people. Nowadays, the majority of hands go up. *Have you ever met a stateless person?* Everyone cocks their head; almost no hands go up. The profile of stateless people is undeniably rising, but the issue still lacks immediacy for most people.

I persevered with my activities, confident that continuing to tell my story would: (1) enable me to inform the general public about the many contradictions and inconsistencies inherent in citizenship and other legal systems; (2) give impetus to deeper thought about the citizenship system as a whole; and (3) increase understanding of and reduce prejudice against stateless people.

Stateless Person Takes Podium for First Time at Symposium in Japan

In November 2008, I organized a symposium entitled "The World as Seen from the Eyes of a Stateless Person." As an anthropologist, I believed that first-person accounts from the mouths of the stateless people themselves carried the greatest persuasive potential. One by one, I wrote to stateless people to ask them to meet with me and consider speaking at my symposium.

I aimed for a maximum diversity of speakers to better emphasize the spectrum of statelessness cases. My lineup included a stateless permanent resident; an undocumented stateless person; a Japan-born, second-generation refugee in a state of statelessness; and the spouse of a stateless resident. Their ages ran from their twenties to their eighties. In addition to stateless speakers, I invited those in the field involved with stateless people, including an attorney, a healthcare worker, and a staffer at the UN High Commissioner for Refugees (UNHCR) to speak at the symposium. I asked legal scholar Kohki Abe to coordinate.

The National Museum of Ethnology (Minpaku) where I worked extended me a grant to organize the symposium, so I went to talk with the UNHCR office in Tokyo's Shibuya district to ask them to host it.

Saburo Takizawa, who then ran the Tokyo office, was cooperative and promptly introduced me to their legal affairs officer. After several discussions, we resolved that the Minpaku and the UNHCR would cohost the symposium.

To the best of my knowledge, this was the first symposium to be held in Japan, and maybe in the world, that was focused mainly on stateless people. This may be why it garnered such a big response. Despite the fact that we held the symposium on a holiday, the 150-capacity space was standing-room only. It took time for the crowd to quiet down. Many newspapers, magazines, TV, and other media organizations covered it.

Participants offered a great deal of feedback. Encouraged by speakers and organizers, we founded the NGO Stateless Network in January 2009, two months after the symposium, thereby launching our stateless aid and awareness campaign.

The Stateless Network provides the support and counsel needed by those facing difficulty due to their stateless status in our nation-based modern society in the belief that those with and without citizenship are equal global citizens. We set up a consultation contact and held events in order to give stateless people a place of refuge. During my stateless years, I had often come smack up against barriers of statelessness and each time wondered where to go for help. Back then, I had wished that there was a place to go for advice.

We transmit information on issues relating to statelessness and on the varied opinions of stateless persons themselves in order to increase more people's understanding of the subject and to eliminate discrimination. We wanted to transmit the voices of stateless people, both at home and abroad, to those who came into little contact with them, while working together to enable stateless people to solve their own problems. We aspired to build a stateless-friendly society.

Stateless Network

Documentary on Statelessness

Around the time that I began these activities, director Masayuki Gen invited me to create a documentary film on statelessness with him. Producer Fumiko Nakamura came all the way out to Yokohama to meet me. She told me she had secured a broadcast slot for a documentary program on NHK, Japan's national broadcaster. This was more than I could have ever asked for. I readily agreed, thinking that the truth about statelessness could be conveyed to more people via a visual medium.

Director Gen tackled the project as if it were about him, particularly since he had experience with nationality and identity conflict, as a second-generation *zainichi* Korean resident of Japan. I spoke as much as possible about stateless people I knew and conscientiously deliberated about which stateless persons to interview in the documentary. I decided on Nguyen Tin Hong Hau, a second-generation Vietnamese refugee born and bred in Japan who had spoken at the symposium; Li Wen Biao, who had lost his citizenship and visa due to administrative discrepancies among the three countries of Bolivia, China, and Japan; a Rohingya resident of Tatebayashi, Gunma Prefecture; a Japanese Filipino Child (JFC); and my own parents, who chose statelessness as a result of the normalization of diplomatic ties between Japan and mainland China.

Li Wen Biao Loses Citizenship and Visa Due to Administrative Snafu

We visited the *qigong* clinic that Li Wen Biao runs in Chiba Prefecture. He has a friendly smile and goes by the name Fumihiko Kimura. He was born in Shanghai on April 16, 1952. He worked in international trade in that metropolis, until moving to the Republic of Bolivia in February 1989, and in April 1990 acquired Bolivian citizenship. On February 28, 1995, he arrived in Japan for business on a 90-day visa. In April, during his stay, he visited the Chinese embassy to ask about restoring his Chinese citizenship. Following the instructions of the embassy staffer, he went to the Bolivian embassy in Japan to renounce his Bolivian citizenship and used that document to apply to restore his Chinese citizenship. However, he was informed shortly thereafter that he could not restore it. Li said,

"A discrepancy between the Chinese embassy and China's Ministry of Public Security in Beijing led to the rejection of my application for Chinese citizenship, resulting in me becoming stateless and with nowhere to stay other than Japan. Eventually, my visa to stay in Japan expired. But I must work to live, so I put my knowledge of *qigong* to use and began working as a *qigong* teacher."

When he contacted me, Li still had no visa and had been laying low for over ten years. He was terrified of getting detained. Since showing up at the Tokyo Regional Immigration Bureau to ask for a special residency permit, he was living alone quietly under Japan's provisional release program. Without a visa, he was not permitted to work. But he couldn't make a living without working. He told me he had not met his family in Shanghai since 1995. When we visited him at his home, he was sitting quietly alone at the table eating.

He tried with all his might to hold back the large tears rolling down his face as he said,

"What I feel most is mental anguish, as I have been stateless for more than 13 years. I have been separated for a long time from my family and relatives, and my mother died last year at the age of 90. Even though I was her eldest son, I was unable to be there with her at the end or even to attend the funeral."

He said he had another source of distress. It was his health. With no visa, he was unable to enroll in health insurance.

"I wonder sometimes what the hell nationality is. Even without citizenship, we have the fundamental human right to life. My whole life is in Japan. I cannot live somewhere outside Japan. So, more than citizenship, I want a visa to be in Japan."

Li had to go once every two months to the Tokyo Regional Immigration Bureau in Tokyo's Shinagawa district to extend his provisional release. Director Gen and I went with him. On the bus ride back after going through the process, Gen asked,

"What is your dream?"

"My dream?" He stared off for a moment, then said with a smile, "I want to live like an ordinary person. That's my dream."

Behind his smiling face and characteristic crow's feet, Li seemed forlorn.

Rohingya Leader in Japan

The Rohingya are known as a "wandering people" and are the stateless people drawing the most attention in recent years. After hearing that they live in high concentrations in Tatebayashi, Gunma Prefecture, we went to visit a Rohingya village there.

Zaw Min Htut, known as a community leader among the Rohingya, escaped Myanmar in 1999.

"Japan is a democratic nation that protects human rights. So, I had high expectations."

After getting off the plane in Narita, he was shoved into immigrant detention for a year. Hope turned to disillusion. He had been out of the detention facilities on provisional release for a decade, had applied for refugee status and had brought over his wife and child.

There was a large-eyed baby wrapped in a towel in a crib at Zaw Min Htut's house. Zaw Nain Htuh had been born in Japan.

I asked what the baby's nationality was. Zaw Min Htut choked on his Japanese words,

"The ward office registered him as a Myanmar citizen, but we are refugees, so the Myanmar embassy won't give us citizenship."

Like this child, children born to refugees in Japan are, in effect, stateless.

"I believe that the Japanese government protects human rights. But it's a different story for foreigners.... We are human beings. The Myanmar government refuses to recognize us. Japan refuses to recognize us. Where on earth should we go? The sky? The ends of the earth? I have felt this frustration for over ten years. Since I was born in Myanmar, I should be a Myanmar citizen. Just as you who were born in Japan are Japanese."

His voice had become agitated in his vexation. Director Gen, who had come with me, asked Zaw Min Htut:

"What does stateless mean to you?"

"I don't believe in the word *stateless*. Anyone born into this world should have a country. Every single person should have a country," he said with fervor.

"I agree in part with your view that the country of one's birth should grant that person citizenship, but.... I also hold a different view. I get that since you were born in Myanmar, you are a Myanma, but how about your children?"

"Uh, hmm, the children, my children were born in this country, so the Japanese government should grant them citizenship."

Zaw Min Htut seemed to be in pain. His eyes darted furtively as he mustered all the strength in his body.

I was exhausted after the interviews that day. Back at the hotel, I organized my notes from the interviews and felt choked up. Gen and I were both second generation foreigners born in Japan. Gen asked me what it was like meeting Rohingya.

"Even though we are both stateless, the stateless problems we face are completely different. It was painfully clear that they believe themselves to have nationality. That affects the nationality of their children who were born and grew up in Japan."

Gen related it to his own experience.

"Those kids will have a tough decision in the future. What country do I belong to? What is my nationality?"

"Yes, they will definitely have trouble with that, whether they get Japanese citizenship or remain stateless.... But I think it's important that we at least secure their legal status conferring sufficient rights in their current lives..."

I said that and felt suffocated, because discussing the trouble-paved path that Gen and I had walked and that those children would walk hit close to home for me.

Second-Generation Vietnamese Refugees and Akatsuki Village

"What is your nationality, Hau?"

"Um, forget that question. I don't accept it. I stopped asking myself that question, so I cannot answer it."

"Why did you stop?"

"Because I started thinking it's meaningless. Because I decided to think about other things instead."

Nguyen Tin Hong Hau was born in Japan to Vietnamese refugee parents. Her older sisters were born in refugee camps in Vietnam and the Philippines. Only Hau was born in Japan.

Her parents reported her birth to their local ward office, and her ID lists her as a Vietnamese citizen. But as the daughter of refugee parents, she is not registered in Vietnam and has no Vietnamese ID.

"I am stateless.... No country gave me citizenship. So, I have no national passport. It's not as if I am officially stateless or anything like that. There's no document that…"

Hau was adept at writing her feelings in candid and evocative Japanese. Her parents' native language was Vietnamese, but she never learned it. She could handle ordinary conversation in Vietnamese, but complex debates, let alone writing, was a different matter altogether. She had seen her parents, who had come to Japan as refugees, struggle in a society in which they had a linguistic disadvantage. They had fled their home country and were treated as foreigners in Japan. She often asked herself,

Did my parents really win their freedom? Did they become happy? What is my national identity? What is my mother country? My maternal language?

"How did you feel when you first realized you had no country?" Gen asked.

"I wondered if that is even possible? And it was my own situation! What the…? I thought my country was Vietnam…. That's what I thought. I felt so alone."

"Alone? Why?"

"For one thing, even though I was stateless, my parents saw themselves as Vietnamese… whatever the law says, regardless…. But I had never had that, so I felt that nobody would understand. I was alone."

We went to Akatsuki Village in Maebashi City, Gunma Prefecture. Hau had begun coming here when she was 18. This Vietnamese refugee camp for former boat people who landed in Japan offered an oasis for those suffering psychologically living in Japanese society, due to language issues, exhausting labor, and personal relationships.

Nguyen was once himself a Vietnamese refugee and now worked at Akatsuki (Jn: dawn).

Gen asked: "What do you think of second-generation Vietnamese refugees like Hau-chan who were born in Japan and grew up among Japanese people?"

"First of all, the children born in Japan face the issue of nationality, which is, after all, the crux of the issue of statelessness. We have raised the issue at many conferences but have yet to find a solution…"

Gen asked, "Hau-chan, don't you want to try to get Japanese citizenship?"

"Well, no, I don't."

"Why not?"

"Hmm. I wonder why not… My parents keep telling me to get it. They say: 'Hurry up and get it. It's too sad not to have any nationality. Hurry up and get citizenship.'"

This second-generation Vietnamese refugee rejected any need for citizenship categorically, adding "I don't mind being stateless for the rest of my life."

First-generation Vietnamese refugees had abandoned their country, their home villages, and wandered into Japan as stateless persons. Now they lived in Akatsuki Village.

"Then, what is statelessness to you, Hau-chan?"

Hau kept her eyes down, without answering.

"What do you intend to do?"

"I plan to continue to live as I have up till now."

"Remaining stateless?"

"Yes."

"Why?"

"I get the feeling somehow that inasmuch as I was denied something called nationality, I can more cherish what I have now. Isn't that the kind of place Akatsuki Village is? Like, well, that's ok. Being stateless is fine."

The village is a place where anybody is accepted, regardless of nationality—a place full of warm, kind people. Tears streamed down her cheek, as she said,

"I am so mad at how there is no place for the generous people of Akatsuki Village in society, at how society doesn't accept them."

"But this is a place for everybody. A place for me to belong. I cherish it. So, being stateless is ok. There are plenty of places for me," she said, wiping away the tears.

A few years later, Hau contacted me.

"I want to get a Schengen visa. Can you tell me some good ways to get one?"

She was heading to Germany for research but had only a re-entry permit and asked me if there was some good way to apply. After I told her my own experience getting a Schengen visa, she spent four months to get one so she could enter Europe. She contacted me again after getting back from Europe.

"I had no problem going to Europe but was stopped in transit at the Dutch border and missed my flight. The experience was unimaginably horrible. I wished I hadn't gone."

She told me she was detained at the border by a two-meter-tall (6.5 feet) man and was terrified.

Several months later, she left graduate school and got a job. Taking it easy at home with her parents until the job started, her parents sounded her out, saying, "Why don't the three of us get Japanese citizenship? This is our last chance. If it doesn't work, your mother and father will give up."

These words cheered Hau. She had just been hired by a TV broadcaster and was insecure about the impact having no passport could have on her work. She imagined it would limit her job travel opportunities and other prospects. She wondered if she would cause the station trouble.

"Of course, I wanted to respect my parents' sentiments. But more than that, I was relieved to hear my parents give me an excuse to naturalize because it felt too humiliating to get citizenship just for my own convenience."

Getting the job helped Hau's naturalization application go smoothly. It took about a year for her and her parents to acquire Japanese citizenship and become citizens.

Today, Hau frequently goes overseas for work. I included her feelings in the book I edited entitled *Passportology* (2016, Hokkaido University Press).

> Nothing happens at airports anymore. World-convulsing, horrific scenes like what I experienced in the Dutch airport disappeared. In their stead appeared ordinary scenes that other people take for granted. My passport put a lid over an uncertain world....
>
> While waiting at the airport passport control, I recall my experience in Holland—how even when I trembled at my precarious existence, a tiny ember smoldered deep in my heart that said, 'even still you cannot deny that I exist here and now.' The only thing that got me through that terrible scene was that certainty....
>
> The nation state seems uncertain to me, even now that I have citizenship and a passport. Agreements between one nation and another are more uncertain. But I should ride atop the wave of my life in the rough

seas of this nation-based system. That ember glows inside me still. And that's fine. As long as I have that, that's enough.

Although citizenship changed how people treated her, what Hau experienced during her years of statelessness couldn't be extinguished so easily.

Defanged Lawyer

Statelessness among second-generation Vietnamese refugees is not a problem confined to Japan. There are Vietnamese refugees born and bred in Thailand. Thailand's nationality law is based on *jus sanguinis*, so these refugees are not able to acquire Thai citizenship and are registered as Vietnamese. They were born and grew up in Thailand, but these second- and third-generation Vietnamese refugees who had been treated as second-class citizens paid large sums for fake passports to work in Japan.

In the 1980s and early 1990s, Japan allowed them in on short-term visas. They were able to earn dozens of times the income they could make back home. They sent money back to their families. After the bubble economy broke in the early 1990s, Japan began to crack down on undocumented and visa-overstayed workers. Many foreigners were deported. The descendants of Vietnamese refugees had been considered stateless by Thailand, so even if the Japanese government tried to deport them to Thailand or Vietnam, those countries refused to accept them as their own citizens. This led to long stays at immigration detention centers.

Attorney Fumie Azukizawa handled a Vietnamese refugee case like this and sued the Japanese government. She was one of the founders of the Stateless Network.

Director Gen asked her,

"What's the most difficult aspect of the law in dealing with statelessness?"

"Japan has no law that protects stateless people. With no legal grounds to protect them, I feel disarmed as a lawyer."

"Won-san, what will you do if they deport you to Vietnam?"

"I don't want to go to Vietnam. I have no home or family there."

"Vietnam is not your country? What is your nationality?"

"I don't think I have one. Whatever nationality people ascribe to us, let me see—it's like discrimination.... Our parents fled the war to Thailand, and we were born there. We have been violating the law since the moment we were born. It's not like we committed a crime—nor did we punch someone or steal something. But the war put us in this position. Sometimes I wonder what the hell I did. I did nothing wrong but have been illegal since birth. We work hard for our families, our parents, and to survive. We save money and send it to our families. Of course, we understand that illegal entry into Japan violates the law. But realistically, what other option do we have?"

Gen asked,

"Azukisawa-san, there is no law on statelessness. As an attorney, why do you want to take on that kind of court case?"

"Illegal from birth. Illegal wherever you go. I don't want people to spend their entire lives being accused of that. Japan is an advanced industrialized country that at least claims to protect human rights. As a Japanese person, I don't want to think that even Japan refuses to recognize them as anything other than an illegal in perpetuity."

After this interview, Atty. Azukisawa brought a suit on behalf of the Vietnamese refugees against the government to void the deportation order. They won in 2010.

The court victory gave them a special residency permit, allowing the Vietnamese refugees, at least for the time being, to avoid being sent to a country not of their choosing and long-term detention. But in a country with laws that remain ambiguous when it comes to nationality, some are registered as Vietnamese, some as Thais, and some as stateless. Japan has no system to certify stateless persons, so where they fit legally in terms of nationality remains uncertain.

Remnant Japanese Residents of the Philippines

There was one group of people I simply had to include in this documentary program—ethnic Japanese left behind in the Philippines. I wanted Japan's people to know not only about what stateless foreigners who come to Japan experience; but also, about the experience of Japanese who become stateless.

I flew to Davao City and visited the local association for ethnic Japanese residents. I traced the history of, and imprint left by Japanese who had gone to the Philippines. We visited the homes of *zanryu* ethnic Japanese. It is well known that many Japanese crossed over to China before the war; that some of their children ended up stranded there after the war; and that those *zanryu* Japanese orphans in China began "returning" to Japan in the 1980s. I found out from Norihiro Inomata, who helped us found the Stateless Network, that many *zanryu* Japanese were left behind in the Philippines as well. I wanted to be sure to visit some of them.

Director Gen, our crew and I headed off to Davao City on Mindanao Island. The sun shone bright that day. Inomata took us to the village, noting that, "It's rare for someone to come here from Japan."

About 20 or 30 villagers gathered under an arbor made of bamboo and tree leaves. When children running around barefoot saw us arrive, they came over to the arbor. A charming old woman smiled and joined the others in receiving us. I shook the old woman's hand.

"Hello. I am Lara."

She brought her mouth next to my ear and in a soft voice said, "Tomeko, Sakagawa, To-me-ko."

"May I ask you your age?"

She covered her face embarrassedly and told me in Cebuano the local language, through an interpreter, that she was 75.

Tomiko Sakagawa (official name) was born to a Japanese father and Filipino mother. Before the war, many Japanese had gone to the Philippines as migrant workers. The Pacific War began when Tomiko was in elementary school. Her carpenter father was killed in an air raid while working at the port. Tomiko moved through the mountains in flight with her Filipino mother and five siblings.

"We fled from one place to the next but had no food. My brothers all starved to death; I was the only one who survived."

Tomiko wanted to get Japanese citizenship. *Zanryu* Japanese in the Philippines like Tomiko had been left behind after their fathers died in the war or were forcibly repatriated to Japan after the war. Their *koseki* family registry was unclear, so they remained stateless throughout.

Norihiro Inomata of the Philippine Nikkei-jin Legal Support Center visits *zanryu* Japanese in the Philippines, interviews them about getting Japanese citizenship, and searches for their fathers' family records. *Zanryu* Japanese like Tomiko had to live in hiding after the war due to the anti-Japanese sentiment among Filipinos. They often destroyed any documents or photos that could demonstrate they were the children of Japanese people.

Inomata slowly climbed the stairs of Tomiko's stilt hut. In the dimly lit space, he asked her about her experience going to Japanese school. He wrote down the interview, clickety clacking the keys of his laptop. He printed it out on a tiny, portable printer and asked Tomiko to sign it.

Tomiko painstakingly formed each syllable of the katakana she had learned as a child. She made some errors, such as angling the ミ (*mi*) of her name in the opposite direction. Then, she pressed a thumbprint onto the document. Tomiko called upon what Japanese she could remember to convey her feelings to Inomata, saying *Arigato. Takusan arigato.* Inomata smiled and answered in Tagalog: *Salamat.*

Inomata took us the next day to a *zanryu* Japanese-Filipino living deep in the mountains. Accustomed to the local terrain, Inomata took off his footwear and rolled his slacks up to his knees. Our shoes sank into the muddy, pathless terrain we ascended, slipping and sliding, until finally reaching a home high up in the mountains.

Saide Takihara, a white-haired man with wheat skin and dignified eyes greeted us.

"I'm Lara."

"Papa is Ōnishi Takihara. Papa, *Hapon.*"

Sixty-seven-year-old Saide cultivated Manila hemp (*Musa textilis*, also known as abacá). His father was Japanese. His mother belonged to the local minority Bagobo tribe. Saide lived in a dugout hut made of bamboo and tree branches, with a floor space equivalent to about six Japanese tatami mats. It lacked running water, electricity, and of course, gas. Illness had taken his wife a few years before. I asked him,

"What kinds of things did your father tell you about Japan?"

"He said Japan was a great place. He wanted to take me, his son, back with him to Japan. But our Filipino family was against it."

After the war ended, Saide's father had been put into a camp. Later, he had been forcibly repatriated to Japan. Saide was five at the time.

Saide's family set out a bamboo table and chairs in the open space next to their hut. They stretched a cloth tent above that; in the back, they arranged stones and twigs to build an open-air fire; and they cooked for us. They climbed soaring palms to knock down coconuts; chopped and cooked chicken to mark our visit even though they rarely ate meat; and filled the long table with a veritable feast. This was genuine hospitality.

"It's so sad to grow old without seeing Japan. When I think of my father, I become so uneasy. I dream of the day that Japanese people will help me get to Japan."

Hearing how Saide felt put me at a loss for words. Looking at his pure, sparkling eyes, all I could do was place my hand on his back.

"Papa, I want to have you go to Japan before you die," Saide's son said.

"I want to go to Japan for my children and grandchildren."

Saide's life in the mountains had been indigent and without any schooling. He wanted Japanese citizenship. Two decades had already passed since applying. I asked him if he thought he would get it. He responded immediately.

"Of course."

"Why do you think so?"

"Because I have my father's Japanese blood," he answered, smiling and confident. Next to him, his son Kinji bowed, with tears in his eyes, and said in Japanese,

"We are still waiting after 20 years. Please help us…"

Then, in the local language, Kinji told us,

"My father looks for mementos of *his* father every morning. Where on earth is his father? He doesn't even remember his face, since he was separated from his father when he was little."

Modern JFCs and Jaime's Nationality?

The saga of Japanese, Filipino, and stateless children continues. Ethnic Japanese left behind in the Philippines, like Tomiko and Saide, were the pre-war version of Japanese-Filipino children (JFCs). There are modern-day JFCs, too.

My crew and I visited stateless persons in many places. JFCs are born to a Japanese father and Filipino mother. Administrative and procedural errors such as registering the birth of the child often cause the child to remain stateless, according to an organization that helps stateless and other children, and a teacher who uses church facilities to provide educational support, both in Mie Prefecture.

I was shown a photo of a girl, taken from an album on the school shelves, as an example. Jaime was deported to the Philippines along with her younger brother and mother who had been arrested for overstaying her visa. She was ten years old. Jaime and her brother were stateless so had no passport. It took a great deal of effort even to get their travel papers in order to get to the Philippines with their mother. When her mother was detained by immigration, Jaime and her brother were also detained in separate cells. Jaime's brother had become mute in the aftermath of his detention due to the terror and stress he felt.

We went to meet Jaime, who was now in the Philippines. First, we met Jaime's mother Annabelle Cruz (pseudonym), and she took us to Jaime's school. As soon as we entered the school, Jaime left the friends she had been chatting with during lunch period and approached us, smiling. Big eyes and jet-black long hair framed an adorable smile. Annabelle noticed Jaime staring at her friends, running her hand through her hair, and asked her in Japanese,

"What are you so embarrassed about?"

Blushing, Jaime said *"yoroshiku onegai shimasu"* in fluent Japanese, bowing her head in deference to us.

Jaime was born in Japan to a Japanese father. She couldn't get Japanese citizenship because her parents were not legally married. While pregnant with Jaime, Annabelle suffered domestic violence from her husband and, feeling in danger, ran away. Jaime had never met her father and was raised by her mother. She had attended a Japanese preschool. A photo shows her making the V sign for peace—a common pose in Japan—with her friend at a Japanese-style field day, with kids wearing red or white hats. The photo illustrates how assimilated Jaime was into Japanese society. Japanese was her native language, and she believed herself to be Japanese. But all of a sudden one day her mother is deported, and she is sent "back" to the Philippines. Jaime and her brother learned then for the first time that no nation recognized their citizenship.

While Jaime was in class, we spoke to Annabelle and asked about Jaime's father.

"He was Japanese. He told me, 'we can get married, but I won't send any money to your family in the Philippines.' Jaime's father drank a lot—from morning to night. At home, he'd go into drunken fits."

I went and watched Jaime and her friends talk. She came up to me and asked,

"When will you go back to Japan?"

"Day after tomorrow."

She looked down, a bit sad. In turn, her friends asked in Tagalog what she had said. Jaime answered in Tagalog what she had asked and how I had answered. One of her friends said,

"Jaime, you really can speak Japanese!"

I understood then how bilingual and bicultural Jaime was.

After class, we visited her house. Annabelle did her best to answer our questions in broken Japanese.

"In her heart, Jaime always wants go back. But sometime I just lie to her and tell her she can go back—she can go back sometime. But she know. In her heart, she know maybe she can't go back. Because she's not in the family register. He wouldn't recognize her either. You maybe can't go back. Myself I think Japan is selfish. The child is half Japanese, half Filipino, no? But they don't listen. I think it is so sad."

Jaime entrusted us with letters she had written in Japanese to her teachers and friends in Japan. Gen asked,

"What is your dream right now, Jaime?"

She tilted her head slightly and confirmed the question—*my dream?* After a moment, she grabbed the towel right in front of her, pressed it against her face with all her might, and let loose the pent-up emotions in her heart. Bawling, she said,

"I want Mama and me to be happy. I'd be happy in Japan. Mama would have a job in Japan. There is no job here."

Gen asked another question.

"Jaime, what is your nationality?"

"I think I am Japanese. Because, I want to go back to Japan. I think I'm Japanese because I was born in Japan."

Gen then trained the camera on me and asked,

"Chen-san, what nationality is Jaime?"

I couldn't respond for a while, being squished between Jaime's dreams and the harsh legal realities. I took a deep breath, straightened my posture, mustered my strength, and searched for the right words.

"I think Jaime's nationality is what Jaime thinks it is. That's my answer," I said, unable to hold back the tears running down my cheek. I looked at her and smiled, adding the Japanese interjection of affirmation *ne*, seeking backchannel confirmation from her. Jaime didn't let it rest there.

"But am I Japanese?" She used the towel to wipe away the tears that welled up in her eyes, then wept as she continued, "Because, my friends told me I'm not Japanese. Am I really Japanese?"

I had also been filming Jaime, but my hand shook as I tried to hold back my own tears. In the end, I broke down and could no longer operate the camera. Jaime pressed me further.

"Will I be able to go back to Japan? Can Mama go with me?"

"Let's do our best. I'll try to find a way."

With that, and keeping the towel applied to her face, Jaime nodded fully.

Stateless—Where is my Country? ran for 90 minutes on NHK's Broadcasting Satellite system. My ties with all those I had met continued after the broadcast. To keep my promise to Jaime, after returning to Japan, I went with Gen to consult with an attorney well versed in JFC cases. After describing Jaime's case in detail, he advised us.

I promised the lawyer that I would return to talk after getting all the necessary paperwork together, as per his instructions. We sent a letter to Annabelle asking her to get together the documents required on her side and send them to Japan. A month, then another month passed, but Annabelle's response never arrived.

"I wonder what happened…"

"Maybe she can't get all the documents."

Indeed, for someone living in the Philippines, even making one copy is quite a task. It would be far tougher to compile many different, complex documents. I wanted to keep my promise to Jaime, but I recognized that there was only so much that we could do.

11 Not Someone Else's Problem

Fall Seven Times, Get Up Eight

After launching the Stateless Network, I spent my days giving consultations to stateless people and searching for solutions. While coming to terms with my own sense of powerlessness, I pressed on, with the support and kindness of many people. It took a great deal of work to give shape to people's ideas, to set up legal consultation contacts, to create pamphlets that raised awareness about statelessness, and to organize seminars, networking events, and photo exhibits. But there was something irreplaceable about the joy I felt when these ideas did take shape.

In part because we were the first ever organization in Japan to support stateless people, we began to get invited to UNHCR consultations held around June each year in Geneva. This increased our contact with other organizations that support refugees and stateless persons around the world.

Beginning in 2014, the UNHCR began pouring energy into issues of statelessness and launched a decade-long campaign to eradicate statelessness globally. This increased the number of support organizations in each country and in one go raised the profile of the statelessness issue. There was an increase not only in aid activists but also researchers. Tilburg University and UNHCR cohosted an international conference on statelessness in The Hague. With all these conference invitations, I began traveling to Europe more frequently. I wore many hats—including that of the leader of an organization that helps stateless people, that of an anthropologist who studies stateless persons, and that of a former stateless person myself. At international conferences, I gave presentations on my own experiences as well as on stateless persons in Japan.

Participating in these conferences, I began to feel uneasy about the stated legal goals of organizations around the world—to eradicate statelessness, to ensure there are no stateless people. I cannot deny that in the modern society based on a foundation of the democratic nation, such a mentality contains a kernel of legitimacy. But as someone who herself experienced statelessness, I worried that calls to eradicate statelessness might foster a negative image of statelessness, as if statelessness itself is somehow bad. Beyond eradication of statelessness, we need to better understand what causes statelessness and come to terms with the constraints inherent in our citizenship system. It is also important to expose each country's contradictions and administrative defects. I felt more than ever a desire that each person be treated equally regardless of citizenship status, rather than trying to eradicate statelessness.

Swamped with work for my main job and the Stateless Network, I increasingly found myself running around both in Japan and overseas, and sitting at my computer late at night. Without realizing it, I came down with insomnia, perhaps due to overwork and stress. Even lying in bed, my head was always filled with this or that thought, and my nerves refused to settle down.

That situation continued for a year, then another year. It built up. I collapsed several times and each time had to be taken to the hospital in an ambulance. I apparently had trouble with my autonomous nervous system. My doctor told me to get proper rest and sleep. I was pushing my physical limits. I couldn't cause my family worry and agonized over whether to continue juggling my work and activism or to step back.

Some people gave up on me and disengaged.

But my friends encouraged me, saying, "What's important is the long haul, even if you go at a slower pace." I slowed down and managed to continue my activities a little at a time, always maintaining awareness of my health.

After considering a number of factors, I left the National Museum of Ethnology, where I had worked for ten years, and transferred to Waseda University in 2013. My university students became involved in Stateless Network activities and events. Young people learned about statelessness, and we worked harder to expand our network.

Greg Constantine is a photographer who captures the daily lives of stateless people around the world. I invited him to photo exhibits and lecture conferences. I also organized refugee film festivals and, with students, ran educational assistance programs for stateless people living in other countries. The students spearheaded the launch of our Stateless Network Youth (SNY). The young students provided powerful support as they propelled us ever forward with their unadorned curiosity and inquisitiveness. During the novel coronavirus pandemic, the students themselves organized online seminars, raised donations for stateless people in trouble due to the pandemic, and posted online the text of statelessness-related interviews. I pondered the importance of passing on our activities to the next generation.

Students formed "Stateless Network Youth" and their activities were covered in "*The Japan News by the Yomiuri Shinbun,*" February 26, 2016

With the Covid-19 pandemic hitting us in early 2020, SNY's new students wondered how they could continue our activism. They asked me to give an online lecture. Off on sabbatical in Malaysia, I had never even met these students. I wasn't familiar with giving online lectures. I was nervous but managed to talk about my experience as a stateless person, the realities of statelessness, and the rainbow metaphor I wove into my doctoral thesis. I also related my dream someday to create a picture book that could readily convey the issue of statelessness to children.

That lecture inspired the students to produce and perform their own *kamishibai* picture-story show in order to raise awareness about statelessness and convey to children the importance of identity, at the first ever online Waseda (University) Festival in November of that year. The SNY students expressed in a way that anybody could understand, each nationality with a different colored muffler, with a rainbow-colored scarf for identity. Those good at drawing handled the illustration, while those good at storytelling wrote the text. Everyone joined in to narrate the video.

The students later showed the video at the Waseda Festival and reportedly won first prize.

I decided to publish it as a picture book. I didn't want to let the *kamishibai* paper picture play go to waste and wanted more people to learn about it. Since then, I have stayed in touch with the students online and on social media. I sent it to my friends with kids and got a wide range of responses.

From Malaysia, I managed to find and contact a picture book publisher. The editor of my previous book *Stateless* introduced me to Miyuki Kimura, a major player in the picture book publishing world, who happened to be my editor's classmate from college. Kimura was a pleasant, lovely woman who knew the picture book industry inside and out.

Kimura and the SNY students then held several online meetings to get things going. She taught us a great deal. "Let's create a picture book with this story based on Lara," Kimura urged. That's how I ended up the protagonist of my own picture book.

Picture book about stateless people, published in July 2022

The students came up with the idea of using mufflers for nationality and scarves for identity. I personally loved the idea, but the publisher said it would be too hard for kids to grasp so we should think up something simpler. The debate and process turned out to be quite fun.

The students did crowd funding for PR purposes, and we raised more than our target from many supporters.

Ōtsuki Shoten published the picture book in July 2022 under the title *Niji-iro-no Pendant—Kokuseki-no-nai Watashi-tachi-no Hanashi* (Rainbow-colored pendant—our story without nationality). It gained media attention as a picture book planned by the students themselves, including from NHK News, radio, and newspapers. After publication, the students continued to raise awareness of statelessness through special story-hour readings of the work.

It was stimulating and edifying to work together across generations and fields of study. The students were so reliable. They included the picture book our desire for students and children, who will take on the responsibility for our future society, to understand nationality and statelessness, and our desire for the shining of the rainbow pendant so crucial for life.

Not Someone Else's Problem

Some people may consider statelessness to be a problem for someone else, namely a foreign someone else. But statelessness is not limited to foreigners, as it has the potential to become personal.

Japanese citizenship is grounded in the *koseki* family register. The Ministry of Justice explains the *koseki* thus:

> Family registration (*koseki*) is the system for recording the kinship of individuals from birth until death. The registration is made for every Japanese national and is the only public document to certify that he or she has Japanese nationality.

The *koseki* is an official record that registers and authenticates social status conferred by Japanese nationality. This register lists each nuclear family as a unit set, with the children retaining the parents' surname until getting married themselves. The general principle is *one surname, one koseki*, so everyone in the *koseki* has the same surname.

One *koseki* contains a *honseki-chi*, which indicates the permanent domiciliary location, and a head of household, who represents the *koseki*. If your legal spouse is a foreign national, then your spouse cannot become a constituent member of the *koseki* and is identified only by the fact that a marriage took place. A child of unwed parents (an illegitimate child) enters a *koseki* headed by the mother, with the paternity field left blank. Each constituent member of the *koseki* has identifying fields that must be filled in to record birth, marriage, divorce, adoption, and other changes. Outside Japan, East Asian countries that use the *koseki* family register system include China, South Korea, and Taiwan.

In this way, the *koseki* verifies one's legal status within the nation state system, and the state of belonging to no *koseki* (known as *mukoseki*) can come about due to many different circumstances: insufficient information, administrative flaws related to marriage and birth, and political and legal discrepancies between nations.

The 300-Day Post-Divorce Problem

The *zanryu* Japanese I visited in the Philippines belonged to no *koseki* because their parents couldn't register their birth in the first place, due to the chaos of war in the country to which they had migrated, or because the documents they submitted were never registered in the *koseki*. One example of becoming *mukoseki* involves the *300-day post-divorce problem*.

Article 772 of Japan's Civil Code (enacted in 1898) stipulates:

(1) A child conceived by a wife during marriage shall be presumed to be a child of her husband.
(2) A child born after 200 days from the formation of marriage or within 300 days of the day of the dissolution or rescission of marriage shall be presumed to have been conceived during marriage.

This regulation drove some mothers to forego registering the birth in order to avoid the child joining the *koseki* of her previous husband rather than of his or her biological father.

Divorce, like marriage, requires the agreement of both parties. Sometimes, it's impossible to get divorced even when the marriage has all but disintegrated. If the wife becomes pregnant during this period of legal limbo, one can guess that the baby the pregnant woman carries is not her husband's. But people living today are bound by this law enacted based on social norms more than a century old.

Some people don't register in resistance to the absurdity and sexism deeply rooted in our society and laws. For example, some children in our society were born to Japanese nationals but are now stateless, because the parents, frustrated by the defects of the *koseki* sysem, didn't register the child's *koseki*. This recalls the discrimination against children born out of wedlock caused by the 300-day post-divorce problem.

Mukokuseki and *mukoseki* (having no nationality vs. no family register) are not identical issues. But since the *koseki* is the only public document to certify citizenship and kinship ties, not having a *koseki* means having no means to prove that you are a Japanese national.

People without *koseki* can register and get citizenship if at the time of birth they *met* the conditions. But *mukoseki* cannot exercise their right to vote in Japan's elections even though they reserve the right to get Japanese citizenship. Not only were stateless persons' legal status precarious due to problems such as being unable to get ID, they may also be cut off from various government and welfare services. In principle, they could not get a *juminhyo* residence certificate, which is created after the birth is registered. Without a *koseki*, even a Japanese citizen was unable get a health insurance card. Without a health insurance card, you must pay hefty sums out of pocket for treatment at a hospital. You cannot get health checks or shots for your infant children. You often cannot receive government childcare allowance or child-raising benefits. You cannot get a passport issued because a prerequisite is submission of a certified transcript or abridged copy of your *koseki* family register. Without a *koseki*, you are legally invisible. As of 2020, the number of Japanese citizens without *koseki* (with no family register) exceeded 10,000.

I too was *mukoseki* from the Republic of China. I lived on the legal basis of my alien registration ID for my country of residence, Japan. Many ethnic Chinese from the Republic of China with no *koseki* reside in South Korea as well as Japan. *Chosen* (associated with the country *Kita Chosen*, or North Korea) residents of Japan are also *mukoseki*. Their ID says they are citizens of *Chosen*, a country that does not exist, rendering them, for all intents and purposes, stateless.

(Note: In Japanese, the Democratic People's Republic of Korea is called *Kita Chosen* or *Chosen Minshushugi Jinmin Kyowakoku*; whereas the Republic of Korea is called *Kankoku* or *Daikan Minkoku*.)

Many people living among us are in a state of *mukoseki* or *mukokuseki*. This cannot be characterized as someone else's problem.

Koseki: From Imperial Subject to Foreigner

In the modern era, a nation demarcating citizen from non-citizen among those dwelling within its territory by granting or stripping citizenship has been considered an ordinary exercise of sovereignty. Inasmuch as this is so, the meaning and function of citizenship goes beyond formality to give the nation unfettered discretion to make an opportunistic political judgment. Its political nature, so to speak, cannot be denied.

> Peculiar to citizenship in Japan is how koseki registration reveals the apparent strong hand of government. That is, one enjoys civil rights as a constituent member of the Japanese nation, and koseki registration has wielded as much and, at times, more normative influence than citizenship. (Endo 2010, 18, 19)

Indeed, the Japanese government relied on the *koseki* registration system to strip Koreans and Taiwanese of nationality rights after the war. Koreans and Taiwanese had lived in Japan as imperial subjects (*teikoku shinmin*). After the war, the government deprived these subjects of that status and rendered them *gaikokujin* foreigners. This action traces back to April 28, 1952, the effectuation date for the Treaty of San Francisco, by which Japan renounced all claim to Korea, Taiwan, and Sakhalin (Jp. *Karafuto*). Nine days before that treaty went into effect, on April 19, 1952, a directive from the Justice Ministry's Civil Affairs Bureau stripped Japanese citizenship from Koreans and Taiwanese, as an automatic consequence of the peace treaty locking in territorial changes.

The Constitution does not define qualifications for *kokumin* citizenship status; Article 10 says only that the "conditions necessary for being a Japanese national shall be determined by law," leaving legal questions about qualifications to the Nationality Act. Nevertheless, what the peace treaty stipulated regarding determining the citizenship of former colonial subjects was the Family Register Act (*Koseki-Ho*), not the Nationality Act. The ministry directive stripped Japanese citizenship from those subjects who, before the treaty went into effect, had been treated as if they should be in *koseki* in the colonies of Korea or Taiwan. They did this by designating them anew as legally Korean or Taiwanese. The directive also enabled those who had had *koseki* in Japan proper to maintain their Japanese *koseki*.

It deserves noting that former colonial subjects living in Japan continued after the war to be excluded from the Family Register Act (1947, No. 224), which was amended after the war. This legal foundation exposed former colonial subjects to discrimination in countless government programs. A glaring example is their exclusion from the locally administered system of residence registration. Until 2009, when the law was finally amended, foreign residents were explicitly excluded by Article 39 of the Basic Resident Registers Act (1967, No. 81).

> This Act shall not apply to a person having no Japanese nationality or a person designated by other government ordinances.

Residents to be registered were Japanese citizens listed in *koseki* family registers. Foreigners had to register at their local government office as aliens, rather than residents, if they stayed more than 90 days in Japan, as per the Alien Registration Act (1952, No. 125). All former colonial subjects without exception were registered anew as *foreigners* and became subject to public security administration. Below I look at a case that illustrates the modern-day repercussions of this distinction between domestic and overseas *koseki* family registers.

Legal Status Contradictions Come to Light During Honeymoon Preparations

Lee Sinhae married a Japanese national and works as a journalist while raising her child. She is a third-generation Korean, who was born and grew up in Higashi-ōsaka. Lee's grandparents on both sides immigrated to Japan, settling in Osaka, during the colonial period. As imperial subjects, they had Japanese citizenship but were registered anew as foreigners (with Korean nationality) in compliance with the 1952 directive. Lee's father's citizenship on his alien registration was listed as *Chosen* (associated with North Korea); her mother's was *Kankoku* (associated with South Korea).

Her parents had no particular political ideology but did identify as *zainichi* Koreans residing in Japan. They had decided to love and live their lives together as fellow *zainichi* Koreans. Lee explains,

"At the time, those with *Chosen* citizenship could not marry someone with *Kankoku* citizenship, so they built a family based on a common law marriage."

When Lee was born, her parents went to register her birth at the local city office. She was recorded as her mother's illegitimate child and inherited her mother's, not father's, name. Her alien registration marked her citizenship and visa in keeping with her mother's *Kankoku* and special permanent resident.

Her second-generation parents raised her and the primary language at home was Japanese. She attended Japanese school but, from the time she was a toddler, identified herself as a *zainichi* Korean. She attended Korean language summer school held by the *Chosen Soren* General Association of Korean Residents, not on the recommendation of her parents, but on her own volition for her own innocent reason: "Because I want to wear that adorable *jeogori* [traditional Korean blouse]."

Around the time of her graduation from university, her father passed away, putting great stress on the family's finances. Lee gave up on getting a job with a corporation and instead began working as a *hosutesu* bargirl to support her family. Speaking good Korean, Japanese and even English, Lee was popular among customers. She was adored as the club's main moneymaker. Later, a frequent client's employee fell in love with her, and they got married.

She and her Japanese husband had no issue submitting the marriage papers to the local city office. The problem arose later. The ecstatic newlyweds decided to go to Guam for their honeymoon, so they went to the South Korean embassy to apply for a passport. The embassy staffer at the counter told her, "I cannot find your *koseki*, so we cannot make a passport." Lee had not expected to hear that.

"I had always just assumed I was South Korean as it said on my alien registration, so that was the first time I found out I was actually *mukoseki* (no family register) and effectively *mukokuseki* (stateless). I cried."

She went home to complain to her mother. The *zainichi* are a patriarchal community, her mother said she had "left everything to Ahppa." But her father had already passed away, so there was no one left to blame. Her parents had felt reassured to have registered her birth at the Japanese city office, so it hadn't occurred to them to apply to the South Korean government. To begin with, her parents had citizenship in different Koreas and so could not get legally married. Even though they had never left Japan and saw themselves as *zainichi* Koreans, other than registering her birth in Japan, they probably never felt a need to register her *hojeog* (South Korean *koseki*). Her Japanese-speaking parents would surely have had great difficulty handling the procedures and getting the information needed to register, considering they didn't speak Korean fluently. It is likely that many others are in the same quandary as Lee.

Lee asked everyone what could she do to be able to go on her once-in-a-lifetime honeymoon. In the end, she got the organization Mindan (Korean Residents Union in Japan) to arrange for her to create a new *hojeog* in South Korea. While researching the information needed to create it, they learned that her mother also had no Korean *hojeog*, so they had to go back and create her mother's *hojeog* in order to create Lee's.

"They asked for a lot of money to create the *hojeog*, but I was able to haggle them down to 150,000 yen for the two of us," Lee recalls.

After getting together all kinds of documents needed to prove her identity, she finally got the Korean *hojeog* set up and a passport issued. Although the honeymoon started much later than originally planned, they went.

The reality of being stateless and *koseki*-less that confronted Lee as she struggled to plan her honeymoon represented the fragility of her ties to the nation state. She is unlikely to forget the experience.

Unable to Acknowledge Paternity

I was approached by a second-generation Vietnamese refugee in her twenties named Ngan Phê (pseudonym) about trouble submitting parental acknowledgement for her child. She explained the whole sequence of events in fluent Japanese that included the western Kansai dialect.

Her visa was *teijusha*, or fixed resident and her nationality was listed as Vietnam. She was born in a refugee camp in Hong Kong, and at 4 moved to Japan, where she grew up. If you didn't hear her name or see her ID, you'd think she looks Japanese. (Incidentally, she's a lovely and stylish woman.)

She dated and got engaged to a Japanese man. They went to their local city office to register their marriage but were told that they could not register it unless she could prove she was single. They later went to the Vietnamese embassy to apply for the documents, but the embassy demanded she show them her Vietnamese passport. She presented her alien registration card, issued by the Japanese government and upon which her nationality was listed as Vietnam.

"I have no Vietnamese passport. This is the only ID I have."

"This is Japanese ID. Please bring us Vietnamese ID."

She had no ID issued by the Vietnamese government. They felt helpless. They began a common law marriage, comforting themselves with the belief that their love was more important than documents.

Phê became pregnant and gave birth prematurely without being legally married. They felt strongly that since Phê had struggled to verify her identity when they tried to register their marriage, they didn't want their child to go through the same trouble and so wanted to get the child's *koseki* properly.

As is, the child would become an illegitimate child on paper, so soon after the birth, they went to their local city office so Phê's husband could officially acknowledge the child as his own. They were told that it would be impossible without the mother's proof of nationality and proof of marriage competency.

Phê was *Vietnamese* according to her alien registration. But the documents for her as a second-generation refugee born outside Japan were not submitted to the Vietnamese government, and she would be unable to get the documents required by the city office from the Vietnamese consulate. She could not hide her bewilderment.

"The first time I found out I was stateless was when the embassy told me *you don't have Vietnamese citizenship*."

Holding a three-month-old, they ran around to various offices, but the paternal acknowledgement process did not go well. They were at their wit's end.

They panicked, thinking the child would end up without a *koseki*. They looked up online and found out about statelessness and finally got ahold of me.

Phê and her one-year-old daughter

I told them about previous cases I had worked on, in which a couple got their marriage application accepted by attaching an official written statement that they were refugees. I advised them to check it the next time they went to their ward office.

They dejectedly reported,

"They told us we needed the documents from the Vietnamese consulate, after all."

"Then, try another city office," I told them.

They called me excitedly a few hours later.

"[We contacted] the ward office of the next town over where my husband's family lives. They told us that if we go there, they might accept the paternal recognition and the marriage application even without the documents from the consulate. Plus, they were so nice; unlike the other ward office."

They scrambled to get all the information together and do all the unfamiliar procedures needed to get their child a *koseki* family register.

Even making every allowance for the slight complexity of the case due to Phê's being a second-generation refugee, the list of required documents should not vary from city office to city office. This slipshod and arbitrary treatment affects whether people can get *koseki*, citizenship or ID.

I would also like to touch upon how much ID cards dominate our lives. Phê and others in her situation get Vietnamese citizenship written on their Japanese IDs even though the Vietnamese government doesn't recognize their citizenship. They get IDs that don't conform to their reality, which even they don't grasp.

To make matters worse, this situation passes on to the next generation. Does the national government simply ignore the problem as if it has no role to play, or is there an active coverup of the issue of statelessness? We must not turn our back on this reality. Stateless persons themselves must also raise their voices.

Double Standard Revealed by Systemic Change

A July 2012 amendment indicated that ID foreigners must carry on their persons from an alien registration card to a *zairyu* residence card. My mother was noted as stateless on her alien registration card. I took her to Immigration to switch over to the residence card.

The law was amended in 2012, exactly four decades after a change in diplomatic relations had rendered my family stateless in 1972. Those who held alien registration cards were notified they must update their ID to the new card. Up until then, foreigners could go to their local city office to handle procedures related to alien registration, but the new ID was under the jurisdiction of the Legal Affairs Bureau. So, I took my mother to Immigration. My mother's new *zairyu* residence card now listed her nationality as *Taiwan*.

Taken aback, I walked back to the counter. I pointed at the nationality field on the card and asked,

"Why did it change from *stateless* to *Taiwanese*?"

The staffer said, "Um, just a moment," and went into the back. She probably didn't know why either. She came back after about ten minutes.

"What we write for nationality or region is based on the passport you hold."

With the change to *zairyu* residence cards, the Ministry of Justice had added Palestine and Taiwan to the categories possible under *Nationality/Region*. This meant *Taiwan* for my mother, who held a Republic of China passport. What had been impossible 40 years before was now the rule.

The staffer had used a casual tone to inform us that my mother's nationality had just changed. She seemed to care nothing about how much people might suffer anxiety and conflict over the change to what was written on that ID, an ID that had for various reasons remained unchanged for four decades.

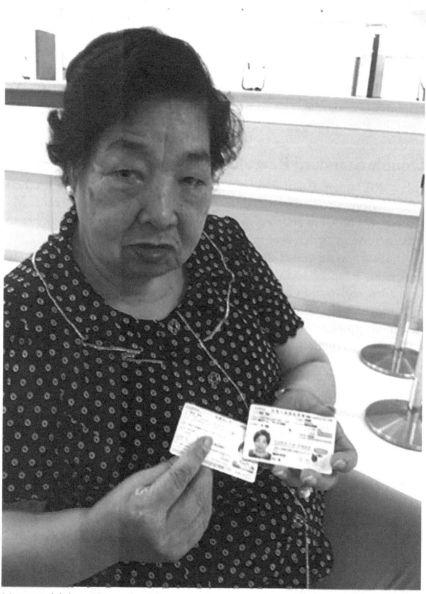

Mama with her ID cards. ID cards shown on the next page: One labeled her as "stateless" (top photo), another labeled her as "Taiwanese"

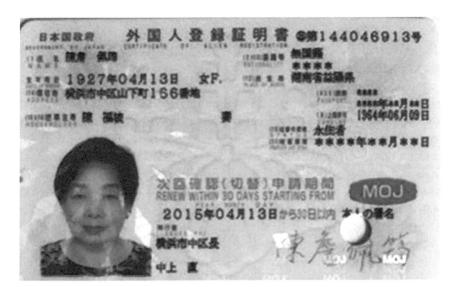

Unsatisfied, I pressed her further. But next to me, Mama said in Chinese, "It's fine, fine. Whatever. I'm over 80. I don't care about nationality." She pulled my hand to leave.

A few weeks later, I accompanied two second-generation refugees living in Kanagawa Prefecture to get their *zairyu* card. On their alien registration cards, one was Cambodian and one, Vietnamese. Like Phê and Hau, they had no Cambodian or Vietnamese passports. When traveling to either of these countries, they used a re-entry permit issued by Japan's Ministry of Justice.

In my mother's case, they had told me that nationality/region is based on the passport held, so I speculated about how the new system would affect what was written on the *zairyu* residence cards of these two, who had no passport. Maybe they would be registered as stateless. Or, would it say *undefined*? If they handled the nationality/region field properly for those without passports, thereby reflecting their statelessness, we would get a clear picture of how many stateless people live in Japan. I had a faint hope that Japan was finally trying *to begin* to introduce a system to recognize stateless people.

They handed in their alien registration cards and re-entry permits, and waited on a bench for the new *zairyu* residence card to be issued.

After a while, they were handed their *zairyu* cards. The nationality/region field had Cambodia and Vietnam.

Taken aback again, I went up to the staffer at the counter.

"What's written under nationality/region on the *zairyu* residence card is supposed to be based on the passport they hold, right? But they don't have passports. Why does it say Cambodia and Vietnam?"

"No, that's what their alien registration cards say, so…"

"What?" My mouth hung open, fed up with this real double standard. I saw how arbitrary the system is with my own eyes, going first with my mother and then with the two second-generation refugees to Immigration to switch from alien registration to the *zairyu* residence card. The experience drove home to me how all the citizenship and other information on your ID lacks credibility while being treated as some sort of sacred verification.

Collaboration with Thammasat University Bangkok Legal Clinic

In 2011, we held an international symposium on supporting stateless people in Japan and invited statelessness specialists from Thailand and France. Bangkok Legal Clinic (BLC), which provides legal aid for stateless people in Thailand, sent Bongkot Napaumporn. Soon after the conference, she came to me to consult about the marriage of a Japanese man named Yukihiro Kudo to a Thai-born stateless woman named Muwangthong Phontip and nicknamed Tip. The two met in Thailand and turned to the BLC for advice. But Kudo couldn't communicate in Thai with the aid worker, and BLC said they didn't understand what Kudo wanted. The clinic told Kudo that there was a group in Japan called the Stateless Network and that since he is Japanese, he should contact them.

According to consultation notes sent to the Stateless Network, Kudo frequently travels to Thailand and began seeing Tip after meeting her in that country. They dined and dated each time he visited Thailand, which was about once every few months. Whenever he was away in Japan, they often spoke online. After going out for a while, they began thinking about marriage.

Around that time, Tip got pregnant. Kudo decided right away to marry her and told his family that he planned to marry a Thai woman. Kudo wanted to bring her over to Japan to live together with his family.

Kudo started to begin the necessary procedures to get a marriage certificate, and it was then that Tip told him that she was stateless.

Kudo had no idea what stateless meant.

Soon after her birth, Tip's mother had entrusted the still-nursing baby to an old woman who babysat in a village in Ayutthaya. *Please take good care of her. I will return in the evening.* But Tip's mother never returned.

"So, I don't know my mother or father. Granny raised me. I didn't go to school."

Granny raised her like her own child, so this story has no tragic-hero aspect. Tip's big, round eyes and smiling face are quite charming.

The couple visited Tip's local government office and the Japanese embassy in Bangkok to try to process the marriage, but they couldn't get the marriage registered because Tip had no birth certificate or any other ID.

At a loss of what to do next, Kudo hired a Thai attorney. The lawyer searched for the parents in an effort to verify Tip's birth, but time passed with no serious leads. Their child was born, and they tried to register the child's birth. But with no ID for Tip, nationality could not be determined, and the child became stateless.

After hearing Kudo's story, we at the Stateless Network held discussions with BLC and conveyed Kudo's intentions. The clinic, for its part, explained to us Tip's circumstances. BLC and the Stateless Network resolved to work together to help with the marriage process and with getting the child's citizenship. Just after we deepened ties and discussion at the international symposium, we built a foundation that facilitated solidarity among Thai and Japanese researchers and aid workers. We divided up responsibilities such as negotiating with the relevant institutions in Japan and Thailand, and accompanying them to various government offices.

A year after they first came to us, Tip managed to complete the ID registration process. Later, they succeeded not only in marriage registration, but also registering the child's birth, paternal acknowledgement, creating a *koseki* family register in Japan, and even applying for a passport.

In January 2012, Kudo and Tip held a well-attended wedding reception in Thailand. BLC's Archan Well and Bongkot Napaumporn, Thailand specialist Kayoko Ishii, and I had all been involved in resolving the couple's issues; and we all attended the wedding. The venue was the house where Tip was left as a baby and then grew up in the pastoral, idyllic Ayutthaya village. The villagers celebrated the couple's marriage. Kudo's family and friends came from Japan to attend.

The couple wore traditional Thai bridalwear with a gold pattern on a white background and held a Thai-style reception. They ate in the garden, launched fireworks, and I wished in my heart for their happiness.

Granny had taken Tip into her arms, waited wondering when her mother would return, and raised her as her own child. Her smile seemed genuinely delighted. She had never dreamed that Tip's life would take such a turn.

The child born to Kudo and Tip acquired Japanese citizenship in April 2012. Today, the family lives in Japan and their second child is already in elementary school. Tip remains stateless. She had a spousal visa as Kudo's wife and now permanent residency. They want nothing. But even if Tip wants to see her family, travel overseas is difficult with no passport.

She has begun preparing to naturalize in consideration of the future. For Tip, reading and writing Japanese is a major stumbling block. Conversation in Japanese is no problem, but she had never even attended school in Thailand, so learning to read and write Japanese is quite a feat.

"How about the application for Japanese citizenship? How about the Japanese for that?"

"It's tough, but I have to *gambaru* for the kids."

With a bright smile, she recounts that she studies Japanese in between child raising and housework, and a few days a week, "I sell *taiyaki* bean-jam pancakes part-time at our neighborhood train station."

 State-Engendered Conceptual Boundaries:
Nationality, IDs, Xenophobia, and COVID-19

The World's Biggest Stateless Population

Many stateless persons try to assimilate in their country of residence. One Rohingya woman acquired Japanese citizenship and is raising children in Japan.

The Rohingya are a Muslim minority of some 80,000 to 120,000, concentrated in Rakhine State (formerly Arakan). They tend to have more chiseled features and darker skin than the Buddhist, Burmese majority. The Rohingya speak Bengali rather than Burmese. They are treated as the *other* by most of the Myanmar population due to religious, linguistic, and ethnic differences.

Rohingya see themselves as Myanmar nationals, but the 1982 Citizenship Law stripped them of that citizenship, rendering them stateless.

Reports from Rakhine State indicate intensifying clashes between the Rohingya and the Myanmar military, including rape, massacres, and the burning of villages. Over the past few years, more than 700,000 refugees have been driven out of their homelands, many now living in miserable conditions in Bangladeshi refugee camps. About 250 refugees fled the hardships there to Japan. Most of them live in Tatebayashi, Gunma Prefecture.

Thidar Lwin is a Rohingya woman who has become involved in Stateless Network activism. When we invited Greg Constantine for the Rohingya photo exhibit, we asked her to give a talk on her own career. She readily agreed.

"But this will be my first time to speak in front of people.... I will be nervous. Can you check the text of my lecture?"

Up until then, women didn't play a very conspicuous role in Rohingya society. Even Thidar Lwin hesitated. She wore a vivid yellow hajib and dress to the lecture and gave a fantastic lecture. After that, she often spoke on the Rohingya issue.

Thidar was born in Rakhine State in 1989. Her grandfather and great-grandfather were also Rohingya born in that state. Her father went to college in the former capital Yangon, then returned to Rakhine to teach high school. He was involved in the democracy movement and became the subject of a military manhunt in 1988. Feeling in danger for his life, Thidar's father left his family and fled to Japan.

Her mother sold off their home, took the kids, and moved to Yangon. Thidar was 3. She lived with her mother and siblings until sixth grade. There are many Buddhists in Yangon; she was bullied and called *kalar*, the pejorative word used against ethnic Bengalis. She suffered not only social humiliation but also legal discrimination. Her Rohingya ethnicity barred her from the citizenship card that Myanmar citizens get when they turn 12.

Thidar's father had gained refugee status in Japan. After consulting with her parents, her mother brought the children to Japan. Thidar had waited a decade to meet her father.

The happy, reunited family initially lived in Tatebayashi, Gunma. At first, Thidar couldn't speak Japanese. She had to carry a curry bento from home because the school lunch was not halal. Her parents made her a different curry each day. She had a tough middle school experience, bullied by classmates who mocked her, gleefully noting that *her bento is always brown!*

Later, she learned Japanese. Her environment changed as she entered high school then vocational school, which were fun for her. At 16, her parents took her to Thailand. The next day she met her Rohingya betrothed and was to marry the same day.

"I was shocked, but my parents chose him, and I trusted them."

The husband returned temporarily to Myanmar, got his paperwork in order, and came to Japan six months later. Thidar noted,

"It wasn't bad. Getting to know someone *after* marriage made every day fresh."

Today, they are happily married with five kids.

When Thidar attended an architectural college, she joined a program to spend six months studying in Spain and Italy before graduation. She went to the Myanmar Embassy to get her passport renewed. The embassy refused and confiscated her passport instead.

Meanwhile, her *zairyu* residence card (issued by the Japanese government) had her as a Myanmar citizen. She inquired about her next course of action and was issued a re-entry permit. The Ministry of Justice issues these travel papers to stateless people, refugees, and other foreign residents who cannot get a passport. She used a re-entry permit to apply for a visa but, in the end, couldn't get the right visa and had to give up on studying abroad.

They held a family meeting and decided to go for Japanese citizenship to avoid ongoing difficulties. But they had trouble assembling the documents required for naturalization. She no longer had a Myanmar passport, yet her residence card showed her as a Myanmar citizen.

There exists no government institution that could verify her identity since she was stateless. Her application for citizenship was initially rejected and it took her six years until she finally got it. Today, she uses the Japanese name Rurika Hasegawa, but with her chiseled features, she's often treated as a foreigner.

Thidar notes three reasons she's happy she acquired Japanese citizenship. One is the "new convenience when going overseas." Another is a new sense of belonging.

"When I was stateless, having only a re-entry permit, if an emergency arose overseas, I didn't know where I would be deported back to. No governmental agency would protect me. I always felt anxiety as if I had no place to come back to."

The third reason is her right to vote.

"That is, that we ourselves choose who will rule us."

"Thidar-san, do you want to return to Myanmar?"

"For me, Arakan [Rakhine] is my homeland, but for my children, Japan is their homeland. Even if I returned to Arakan, it would be hard to live there because I don't belong anywhere. So, I'm not thinking of going back."

Thidar expressed her attachment to and the challenges of life in Japan.

"We love Japan. But we are not treated completely as Japanese because of our appearance. Honestly, I wish people would stop focusing so much on appearance."

She declared her identity with finality.

"I am a Rohingya with Japanese citizenship. I want to pass this identity on to my children. And I want more people to learn about the Rohingya issue and about what's going on with statelessness."

There are stateless children who were driven out of their homelands with no place to return. To construct a society in which they at least can live in peace, we need a new perspective that transcends nationality, religion, and ethnicity. We might be able to find that via the voices and lived experiences of children who have crossed borders.

Revisiting the Life Permitted by the Pre-modern State

With the advance of globalization, global phenomena arise that don't fit into the narrow confines of the sovereign state. Yet people continue to confine themselves in a mentality founded on the familiar nation state to which they have become so accustomed. The very nature of the sovereign state is such that it cleaves the population into *citizens* and *foreigners*. The citizens are given a set of rights and obligations such that they are protected when unforeseen events take place.

Each country has a nationality law that stipulates who is a citizen. As a reminder, in broad strokes, the system of determination is either *jus sanguinis*, which gives the child the nationality of the parents, or *jus soli*, which gives the child the nationality of the country of birth. Citizenship can then change for reasons other than conditions of birth, such as diplomatic relations or changes to territory or sovereignty. When a colony breaks up or achieves independence, what happens to those former colonials now living within the borders of the former suzerain?

There are those who don't live within the confines of the nation state or nationality. In 2017, I got the following Facebook message:

"I read your book. We run a school for stateless children in Tawau [Malaysia]. I want you to come visit the children here."

The following year, I prepared to go meet this group of stateless children. When I told my students, they said they wanted to go with me. I asked them to create a program to provide education to stateless children.

We visited islands in national border zones around Malaysia, Indonesia, and the Philippines. It was like paradise—blue sky, azure sea, and white sand.

Many stateless children live in Tawau, located near the Sulu and Celebes Seas.

Before going, I read *Border-Crossings from the Sulu Maritime World*, in which cultural anthropologist Ikuya Tokoro details the Sulu Sea region. Commenting on the traditional political system of Southeast Asia, Tokoro touches upon theorist Benedict Anderson's reflection that, "A nation is represented at its center, not at the periphery. The nation's territorial extent is always in flux."

To Tokoro, this means that although national *borders* between modern states have conventionally been defined by their territorial dimensions, the traditional Southeast Asian state has no borders in a strict sense. In today's nation state, changing nationality is strictly controlled, and multiple citizenship is frowned upon; considered the exception to the rule. More and more people are forced to choose among multiple nationalities. In modern society, the various peoples and lands of the earth are presumed to belong exclusively to one or another of the nation states. The nation's requirements that *national territory* and *national people* represent inflexible, exclusive belonging was an alien principle for the Southeast Asian maritime world during the colonial era. During that period, people and territories frequently changed hands as a matter of course. Tokoro notes how common it was for people and territories to belong to multiple nations or no nation at all (*terra nullius*). His people who belong to no nation correspond to stateless people.

Stateless children in the Sulu and Celebes Seas

"The society we live in today may be rather unnatural."

The Bajau Laut are often introduced as sea nomads, sea gypsies or a floating people. Their lifestyle is an anomaly even among the seaborne peoples of the Sulu Archipalego. Typical sea gypsy families live on their houseboats with no home on land. They move from one fishing ground to the next, never staying long in one place.

Speakers of Sinama (the language of the Sama-Bajau) are spread throughout the islands of Southeast Asia—from the southern part of the Philippines, to the Bornean coast, Indonesia's Sulawesi and the Maluku Islands. David Kim knew a lot about the area and took me from Semporna in Tawau on a 40-minute speedboat ride to where the Bajau Laut are.

The people who lived on the island were far removed from any notion of nation or nationality. Their lives revolved around fishing every day with no opportunity to use anything as identification. Even to get ID, they would first have to go all the way to Semporna or other towns in Tawau to register the birth. The travel costs alone to go from island to town would set them back a month's earnings. Even if they registered the birth and got an ID, it's not like these islanders could avail themselves to any great service from the government. Bajau Laut residents thus had little desire to get ID or citizenship. They continue to live stateless lives. That is natural to them.

But capitalist society has pushed its way in recently, step by step. A resort hotel went up on a nearby island; contact with the outside world has grown; and the number of jobs catering to tourists increases. As a result, the number of Bajau Laut islanders trying to get ID in order to learn English and get jobs has gradually begun to increase.

In addition to the island, we visited Grace Training Center (GTC) in a Tawau town about 60 kilometers from Semporna. GTC has educated over 500 stateless children since it was launched in 2010. The program is run by the Calvary Love Foundation, itself run by a Christian church. Today, about 300 children aged 5 to 16 attend each year. In 2018, when I visited, there were 300 children, a number that rose to 371 in 2019.

The children who learn at GTC often have parents who migrated from the Philippines or Indonesia to work in Tawau, according to Thu Esther who runs the center. The parents take irregular routes to Tawau, sailing on ocean routes then drifting ashore. They are undocumented, so even if they become pregnant and give birth in Malaysia, they cannot register the child's birth. I learned that they often either end up as legally invisible or they register the birth with the Malaysian authorities but cannot acquire citizenship to any country.

Another pattern is that one parent (usually the father) is a Malaysian national, but the other parent (usually the mother) is undocumented. The parents are not legally married, so the child cannot get Malaysian citizenship despite inheriting a parent's Malaysian "blood." The official line is that the government will give citizenship if one parent is a Malaysian citizen, but the reality is that the application process often doesn't work.

During our visit, we ran a program conceived and organized by Stateless Network Youth students, with group dancing, folding paper airplanes, and classes. I was so proud to see the sparkly-eyed GTC children intently watch the young university students at the podium—raising their voices, stretching out their hands with all their might, and bombarding them with questions.

Rei (pseudonym) is a 13-year-old student at GTC. He is a bit smaller and thinner than other kids his age, perhaps due to nutritional deficiency. He showed us and the GTC teachers his home and the route he takes from his home to GTC. His mother Sherry (pseudonym) is 32. Rei is her oldest son. When we visited Rei's house in March 2018, Sherry had just given birth to her ninth child two weeks earlier. Both she and her husband had come to Tawau from Mindanao by boat. The husband was looking for work. When we were at the home, he was out on a job interview. Sherry said, "Our finances will stabilize a bit if he can manage to get a job in logging."

Rei's prefabricated bungalow was in a riverside Mangrove forest. On his way to school each day, he had to get past the cacophony and dust released by a tanker operating at a nearby site that processed oil palm. This made for appalling living conditions. Rei explained how he had previously commuted to school on a boat, plying a nearby river populated with alligators and snakes. Recently, a concrete road had been built that ran near his home, so he finally heeded his mother and began taking an overland route to school. But the new land route tripled his commute time, compared with by boat, and now takes 90 minutes. So, Rei must leave home an hour earlier, with his little brother and sister in tow. They walk an hour and a half each way under the blazing Tawau sun, not an easy task.

As the eldest among nine siblings, Rei naturally took care of his younger sisters and brothers. But he also, without a hint of reluctance, took excellent care of his mother who a fortnight prior had gone through childbirth. When asked what he wants to be when he grows up, Rei blushed and answered with an innocent, smiling face: "I want to be a singer."

In nearly every case, the children became stateless due to their parents' international marriage, to border crossings or administrative procedural oversights. Since such children are treated as illegal aliens, they cannot attend regular school, thereby losing their right to get an education. GTC was founded in order to ensure children in a state of statelessness at least have the opportunity for education.

The system of nationality and the nation state often produces stateless children, with nationality further creating barriers to education and jobs, undermining their futures. We who live in peace under the modern nation-state system have no qualms distinguishing ourselves from others using the yardstick of nationality, but we need to become aware of how that same system leads to the suffering of many. It is inappropriate to deny children the right to education and a life because they are stateless.

Human beings cannot choose their parents or where they are born. Yet, they are assigned a different nationality and afforded different rights depending on where they are born and who their parents are. The major part of their entire lives is already determined. Are we ok with such a system?

The stateless children I met on the islands of Semporna have such sparkling eyes. Some people might feel sorry for them because they are stateless. They might then tend to solve the problem by demanding they be granted citizenship. But is that really the right way forward? We must understand the limits and sheer infeasibility of the current system that crams people with no concept of nation or nationality and people who repeatedly cross borders into the rigid framework of the nation state. This is the system that drives these maritime people into the painful predicaments in which they find themselves.

The Doctor Who Genuinely Relished Statelessness

"I became stateless with the collapse of Manchukuo [Japanese puppet state] in 1945. Since I was stateless and could speak Japanese, I was lucky to get the chance to work at a US military hospital. Thanks to that, I was able to study American medicine in Japan. I became a physician and economically well off, so I went on a trip with my family. I was the only stateless member of my family, so getting a visa, getting in and out of the country was inconvenient. I'm 84. I have no desire for citizenship, because I can be free. What I want is to stay healthy and serve society as a physician as long as possible and some day for the world to be as one in peace."

This was the comment of my interview subject Eugene Aksenoff (Jp: エフゲニー・ニコラエヴィチ・アクショーノフ; Russ: Евгений Николаевич Аксёнов), a stateless resident of Japan. His cheerful character, liberated ideas, and positive thinking provided a dramatic contrast to the negative way people generally conceive of stateless people. It truly removed the scales from my eyes.

As a former stateless person, I felt a sort of empathy and reassurance that such an appealing stateless person exists in the real world.

Aksenoff was known simply as Doctor and sometimes as *Aoime-no Akahige* (Blue-eyed red-beard; *Akahige* is a Japanese term meaning skilled doctor). He opened an International Clinic for foreign patients in 1953.

Aksenoff was born in Harbin on March 5, 1924. The city was then under the rule of imperial Japan's puppet government Manchukuo. After the Russian Revolution, his White Russian father fought the Red Army in Siberia as a commissioned officer. Captured by the Red Army, he was saved from being shot by a friend he happened to run into. His father fled on a horse given to him by a friend and escaped to Harbin, where he later

Dr. Eugene Aksenoff, 1924–2014

brought his mother. Born and raised in Harbin during the Manchukuo period, Aksenoff was comfortable with Japanese and Chinese. At 18, he met the noble Yoshitaka Tsugaru, who had come from Japan. Tsugaru urged Aksenoff to study in Japan, so he came over to Japan in the middle of the Pacific War. He took a preparatory class in Japanese at Waseda University's international school, then studied medicine at Jikei University School of Medicine.

As the war heated up, prejudice against foreigners grew. Against that backdrop, Aksenoff stood 183 cm tall with a sweet face. He appeared in several movies of the time. The Army even had him play a spy in one war propaganda film. His film work paid for his college and helped him get through a tough time.

With Japan's defeat in 1945, Manchukuo was dismantled, rendering Aksenoff stateless. He forewent naturalizing to Japanese citizenship or returning to the Soviet Union, and instead chose to live in Japan in a state of statelessness. He chose freedom unencumbered by nation or ideology.

After the war, he went to see the landing of the occupation forces. He was mistaken for an American prisoner of the Japanese military and hired as a GHQ interpreter for the military and as a medical worker at the US Army hospital. At that time, being stateless was a fortunate happenstance that led him to work, he says. But he faced a mountain of inconveniences: he was suspected of espionage, prevented from getting married officially due to lack of ID, and had great difficulty getting visas for overseas travel.

Aksenoff traveled to the Soviet Union in 1979, in the middle of the Cold War. While there, he was suspected of being a US spy and arrested by the KGB. In November 1980, Soviet radio equipment was discovered in a Yokohama factory. This time, he was suspected of being a Soviet spy. Where the equipment came from was never explained.

In both cases—when he was detained in the Soviet Union and again in Japan, he was cleared and released for lack of evidence. Each of these countries for which he felt great affinity could only look at him with suspicion. Was that unrelated to his stateless status? He surely felt humiliated and depressed by the experience.

For good or bad, Aksenoff's affability and linguistic proficiency may have had an impact. In addition to Japanese, he spoke English, Chinese, Russian, Greek, French, and other languages. His clinic had no language barrier, and he saw many embassy personnel, celebrities, VIPs, refugees, and migrant workers. He even made house calls in emergency cases. He didn't care if a patient seeking his help was famous or a nobody, a citizen or non-citizen, a legal or illegal resident. He came to be known as a doctor who accepted patients with total impartiality. Rumi Yamamoto,

Aksenoff's right-hand nurse, said, "Sometimes he saw patients of more than ten different nationalities in a single day." He also saw indigent patients free of charge, prescribed medicine and, if the patient asked him, even gave some financial aid.

Aksenoff's upbringing was the starting point that led to his medical practice, examining and treating all ill people equally—regardless of nationality, race, or religion. Although he was born in Harbin, he spent most of his life in Japan. Even had he received Japanese citizenship, his European features would have meant that society would treat him as a foreigner anyways. So, he probably figured that he might as well live free and unfettered by the nation state. In recognition of his practice and lifestyle, he won the Yoshikawa Eiji Cultural Award in 1998, and then received an award from the Foundation for Social Contribution for his contributions to society in 2007.

The recognition extended beyond the borders of Japan. President Vladimir Putin invited him to Russia, where, "President Putin offered me Russian citizenship. I said no, I'm good staying stateless." Aksenoff winked and smiled when he told me this.

Snapshots of the good doctor with patients crowded the wall of the examining room where he had spent his entire career, and illustrated how much he was loved and revered. He can be seen in photos with Michael Jackson and French President Jacques Chirac.

In a sense, Aksenoff savored his statelessness during the 70 years he lived in Japan. He was both a founder and an honorary consultant of the Stateless Network we founded in 2009. His carefree smile and his quip that "a borderless clinic deserves a stateless doctor" remain seared in my brain even today.

After a full 90 years of life, this physician that I so admired passed away on August 5, 2014. He lived informed by a turbulent past as well as a spirit of tolerance and harmony. His life teaches us the importance of pursuing not national or other interests in a narrow sense; but rather to use your position to ensure you make at least a small contribution to the happiness of all.

Statelessness and the Ravages of War

Florim Ademaj was born in 1970 in the autonomous province of Kozovo, in the former Yugoslavia, to an Albanian father and a Croatian mother living in Bosnia-Herzegovina. In 1976, when he was six, his parents left Kosovo for Bosnia. Florim spent his school years as a ward in the home of his father's friend. In 1988, he graduated school in Kosovo and went to Bosnia to live with his parents. But his happy family life was short-lived. In 1990, war erupted, and in 1991, Croatia, Slovenia, and Macedonia seceded as ethnic strife intensified. In 1992, Bosnia-Herzegovina also became independent amidst worsening ethnic conflict between secessionist Croatians and Muslims on one side and unionist Serbs on the other.

When the horrors of war arrived in Zvornik, where Florim lived, Serb forces placed him and his parents in concentration camps in 1992.

> Serbs came into our apartment at 5am and checked our ID cards.... During about ten months in the camps, I saw them kill about 700 with my own eyes. I went from nearly 90 kilos when I went in, down to 35 kilos when I got out.

Records indicate that more than 2,000 civilians were killed in Zvornik. Florim said in a heavy, painful tone, "My parents were killed right in front of me... My days spent in the concentration camp were truly a nightmare."

Florim alone barely escaped with his life. He moved around Poland, Hungary, Germany and other European countries, landing in the Netherlands in 1996. There he applied for asylum and was told he would get it soon. The Dutch court asked him to testify that many civilians were killed in the camps.

> They asked me to testify about the massacres but reliving the nightmare of war was painful. Testifying meant that, at any time, someone, a Yugoslavian, might take revenge against me. I didn't want to betray anybody. Someone advised me that it would be safer to get away from Europe and go to the Far East where there were few Yugoslavians.

Florim wanted liberation from this unending nightmare, and just around that time an acquaintance came to him with an idea. "In exchange for you carrying this bag, I will give you a passport and a ticket to Japan."

I can go to the Far East!

Florim grasped at the straw that became his ticket to the Far East. He agreed to the proposition and left the Netherlands, where he had lived for four years. He had received an Italian passport, the air ticket, and the bag. He thought that if only he could get to Japan, he would be able to escape this suffering and live free.

From One Hell to Another

> When I got to Narita (International Airport) and pulled my luggage off the baggage conveyor belt, two people quickly approached me.
> "Is this your luggage?"
> "Yes."
> "Ok, please come with us."
> They took me into a room to interrogate me. Without ever seeing the streets of Japan, my life behind a fence began. I had left one hell, only to end up in another one.

Suffering from the trauma of war, Florim ended up being used by organized crime. He spoke bitterly about the man he had been two decades earlier:

> I had no idea what had been in my suitcase. After pulling it off the belt, I carried my own bags for the first time. *Wow, it's heavy,* I thought. When I was first given the task, I had a vague awareness that it might be dangerous. But I was in such a bad place then.

A quick search of Japanese media revealed that in fact the papers in 2000 had covered the story of a Kosovar refugee detained on suspicion of smuggling drugs. He stayed in detention for a year as his criminal trial progressed. He was sentenced to seven and a half years of prison.

> I lived like a slave day after day in Fuchū Prison. In addition to prison labor, I sat and hugged my knees every day. I couldn't relieve myself unless I pushed a button to call the guards. I couldn't take that life and just lost it.

After finishing his prison term, Florim was transferred to the Shinagawa Detention Center.

> During my eight months in Shinagawa, the Japanese government contacted Serbia, Holland, the UN and elsewhere to try to deport me. While inside, my homeland Yugoslavia had collapsed. In the end, no country would accept me.

Immigration drew up documents for Florim and designated him *stateless*. Florim noted, "That was when I first learned the word *stateless*." He was then sent to the Higashi-Nihon immigration center in Ushiku for two more years of detention. Florim suffered PTSD from the trauma of war and the long years of detention. The detention facilities overmedicated him, starting with sleeping pills and including a wide range of drugs.

In May 2009, I got a call from Florim at the Ushiku detention facility. "I am stateless. I have no country to go back to. An activist who works with refugees gave me your number. I need your help."

I made the time to travel from Osaka to Ushiku in Ibaraki Prefecture. I first met Florim in the visiting room at the detention center. I presented my ID at the entrance and wrote down his name. While waiting for my number, I bought coffee, tea, and cakes for him at a little kiosk next to the reception counter.

When my number was called, I entered the visiting room. An immigration guard sat in the corner of the room on the other side of the glass. The atmosphere seemed tense. I had only seen this kind of scene in TV dramas and movies, so I was a bit nervous. After a while, a guard brought Florim in through a door on the other side of the glass. He greeted me cheerfully in slightly idiosyncratic Japanese.

"*Hajimemashite.*"

He was a middle-aged man, far more spirited than I had imagined. While wiping sweat from his head and neck with a worn-out towel, he said, this time using idiosyncratic English,

"I was exercising."

During our limited visiting time, I asked him about his history before coming to Japan, including why he was stateless. He opened up about his background, his suffering from PTSD, and his very painful memories.

"I want to get out of here [detention center] as soon as possible and live a normal life."

"Well, I think your life will be very hard in Japan, even if you do get out."

"Still, please help me."

Having received that entreaty, I took on that truly heavy burden and returned home. I struggled to find some way forward.

As I looked into options, I frequently received calls from the detention center's public phone. I learned from those with long years' experience helping refugees about procedures for the *kari homen* provisional release program, and about finding lodgings and other living basics for Florim after he got out. In addition to NGOs, those involved with the Catholic Church also helped me enthusiastically. Of particular help was Kenji Arikawa of the Catholic Tokyo International Center (CTIC), which had a great deal of experience with refugees and provisional release. After consulting with him, he arranged for Florim to stay at a monastery and a seminary for several months after getting out to learn about life in Japan and get back on his feet.

Atty. Fumie Azukizawa readily agreed to help with preparing the legal documents for his asylum application and to get a special residence permit. In the end, Atty. Azukizawa and I put up a 500,000 yen surety for Florim's provisional release. Arikawa drove me up to Ushiku on the day of his release.

"I am very happy to be able to see Japanese scenery. It took me many years to see the *real Japan*. Thank you for getting me out."

Arikawa responded to that without skipping a beat.

"No. Now's the hard part."

Florim's heartfelt smile lit up his entire face.

"No problem. I will *gambaru* [work hard]."

Harsh Reality and the Great East Japan Earthquake

In a short time, Florim's initial relief at being liberated turned to stress over the harsh realities of daily life. Unlike prison, there was no food unless he prepared it. He had to work to get the food. Yet, legally he was not permitted to work. Without work, there'd be no money to buy food or coffee. With limited proficiency in the language, he found little work. For someone suffering from PTSD, it was surely a one-two punch.

To nobody's surprise, he ended up unable to endure life in Japan. His desperate phone calls begging for help became more and more frequent. His health visibly deteriorated, until he ended up attempting suicide and was taken to the hospital in an ambulance. With no visa or insurance, his hospital bill exceeded 1 million yen. I grabbed my head when I saw that bill.

The stress gave me many sleepless nights. What could I do to rescue him from this storm of anxieties? Luckily, Florim had a powerful sympathizer and ally in Fumio Noda, who provided mental health support to refugees and migrants at Yotsuya Clinic in central Tokyo.

Ironically, what provided the catalyst for him to escape his depressive state was the Great East Japan Earthquake of March 11, 2011. He had gone to the affected area to support reconstruction. He was called a hero and made many friends who asked him to come back. He seemed so happy, and said: "If possible, I want to move to Fukushima."

He had lost his country in conflict, then, after a period of wandering, washed up in Japan. He had escaped the horrors of war, so he instinctively knew what to do to help with the reconstruction in the Tohoku region and how to create a comfortable place for evacuees. The children in the region saw him taking action and started to call him by the English sobriquet *Hero*. Florim told me that made him so happy.

Seeing him like that brought me to the realization that in the end, what is most important for people in their lives may be to have somewhere to belong. Having someone with whom you have a real connection and someone who needs you is the key for people. Being needed and having somewhere to belong gives us the strength to live. I feel that this enriches our minds in a far more exalted manner than the legal bonds of citizenship.

Visiting Stateless People in the Middle East

Giving consultations to stateless residents of Japan deepened my understanding of their lived experiences. I learned that there are myriad reasons someone becomes stateless, just as the positions they find themselves in are diverse. But I wondered about the stateless residents of other countries. I wanted to continue to meet the stateless in each of the world's countries to learn about their circumstances. I began to think that in addition to East Asia, I wanted to go as much as possible to the Middle East and other places where there are stateless people.

In the back of my mind, I couldn't seem ever to separate myself from statelessness. Even when I was watching movies. *The Syrian Bride* (Hebrew: הכלה הסורית) is a 2004 film about one day in the life of a stateless Druze bride living in the Golan Heights under Israeli occupation. The film captures issues of nationality, national borders, the nation state, and a family's love. Palestinian screenwriter Suha Arraf collaborated with Israeli director Eran Riklis on the film. That itself is extraordinary, but I was immediately drawn to it when I heard that the work was created based on true stories of stateless people living in the Golan Heights.

I planned a screening and a lecture at the Minpaku (National Museum of Ethnology) where I was still working at the time. In autumn of 2011, Aiko Nishikida, a Mideast expert who had lectured at the screening, went to Israel on research. I visited her and suggested we go to the Golan Heights together.

To the north is Lebanon. To the south, Jordan. To the west, Israel. To the east lies the Purple Line ceasefire boundary between Syria and Israel, which both monitor the decades-long ceasefire. International law designates the Golan Heights as Syrian territory, but Israel occupied most of the region during the 1967 Six-Day War and effectively annexed it in 1981. Syria continues to claim it as part of its territory, Southwest Syria. Some 20,000 Jews and 20,000 Druze, who are a minority in Syria, for a total population of 40,000 to 50,000 people, live in an area of 1,200 square kilometers. After it incorporated the heights into its legal system in 1981, the Israeli government offered Israeli citizenship to Syrians left over in the Golan Heights. But many Druze refused Israeli and Syrian citizenship and became stateless.

I desperately wanted to meet and interact with stateless residents in the Golan Heights: see with my own eyes how they lived day to day, learn what kinds of IDs they carried, ask how they felt about the national state, nationality, and what their experience of the world was. I flew to Israel and traveled 180 kilometers north from Tel Aviv to Golan Heights on a bus, then spent several days in the village of Majdal Shams.

The Golan Heights is a wine-producing region with fertile soil and water resources. The elevation above the village looks out over Mt. Hermon between Lebanon and Syria, and from there 60 kilometers east to the Syrian capital Damascus and the Bay of Haifa on the Mediterranean Sea in the West. For the Israeli military, the heights provide a vital strategic anti-Arab vantage point. This territory is disputed by Syria and Israel and thus surrounded by a steel fence and peppered with buried landmines, obstructing free movement in some areas. It also provides a bird's-eye view of the pastoral vineyards below. Beyond the fence is undisputed Syria. The UN Disengagement Observer Force (UNDOF) keeps the peace in this zone that seems to juxtapose a pastoral scene with high tension. I looked at the bright blue sky and white clouds, grey walls and lines of red roofs on an incline, and couldn't help wondering what the people living here thought and felt day by day.

Long ago, when villagers were divided between Syria and Israel, they approached the fence from each side and communicated by screaming through megaphones. This sight has disappeared since mobile phones started facilitating cross-border communications. As captured in the *Syrian Bride*, Druze have a custom of marrying cousins, so sometimes a woman in Majdal Shams marries someone on the other Syrian side of the fence. Since Israel and Syria don't recognize each other, villagers can't move freely between the two areas. Celebrations are held on each side, after which the bride walks across the border to join her new husband. Once you cross over into Syrian-held territory, you have no idea when you will be able to return and see your family again. The fates of these families have been torn apart by international strife.

Israeli-issued ID: Nationality Listed as Undefined

We walked through the center of the village, men chatting in front of their shops spoke to us in kind voices.

"Why did you come to Majdal Shams?"

"I saw *The Syrian Bride* and just had to come."

"Oh, that was a movie made about my family!"

"Huh? Really?"

By extraordinary serendipity, I met the family that was the main subject of the film. Majdal Shamsians are friendly and sociable. They asked us many questions about East Asia, perhaps because they cannot travel abroad.

To learn about how these villagers lived, we interacted with as many different people as possible during our time there. We met a woman who uses art to teach children of the terror of landmines. We went to a live concert given by youth who express their thoughts and feelings in song.

"I run a café right over there. You should come." At the café, Zeid Mahmud made us his special sandwich. Other patrons were relaxing, smoking a hookah.

"I was also stateless, so I am interested in the people of the Golan Heights," I said. Mahmud showed me his ID.

"I'm also stateless. See…"

In the nationality field was written *Undefined*. Hmmm. I thought that maybe this way made more sense than the Japanese way of writing a country name even though the person had no ID to verify their nationality.

"What do you do when you go overseas?"

"Israel issues a travel document for stateless people. I use that to get a visa to the country I'm going to. It's really a hassle because I gotta go to Tel Aviv each time I do this."

Stateless residents of the Golan Heights use a travel document similar to the re-entry permit I once used. Our feelings about the nation state and national borders seemed rather similar.

In 2018, Nishikida invited me to speak about Chinatown and ethnic Chinese in Japan at a symposium held in Lebanon. I went to Beirut and had the chance to exchange views with local academics and visit a refugee camp.

We drove to the agreed upon location and Mohamad, a third-generation Palestinian refugee with the NGO Dream of a Refugee Association, showed us around Shatila refugee camp. Only residents could bring outsiders into the camp. Apparently, even Lebanese government officials and police officers were prohibited from entering.

As we walked the streets, the atmosphere altered subtly. As the population density rose, a web of black electric cables began to connect the decrepit buildings. The writing on store signs also changed.

"The camp begins here."

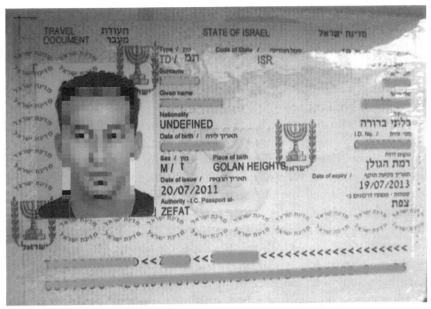

Zeid Mahmud's ID had "Undefined" in the nationality field

Palestinian flags flew and there was an unspoken feeling of *now you have entered* our *territory*. The refugee camp provides no running water, electricity, or other basic utilities. Refugees must run their own electric cables. The view from windows shows nothing but electric cables, a situation that has sparked fires multiple times.

Shatila refugee camp is said to be famous for having many junkies. A group of five Palestinian youths who grew up in the camp have begun a program to increase educational opportunities so residents themselves can improve their own lives and those of their children. We visited a school opened thanks to funding they got from Europe. In the small classroom, toddlers at their desks did their best to learn writing.

Hundreds of thousands of Palestinians live in refugee camps. Unofficial estimates put the number as high as half a million. Their ancestors fled the founding of Israel in 1948 and have been forced to live in camps for more than seven decades. They are already third- and fourth-generation stateless persons. I asked them what kind of ID they carry, and they removed a laminated but tattered ID card from their wallet and showed me. It has a photo affixed to a light-blue piece of paper. When they want to travel overseas, they get a travel document issued by the Ministry of Interior's security bureau.

"We have lived stateless for many generations…"

COVID-19, National Borders, and Statelessness

The spread since late 2019 of the novel coronavirus has dramatically changed the lives of humanity. People have been asked to stay home. Even when it became acceptable to leave our houses, we had to maintain social distance. We can no longer shake hands when greeting people. And for now, masks are a must.

Children who have studied and learned how to handle personal relations in the schoolhouse, now hunker down at home for online classes. We don't get enough exercise. When will this war on corona pass?

My father became a centenarian in 2022. Born in Heilongjiang Province, he of course learned the horrors of World War II and the civil war in China. In the 1950s, after the war, he moved to Japan, then lived the next seven decades as a minority, and four of those decades as a stateless person. My father said, "In my life spanning almost 100 years, corona is the most terrifying experience I have ever had. The fight against this invisible enemy is far more terrifying than war."

It's true that the coronavirus has eaten into our psyches and expectations. Am I the only one who fears not so much getting infected and sick, but creating a world in which we are all suspicious of each other?

The Lebanese government says it has taken in 1.5 million Syrians since the civil war erupted there in 2011, and about 1 million have registered with UNHCR as refugees. Lebanon's population of 4.5 million has increased by a third since the war started, just from refugees. Many Lebanese blame Syrian refugees for their economic woes and frequently urge them to go back to their country.

On top of that, some local governments in Lebanon were told by some media coverage of a connection between coronavirus and refugees living in squalid conditions. Their response has been to restrict the movements of refugees and set mandatory curfews and stay at home orders, justifying such measures to prevent the spread of corona.

Palestinians have lived in Lebanon for generations, yet their freedom of employment is restricted. They live day to day, paid daily, as do many Syrian refugees. Urban lockdowns around the country to contain the virus have caused further damage to the economy, and many Palestinians are struggling, unable to find work.

This type of xenophobia is not confined to Lebanon. Corona has carried this companion scourge with it around the world. At the start of the pandemic, in March 2020, Japanese news covered how multiple long-established Chinese restaurants in Yokohama's Chinatown received an anonymous letter with a racist rant in red ink: *Chinese people are garbage! They are germs! Devils! Nuisances! Get the f… out of Japan!*

Xenophobia against ethnic Chinese spread around the world because the coronavirus originated in the city of Wuhan in Hubei Province. Beyond Yokohama's Chinatown, there have been a string of cases in Europe, Australia, and the US of abusive insults hurled at ethnic Asians who were born and bred locally and can't even speak Chinese. Human beings faced with crisis descend into paranoia and suspicion, smearing innocent people. This dumb foible of our species raises its ugly head in times of major earthquakes, wars, the corona pandemic and other emergencies.

Sabbatical in Malaysia

The pandemic arrived out of the blue. I had been on sabbatical from Waseda University since September 2019 and was working as a visiting scholar at the National University of Singapore. My child's school was a factor, but I set down roots in Johor Bahru, a Malaysian city that straddles the border with Singapore. About 300,000 to 400,000 people commute across the border between Johor Bahru and Singapore for work or school. For them border crossing is a daily occurrence. I too crossed the border each day, like they did. If you share a taxi, you can go one way for less than 1,000 yen; by bus, about 150 yen. If the traffic is clear, you can go to the other side in 15 or 20 minutes. With traffic, it can take one or two hours. Those who go back and forth during rush hour naturally get used to it and watch dramas on their phones with buds in their ears. They make it seem like we are all relaxing in the living room.

In a shared taxi, when you come to an immigration point, you just hand over your passport via the driver. You don't even have to get out of the car. Customs inspection in your *living room* doesn't have to distract you from your drama. You just drive right through. On a bus, however, you must get off at immigration and wait in line for the inspection. You might wait one or two hours. I've stood in this line. It's mentally and physically fatiguing. As we waited in a line at customs, I watched a stray cat wag his tail and lazily swagger across the border. How envious I was of that cat. The cat must have mocked us for all the trouble humans make for themselves.

Singapore-Malaysia border crossings were a daily occurrence, but with the increase of corona patients after 2020 Chinese New Year, restriction of people's movement began to curb the spread of infection. Malaysia went into lockdown on March 18, and the border with Singapore was shut down. The city state depended on Malaysian laborers, so just before the lockdown they made workers go back to their homes to get the luggage they would need to stay in Singapore for a while. So, on March 17, a maelstrom of motorcycles crammed the streets between Singapore and Johor as workers went home to get a change of clothes and other supplies.

Singapore also closed its border. People were prohibited from going outside for non-essential work. The dead stop to daily border crossings meant people could no longer get to school or work and in fact couldn't even leave their homes.

I could see the immigration checkpoint from the window of my place near the border. Usually jammed with cars, motorcycles, trucks and other vehicles crossing the border, the international bridge had become empty. Not a few families, for whom border-crossing commuting was part of their daily existence, found themselves suddenly separated. Students who had crossed the border to get to school were taking online courses even six months after the lockdown. Even physical education was provided online. Fortunately, families and friends could "meet" online as video chat became easier.

Corona advanced our virtual connection.

On the night of March 16, when Malaysia announced the imminent lockdown, I happened to be in Kandy, Sri Lanka. I was a mess when I found out the border would close in 30 hours.

It was a real emergency. I had to get back to Malaysia where my son was. I checked out of the hotel I had just checked *into* and spent the night traveling to the airport in Columbo. Told to discard the ticket I had to Singapore, I had to buy a ticket back to Johor Bahru. There was a new tension in the air at the airport. Once the border closed, I would no longer be able to enter Malaysia. The corona lockdown brought back the fear from when I had been stateless.

What am I going to do if I can't get in?
Where am I supposed to go? To go back to?

From a Borderless Society to a World Full of Borders

The restricted movement caused a different sort of fear from when I had been refused entry to the country due to my statelessness. This time around, I wondered what would happen to humanity.

The corona pandemic has vastly constrained border crossing. We live in a world full of borders founded on an unchallenged principle that the nation state can cling to the authority to close the border and run customs, immigration inspection, and quarantine. *To protect the people* has become an accepted justification for any action. But does it really make any sense at all to sort who can or cannot cross the border based on their citizenship?

A recent opinion piece, with which I wholeheartedly agree, appeared in *Asahi Shimbun* (July 5, 2020, Catherine Ancelot).

> The corona border policy continues refusing entry to foreigners and denying re-entry to documented and permanent residents once they leave the country, barring special circumstances.
>
> The national government naturally takes measures to prevent infection, but some call for clear criteria to rescind major constraints on permanent residents, such as number of infections. Otherwise, people will naturally think that the measures are just arbitrary, rather than an unavoidable insurance policy. Governments and specialists need to explain why the measures used for returning citizens—PCR test at the airport and two weeks quarantine—can't be applied to those who have lived many years in the country.
>
> I am from France and have lived in Japan for 32 years. I participate in society through my work and contribute in my own way. I have integrated into the community. I of course am a good citizen and pay my taxes. This current unfair treatment leaves me despondent that despite being a permanent resident, I am, after all, just a second-class citizen.

This Earth is Like the Titanic

How about Florim and other residents on *kari homen* provisional release? Those on provisional release cannot legally work. This commonly results in great economic hardship. Only those with a *juminhyo* residence certificate are eligible for Japan's special one-time aid program, excluding Florim and others on the provisional release program since their residence is not registered.

Florim has lived in Japan for 20 years straight. Corona makes no distinction based on nationality or residence registration. All residents in the same country face the same risk.

Florim compared the situation to the Titanic.

> This earth is like the Titanic. Who will be saved? The rich. The poor will sink first. Corona does not discriminate. But the national government does. Japan claims foreigners and stateless people are eligible to receive the aid, but I have received nothing. [Governor] Yuriko Koike says *Stay in Tokyo, Stay Home*, so I am complying with that completely. I think I have to fight corona along with everyone in Japan. I have been in Japan for 20

years. I have been applying to become a member of Japanese society, but I continue to be kept out.

Some grumble about the lack of freedom from corona, not being able to walk around for a month or two. But I want that experience to help people understand what it means for refugees and stateless people like me under provisional release to be unable to move freely for decades. I want people to empathize even a little. This corona is a problem facing humanity on a global scale. It's not time to look to assign blame to this or that country or to look for the location of the origin. Isn't it time for humanity to overcome it together?

The earth's population is over 7.8 billion.

The number of people driven from their homes due to conflict or persecution had grown to nearly 80 million by the end of 2019. But who will protect stateless people and refugees? The global spread of this pandemic that aggravates their already weak position has made the answer to that question more urgent than ever.

Epilogue

We who live in this era make full use of the nation-state system. The construction of the modern national state at the end of the eighteenth century engendered the birth of the notion of nationality and citizenry. Nationality based on the nation-state system functions as a system both to exclude and to subsume, sorting those who belong from those who don't. The system of nationality and citizenship conceals an exclusionary aspect that may not at first be obvious. The state system itself is what engenders statelessness. More frightening still is the recent rise of xenophobia in Europe, the US, and elsewhere.

People cannot choose their parents or where they are born. Yet, most people's nationality is determined by *jus soli*, based on where they are born or *jus sanguinis*, who their parents are. Most of us receive our nationality pre-packaged, just as we naturally receive our body parts when we are born. Few raise questions about their own nationality and our system of citizenship.

Nationality is something given to you by the nation state. It is not something that comes with you when you are born but rather given to you after birth to verify your relationship with the nation state. Your hair, eyes, and skin color all come fixed at birth and are not easy to change. But nationality given by the nation state can change in response to national fluctuations as well as due to migration or naturalization. People can have multiple citizenships or no citizenship.

Until now, we have used citizenship given by the nation state to designate group affiliation and identity as well as to distinguish others as "foreigners" or those belonging to a particular country.

Citizenship verifies a person's existence and legal status. But there is no unified system around the world. Rather, each country determines to whom to grant citizenship, based on their national circumstances.

As globalization advances, border crossings increase, making individual nationality and identity increasingly complex. More people migrate abroad; more move frequently; more enter international marriages. This has become an intimate reality for most of us. In the era in which we live in the world today, we have no way to know when our own children, grandchildren or friends will fall into statelessness, an issue that thus far has failed to capture our attention.

Fortunately, the number of people who have come to be able to cleave apart their identity from their nationality has slowly begun to increase. People move, migrate, and come to feel attached to many different places where they live. This is a natural state of affairs, and there is no need to cling to a particular nationality and try to protect something while denying other nationalities. There is no need to affiliate to one particular nationality. It's natural that some people cannot do that.

Migrants, refugees, stateless persons, and others caught in the cracks between nations feel affection to many different countries, so they naturally want those countries to be at peace. There is no way they can choose one of the countries. They naturally want those countries to be prosperous and co-exist. They tend to be victimized by the xenophobic and ostracizing trend spreading around the world, but it's high time the world realized that they have the potential to serve as cultural bridges.

Those caught between the cracks themselves must become aware of the role they have to play. Tennis star and holder of two passports, Naomi Osaka, recently and publicly endorsed the Black Lives Matter movement.

Human beings live connected not just by nationality, but also by where they are born, the language they speak, and many other things. I lived as a stateless person for more than three decades and then gained citizenship. But nationality did not change me. If anything, I live with affection for many different places, using many different identities. I have come to the realization that regulating and binding people using citizenship is nothing but an unrealistic anachronism.

> *What is my nationality?*
> *The answer is I don't really know.*
> *But I discovered one thing about myself.*
> *I am Lara, born in Yokohama's Chinatown.*
> *Nationality and national borders are irrelevant.*
> *Stateless or with some nationality, I am still me, Lara.*

Being surrounded by my family who raised me, my kind friends, my loved ones, and many others is where I belong. Cherishing that, I will continue to live as a woman named Lara.

Many stateless people find themselves in difficult situations, facing discrimination and separation due to a system based on the nation state and nationality, which has spread throughout our modern society. The result is a tendency to strive to eliminate statelessness from the world, due to the negative image we have of stateless as pathetic or pitiable. But the problem of statelessness will persist unless and until we transform nationality and the nation-state we use fully as well as the system of citizenship we created based on those concepts. What we really should do away with is discrimination against stateless people and nation-based prejudices.

Is being stateless really so pathetic and negative? I see rather a great deal emerge from that suffix *-less* that enables stateless people to perceive the truth about society: purity; hunger for self-betterment; an independent world view with some objective distance between themselves and the nation state.

Migrants, refugees, those with multiple nationalities, stateless and others caught between nations have attachments in many areas, making them desire peace in their relevant countries. They are incapable of choosing just one nation. They only seek a prosperous coexistence. The world has so many people in this situation who tend to become victims of exclusion. Yet, they are situated in precisely the perfect position to suss out the contradictions inherent in the nation state. The world should come to realize that they harbor the potential to serve as bridges between multiple cultures.

Our system of nationality and nation state no longer fits today's transnational era. The Russia-Ukraine situation shows us how fixation on the nation state engenders conflict, war, and produces countless victims. Isn't it time for humanity to pull away from nationality-based discrimination, exclusion, and move toward a truly *stateless society* that transcends nationality?

As I am writing this, almost a year has passed since Russia invaded Ukraine on February 24, 2022. The war shows no sign of ending and will continue to victimize civilians for a long time to come. In addition to humanitarian and material support, Ukraine continues to receive military aid. When will this cycle of violence end? What will become of the world? This war has sent prices skyrocketing and made our daily lives that much tougher.

My family still runs a restaurant in Yokohama's Chinatown. The restaurant has served as a place of rest and relaxation for the family—an oasis that my mother had always cherished and treasured. Today, my older sisters have taken over that role. I visited the restaurant one afternoon in mid-April to find a group of female customers sitting at a table with their family, stuffing their mouths with Chinese food. Their faces looked strained, and they were speaking what sounded to me like Russian.

I had studied Russian in college and trained in Moscow and St. Petersburg. I'm ashamed to admit that I have forgotten all that I learned, but I recall that day in the restaurant familiar sounds entering my ear. I approached the table and greeted them in Russian. One said, "Our family fled Ukraine last week."

My sister had said that the customers were Russian, but at that moment I realized they were Ukrainian. She told me that her older brother came from Crimea and her elder stepsister, from Mariupol. I introduced myself in very broken Russian, and her mother sitting next to her smiled and said *hajimemashite* in Japanese.

I asked about the situation back home. The brother made a gun-shooting gesture and said they were able to hear gunfire nearby. The woman deftly translated his comments into Japanese. She said they had family in Ukraine and Russia and simply wanted peace to return as soon as possible.

Steeped throughout our lives in the notion of the nation state, we tend to describe war in terms of nation versus nation, such as "Russia vs Ukraine." But speaking to actual people about their real-life experiences makes it clear that it's impossible to draw a clear line between who is "Russian" and who is "Ukrainian." The conflict between Russia and Ukraine is—forgive the poor analogy—a fight between blood brothers. Meanwhile, other parties egg on the two sides to continue the fight… For nations' policymakers, gaining authority, land, and resources might be important, but to sacrifice civilians for that purpose is intolerable.

The conflict in Ukraine somehow reminds me of the trouble between China and Taiwan. In April 2022, China launched missiles into the Taiwanese Strait when US House Speaker Nancy Pelosi visited Taiwan. It was the fishers and other ordinary civilians who ended up suffering from this US action.

World War II led to the deaths of countless people, the bifurcation of China, and the breaking up of my family. My father left his hometown Heilongjiang more than 70 years ago due to the war. He moved to Taiwan and then on to Japan. I was born in Japan. I was impacted by the split of China and Taiwan and particularly by the diplomatic changes with Japan. Soon after birth, I became stateless, exactly 50 years ago. I continued my stateless status for more than three decades and then in 2003 acquired Japanese citizenship. For me, nations and people; nationality and identity; the movement of people across borders are all important themes of discourse.

I have been researching nationality for about a quarter of a century. To be honest, I have no simple answer. What I *have* learned is that the current system of regulating each individual with a particular citizenship is unworkable. Most people living in Japan today believe in the principle that each person has one nationality and identifies each based on their nationality (for example, *she is xxx-ese* or *she is xxx-ian*). The experiences of various types of real-life people suggest that this will no longer cut it.

I wrote this book because I want as many people as possible to understand the suffering and trouble that these preconceptions cause.

Many stateless people and those involved in the issue have helped me a great deal, including agreeing to interviews. It was impossible to name them all in this book, but I want to express my heartfelt gratitude towards all who helped me in my research. Let me use this opportunity to thank the Stateless Network and all my partners in joint research up until now for their great intellectual, spiritual support, and stimulation.

This book was based originally on *Mukokuseki* (Shinchosha 2005; Shincho Bunko 2011) as well as *Mukokuseki-to Fukusu Kokuseki—Anata-wa Nanijin-desu-ka?* (Kobunsha 2022), but with major additions. Louis Carlet translated my book for the English version. Beginning in September 2019, during my sabbatical, I became a visiting scholar at the Asia Research Institute at the National University of Singapore. I had planned field work based in Singapore and Malaysia, but Covid-19 shut down the national border and the government locked us down in our homes, forcing me to abandon my fieldwork. This ended up enabling me—for better or worse—to spend some time on this book. I have thoroughly enjoyed my collaboration with Carlet and would like to take this chance to thank him.

I have discussed in this book organizations, study groups, activities, and programming with which I am involved. This book was written ultimately based on my personal views. Any mistakes and unsuitable points are entirely my personal responsibility.

Finally, let me convey a message from my heart to my husband who always supports my health; to my son who is growing day by day in his dorm back in Malaysia; to my sisters and family who are upholding the family home and restaurant; and most of all to my sprightly father who turns 102 in 2023: *thank you, xie xie, I love you.*

My wish is that this book reaches as many people as possible and plays even a small role in helping us all transcend nationality, acknowledge each other's diversity, and build a society of peace.

Bibliography

Anderson, Benedict. 2016. *A Life Beyond Boundaries*. London: Verso.
———. 1991. *Imagined Communities: Reflections on the Origin and Spread of Nationalism*. London: Verso.
Appadurai, Arjun. 2001. *Globalization*. Durham: Duke University Press.
Bhabha, Jacqueline. 2011. *Children Without a State: A Global Human Rights Challenge*. Cambridge: The MIT Press.
Bianchini, Katia. 2018. *Protecting Stateless Persons: The Implementation of the Convention Relating to Status of the Stateless Persons across EU States*. Leiden: Brill Nijhoff.
Blitz, Brad K. and Maureen Lynch. 2011. *Statelessness and Citizenship: A Comparative Study on the Benefits of Nationality*. Cheltenham: Edward Elgar.
Bloom, Tendayi, Katherine Tonkiss, and Phillip Cole. 2017. *Understanding Statelessness*. New York: Routledge.
Castles, Stephen and Alastair Davidson. 2000. *Citizenship and Migration: Globalization and the Politics of Belonging*. New York: Routledge.
Castles, Stephen. 2017. *Migration, Citizenship and Identity: Selected Essays*. UK: Edward Elgar.
Chapman, David and Karl Jakob Krogness. 2014. *Japan's Household Registration System and Citizenship: Koseki, Identification and Documentation*. London: Routledge.
Gracia, Jorge J.E. 2005. *Surviving Race, Ethnicity, and Nationality: A Challenge for the Twenty-first Century*. Rowman & Littlefield.
Hayden, Patrick. 2014. *Hannah Arendt: Key Concepts*. Durham, Routledge.
Hunter, Wendy. 2019. *Undocumented Nationals: Between Statelessness and Citizenship*. Cambridge: Cambridge University Press.
Isin, Engin F. and Patricia K. Wood. 1999. *Citizenship and Identity*. London: SAGE.
Kaneko-Iwase, Mai. 2021. *Nationality of Foundlings: Avoiding Statelessness among Children of Unknown Parents under International Nationality Law*. Singapore: Springer.
Kondo, Atsushi. 2001. *Citizenship in a Global World: Comparing Citizenship Rights for Aliens*. New York: Palgrave.
Kymlicka, Will. 1995. *Multicultural Citizenship: A Liberal Theory of Minority Rights*. Oxford: Clarendon Press.

Lawrance, Benjamin N. and Jacqueline Stevens. 2017. *Citizenship in Question: Evidentiary Birthright and Statelessness*. Durham: Duke University Press.
Lee Tang Lay. 2005. *Statelessness, Human Rights and Gender: Irregular Migrant Workers from Burma in Thailand*. Leiden: Brill.
Miller, David. 1995. *On Nationality*. New York: Clarendon Press.
Minahan, James. 2002. *Encyclopedia of the Stateless Nations: Ethnic and National Groups Around the World*. Conn: Greenwood Press.
Münch, Richard. 2001. *Nation and Citizenship in the Global Age: From National to Transnational Ties and Identities*. London: Palgrave Macmillan.
Ong, Aihwa. 1999. *Flexible Citizenship: The Cultural Logics of Transnationality*, Durham: Duke University Press.
Oommen, T.K. 1997. *Citizenship, Nationality, and Ethnicity: Reconciling Competing Identities*. Cambridge, Mass: Blackwell Publishers.
Said, Edward W. 1999. *Out of Place: A Memoir*. Vintage Books.
Soysal, Yasemin Nuhoğlu.1994. *Limits of Citizenship: Migrants and Postnational Membership in Europe*. Chicago: The University of Chicago Press.
Tan Chee-Beng. 2013. *Routledge Handbook of the Chinese Diaspora*. Routledge.
Wang Gungwu. 2018. *Home is Not Here*. Singapore: NUS Press.
Wang Gungwu with Wang, Margaret 2021. *Home is Where We Are*. Singapore: NUS Press.
Weis, Paul. 1956. *Nationality and Statelessness in International Law*. London: Stevens & Sons.

阿部浩己. 2010.『無国籍の情景──国際法の視座、日本の課題』UNHCR駐日事務所.
新垣修. 2015.『無国籍条約と日本の国内法──その接点と隔たり』UNHCR駐日事務所.
荒牧重人他編. 2017.『外国人の子ども白書──権利・貧困・教育・文化・国籍と共生の視点から』明石書店.
蘭信三他編. 2022.『帝国のはざまを生きる──交錯する国境、人の移動、アイデンティティ』みずき書林.
アンダーソン・ベネディクト、白石さや・白石隆訳. 1997.『想像の共同体──ナショナリズムの起源と流行』NTT出版.
石井香世子・小豆澤史絵. 2019.『外国につながる子どもと無国籍──児童養護施設への調査結果と具体的対応例』明石書店.
井戸まさえ. 2016.『無戸籍の日本人』集英社.
大田季子・谷合佳代子・養父知美. 1994.『戸籍・国籍と子ども人権』明石書店.
江川英文・山田鐐一・早田芳郎. 1997.『国籍法（第三版）』有斐閣.
遠藤正敬. 2017.『戸籍と無戸籍──「日本人」の輪郭』人文書院.
―――. 2010.『近代日本の植民地統治における国籍と戸籍──満州・朝鮮・台湾』明石書店.
奥田安弘. 2017.『家族と国籍──国際化の安定のなかで』明石書店.
―――. 2002.『数字でみる子どもの国籍と在留資格』明石書店.
木棚照一. 2021.『逐条 国籍法──課題の解明と条文の解説』日本加除出版.

国際問題研究会編. 2019.『二重国籍と日本』ちくま新書.
近藤敦. 2001.『外国人の人権と市民権』明石書店.
_____. 2019.『多文化共生と人権――諸外国の「移民」と日本の「外国人」』明石書店.
佐々木てる. 2006.『日本の国籍制度とコリア系日本人』明石書店.
佐々木てる編著・駒井洋監修. 2016.『マルチ・エスニック・ジャパニーズ――○○系日本人の変革力（移民・ディアスポラ研究5）』明石書店.
スーザン・ストレンジ著・櫻井公人訳. 1999.『国家の退場――グローバル経済の新しい主役たち』岩波書店.
田中宏. 1991.『在日外国人―法の壁、心の溝』岩波新書.
戴国煇. 1980.『華僑――「落葉帰根」から「落地生根」への苦悶と矛盾』研文出版.
宏1999『在日外国人―法の壁、心の溝―』岩波新書.
田所昌幸ほか. 2018.「特集　国籍選択の逆説」『アステイオン』89:12－125、CCCメディアハウス.
陳福坡. 2015.『人間正道――九十自述』新華時報社.
陳天璽. 2022.『無国籍と複数国籍―あなたは「ナニジン」ですか？』光文社新書.
陳天璽. 2009.「『Where is Home?』から『Home Everywhere』へ――漂泊する華僑・華人たちのネットワーク」『国立民族学博物館調査報告』83: 29－39、国立民族学博物館.
_____. 2005.『無国籍』新潮社.（2011年新潮文庫）.
陳天璽編. 2014.「世界における無国籍者の人権と支援――日本の課題――」『効率民族博物館調査報告』118、国立民族学博物館.
_____. 2010.『忘れられた人々　日本の「無国籍」者』明石書店.
陳天璽・近藤敦・小森宏美・佐々木てる編著. 2012.『越境とアイデンティフィケーション――国籍・パスポート・IDカード』新曜社.
陳天璽・大西広之・小森宏美・佐々木てる編著. 2016.『パスポート学』北海道大学出版会.
陳天璽・由美村嬉々. 2022.『にじいろのペンダント　国籍のないわたしたちのはなし』大月書店.
丁章. 2009.『サラムの在りか』新幹社.
――. 2017.『在日詩集　詩碑』新幹社.
――「なぜ無国籍の「朝鮮」籍を生きるのか？」李里花編. 2020.『朝鮮籍とは何か――トランスナショナルの視点から』明石書店.
土井たかこ編. 1984.『「国籍」を考える』時事通信社.
床呂郁哉. 1999.『越境――スール―海域世界から』岩波書店.
西川武臣・伊藤泉美. 2002.『開国日本と横浜中華街（あじあブックス）』大修館書店.
錦田愛子編. 2020.『政治主体としての移民/難民――人の移動が織り成す社会とシティズンシップ』明石書店.
_____. 2016.『移民/難民のシティズンシップ』有信堂高文社.
根本敬. 2014.『物語　ビルマの歴史――王朝時代から現代まで』中公新書.
無国籍研究会編. 2017.『日本における無国籍者――類型論的調査』UNHCR駐日事務所.
李里花編2020『朝鮮籍とは何か――トランスナショナルの視点から』明石書店.

ロジャース・ブルーベイカー、佐藤成基他編訳. 2016.『グローバル化する世界と「帰属の政治」——移民・シティズンシップ・国民国家』明石書店.
山下清海. 2021.『横浜中華街——世界に誇るチャイナタウンの地理・歴史(筑摩選書)』筑摩書房.
山村淳平・陳天璽編、無国籍ネットワーク協力. 2019.『移民がやってきた——アジアの少数民族、日本での物語』現代人文社.
横浜開港資料館編. 2009.『横浜中華街150年——落地生根の歳月横浜開港150周年記念』横浜開港資料館.

Index

300-day post-divorce problem, 182–3

Abe, Kohki, 162
Ademaj, Florim, 205
Aesthetics and Politics, 72
Akatsuki Village, 167–70
Akino, Yutaka, 34
Aksenoff, Eugene, 202–5
alien registration, xi, 8, 11, 29–30, 47, 81–2, 89, 94, 101, 105, 120, 123, 126–7, 131–3, 183, 185, 187, 192
Alien Registration Card Surrender Report, 133
AmerAsian School, Okinawa, 92
Analects, 27
"Applying for Citizenship" pamphlet, 124
Arikawa, Kenji, 208
Asahi Shimbun, 217
asylum seekers and refugees, migration of, 100
Azabu, Tokyo, 10
Azukizawa, Fumie, 170, 209

Bajau Laut, 199–200
Bālu-jūn (Eighth route army), 96
Bangkok Legal Clinic (BLC), 192–4
Bangladeshi refugee camps, 195
Beijing, 2, 7, 37, 164
Beitou, 2
Berlin Wall, fall of, 31
birth registration, 104, 124, 127
Black Lives Matter movement, 220
Bolivia, Republic of, 164

Border-Crossings from the Sulu Maritime World, 198
borderless society, 216–17
Borders and Identity for People without Borders, 91
Borneo, 119–20, 142–3, 154
Bosnia-Herzegovina, 205–6
Brattle Theatre, 74
Brazilian citizenship, 90
Brunei, 120
Brunei, statelessness in, 142–6
bubble economy, 170
Bush, George H.W., 33

Calvary Love Foundation, 200
Canada, 90
Catholic Tokyo International Center (CTIC), 208
Certificate of Alien Registration, 29
Certificate of Loss of Nationality (CLN), 10
certificates of identity, 100
Changsha City, Hunan province, 35
Charles de Gaulle Airport, Paris, 146–8
Chen Fu Poo, 1, 52
Chang Chak Yan, 61
Chiang Kai-shek, 30
child's citizenship, factors for determination of, 90
child statelessness, causes of, 95
China (People's Republic of China), 2, 164
  Bālu-jūn (Eighth route army), 96
  citizenship of, 8
  closed socialist system, 37

228

Cultural Revolution in, 7, 38, 74
education system in, 52
founding of, 52
launching of missiles into the Taiwanese Strait, 222
Ministry of Public Security, 164
one-China policy, 37
reformist economy of, 37
relationship with
 Japan. *See* Sino-Japanese relations
Taiwan, 37, 51–2
Tiananmen massacre, 31
Chinatown (Yokohama), ix, 1–2, 7, 51, 215, 221
 Chinese community living in, 51
 Chinese education in, 52
Chinese Communist Party (CCP), 2, 7
 power struggle with Kuomintang, 51
Chinese diaspora, 85, 123, 139
Chinese education, 15–16, 52
Chinese entrepreneurial networks and identity, 62–3, 71–2
Chinese entrepreneurs, 60, 71
Chinese Guild Hall Foundation (Zhonghua Huiguan), 80
Chinese identity, 13, 17, 59, 70, 84
Chinese nationalism, 8
Chinese New Year, 215
Chinese school, 15–17
 learning in, 30
Chinese University of Hong Kong, 56
Chirac, Jacques, 205
Chosen citizenship, 185
Chosen Soren General Association of Korean Residents, 185
civil war, 41
Cold War, 31
Constantine, Greg, 178, 195
Covid-19 pandemic. *See* novel coronavirus pandemic
cross-border communications, 211
Cross-Strait Relations and the Role of Huaqiao, 53

daiken exam, 24
Daisuke, story of, 108

Davao City, 171
DAWN Theater Akebono stage production, 111
de facto stateless children, 91
de jure stateless children, 90–1
Democratic People's Republic of Korea (DPRK), 101–2
Democratic Progressive Party (Taiwan), 50
Development Action for Women Network (DAWN), 109–10, 112
Diên Biên Phu, 141
Diet, 93
Disneyland, 60
documentary films
 Mukokuseki—Stateless, 118
 to promote human rights, 75
 shooting of, 74, 79, 117–19
Donner, Jan Pieter Hendrik, 150
double breeds (daburu), 89
dual citizenship, issue of, 89–90, 93
Du Fu, 27

Eastern Europe, 65
economic globalization, 88
employment, proof of, 128
English language, 59
English-Speaking Society (ESS), 42–3
entertainment visa, 108–9, 114
entrance exam, for Japanese high school, 24

family register, xi, 127, 131–2, 134–5, 175, 181–6, 194
filmmaking
 idea of, 76
 schools, 74
film productions and techniques, 74
Florida, 70, 108
foreign nationals, in Japan
 acquisition of Japanese nationality through naturalization, 83
 who overstayed their visas, 103
Four Asian Tigers (the Four Dragons), 56
Frank, Anne, 149–50

gaikokujin foreigners, 184
Gen, Masayuki, 163
German citizenship, 149
global citizens, 123, 161, 162
Golan Heights, 210–12
Golden Week holiday, ix
Goncharoff, Makarov, 100
Gorbachev, Mikhail, 33
government childcare allowance, 183
Grace Training Center (GTC), Tawau, 200
Great East Japan Earthquake (2011), 209–10
Great Leap Forward, 7
Guangzhou, 35

half-breeds (*hafu*), 89
Hamao, Stephen Fumio, 76–8
Haneda Airport (Tokyo), ix, xi
Harvard Film Archive, 74
Harvard Kennedy School, 75
Harvard Law School's East Asian Legal Studies Program, 88
Harvard University, 62
    Fairbank Center for East Asian Research, 62
Hasegawa, Rurika, 197
health insurance, 135, 165
Hemming, Fujiko, 100
Hepburn, James Curtis, 137
Higashi-Nihon immigration center, in Ushiku, 208
high school equivalency test, 24
Hirata, Masayo, 92–3, 95
hojeog (South Korean *koseki*), 186
Honda, Hideo, 95–6, 123
Honda, Toru, 96–7
Hong Kong, 35, 59–62
    General Chamber of Commerce, 61
    studying in, 56–8
Hong, Madame, 98–100, 123
hosutesu bargirl, 185
huaqiao (overseas Chinese) community, 16, 50–3, 59, 79, 82, 87, 120
human rights, protection of, 75

Ichibadori market street, 6
ID cards
    Israeli-issued, 211–13
    Japanese, 189–91
identity conflicts, 49, 163
illegitimate children, 185, 187
    born from foreign women, 130
    child of unwed parents, 181
    nationality of, 107–8
Imaizumi, Masatoshi, 160
Immigration Control Law (Japan), 81, 108
immigration detention centers, 170
Inomata, Norihiro, 171–2
International Christian University, 31
international marriages, xiv, 90, 219
International Okinawa Office, 93
International Organization for Migration, 147
international relations, xiii, 33, 43, 48–9, 54, 101
International Year of the Child (1979), 93

Jackson, Michael, 205
Japan, ix, 60
    Basic Resident Registers Act (1967), 184
    bubble economy, 23
    Civil Code (1898), Article 772 of, 182
    Constitution of, 83, 92, 116
    economic development of, 103
    Edo period (1603–1868), 16
    entertainment visa, 114
    ethnic Chinese community of, 3
    Family Register Act (*Koseki-Ho*), 184
    high school entrance exam, 23–5
    Immigration Control Law, 81, 108
    Legal Affairs Bureau, 81, 84, 104, 123, 131, 159, 189
    Ministry of
        Education, Culture, Sports, Science and Technology, 129–30

the Interior, 10
Justice Civil Affairs Bureau, 10, 83, 131, 184, 192
Nationality Act, 83, 89, 106
overseas Chinese residents of, 7, 10
panda diplomacy, 7
ratification of Convention on the Rights of the Child, 106
re-entry permit, 22–3
research on foreign residents of, 53
stateless residents in. *See* Japan's stateless residents
surrender of, 30
Treaty of Mutual Cooperation and Security with United States, 95–8
US-led occupation of, 30
Japanese citizenship, xiii, 8–9, 13, 41, 92, 105, 123, 152, 173, 197
acquisition of, 83–4
jus sanguinis principle for, 89–90, 92, 107
jus soli (right of soil) principle for, 89–90
nationality law for, 93
of AmerAsians living in Okinawa, 90
applying for, 79–86
and Chinese identity, 84
Chosen (associated with North Korea), 185
got Rohingya woman, 195
issues concerning dual citizenship, 90
for Japanese-Filipino children, 108–10
Kankoku (associated with South Korea), 185
matrimonial citizenship principle, 93
Nationality Act's rejection of, 116
patrilineal preference system, 93
rules to determine, 90
for stateless residents, 87–8
through naturalization process, 83, 126
zairyu residence card, 197
Japanese-Filipino children (JFC), 164
citizenship of, 108–10
nationality of, 174–6
problems related to statelessness, 109

Japanese language school, 80
Japanese nationality, 83, 90, 92, 101, 181, 184
Japanese Red Cross, 101
Japanese society, 14, 21, 24, 26, 32, 54, 60, 62, 66, 85, 101, 167, 175, 218
Japan Immigration Association, 103
Japan News, 179
Japan Society for the Promotion of Science (JSPS), 76, 91
Japan's stateless residents, 86
acquisition of Japanese nationality through naturalization, 83
huaqiao (overseas Chinese) community, 50–3, 59, 87
issues concerning citizenship, 87–8
in Okinawa, 89, 91–4
relation between individual and the State, 94–5
research on, 88–91
stateless children
de facto, 91
de jure, 90–1
Japanese-Filipino children, 108–10
problem of, 93, 95
Uchinanchu Ryukyuans, 95
Vietnamese refugees, 95
White Russians, 100
jeogori (traditional Korean blouse), 185
Jikei University School of Medicine, 204
job hunting, idea of, 54–5
Johor Bahru, 215–16
JR Ishikawacho Station, 25
juku cram schools, 23, 31
juminhyo residence certificate, 131–2, 134, 183, 217
jus sanguinis principle (right of blood), of citizenship acquisition, x, 89, 92, 105–7, 119, 170, 219
jus soli (right of soil) principle, of citizenship acquisition, 89, 105–6, 119, 219

K–12 school, 17
kakyo-go, 21

Kalabaw-no Kai (Association in Kotobuki for Solidarity with Migrant Workers), 150–1
Kalimantan. *See* Borneo
kamishibai paper picture, 179
kamishibai picture-story show, 179
Kankoku citizenship, 185
kari homen (provisional release), 141, 208, 217
katakana syllabary, 26
kikokusei, 13, 33
Kim Dae-jung, 132
Kim, David, 199
Kimura, Fumihiko, 164
Kimura, Miyuki, 180
Kinjo, Kiyoko, 91
Koike, Yuriko, 217
kokuseki, 9
Komoro City, 104
Korean Peninsula, 50
koseki family register, 131–2, 134, 136, 172, 181, 183, 188
    Alien Registration Act (1952), 184
    certificate, 127
    from imperial subject to foreigner, 183–5
    Japanese citizens listed in, 184
Kosovar refugees, story of, 207
Kosuge, Etsuko, 141, 150
Kota Kinabalu, Malaysian city of, 121
KRO (Dutch TV network), 149
Kroengyu, Wuyi, 150, 156
Kudo, Yukihiro, 193
Kuomintang (Nationalist Party of China), 2–3, 7, 50
    power struggle with Chinese Communist Party, 51

Labuan Island, 120
La Campanella, 101
language proficiency, 33, 41, 44
League of Nations' High Commissioner for Refugees, 100
Lee, Bruce, 11–13
Lee Sinhae, 185
Lee Teng-hui, 50

Li Bai (aka Li Bo), 27
Li Wen Biao, 164
    loss of citizenship and visa due to administrative Snafu, 164–5
Lwin, Thidar, 195, 196

Malaysia, 120, 142
    sabbatical in, 215–16
Malcolm X (film), 49
Manchukuo (State of Manchuria), 3, 8, 202
Mandarin language, 57, 59–60
Manila hemp (*Musa textilis*), 173
marriage certificates, 124–5, 127–8, 158, 193
marriage registration, 151, 158, 194
martial law, 37
Mehran, Alfred, 146
Meiji Gakuin University, 137
Meiji University, 16
Metaphor and Politics, 72
Mexico, 90
Mahmud, Zeid, 213
Middle East, 54
    stateless people in, 210–12
Mindan (Korean Residents Union in Japan), 186
Minority Children (1998), 106
Minpaku National Museum of Ethnology, 178, 210
mizu shobai nighttime entertainment industry, 115
Mong Kok district, 58
Morozoff, Fedor Dmitrievich, 100
Mudanjiang Station, 38–9
mukokuseki (stateless), xiii, 21–2, 161, 182, 186
Mukokuseki—Stateless (documentary), 118
mukoseki (no family register), 182, 186

Nagano Prefecture, 104
Nakagawa, Akira, 106
Nakajima, Teruko, 98, 123
Nakamura, Fumiko, 163
Nansen, Fridtjof, 100, 148

Nansen International Bureau, 100
Nansen Passport, for stateless persons, 100, 148
Napaumporn, Bongkot, 192, 194
Narita Airport, 21, 37
Nasseri, Mehran Karimi, 146
National Chengchi University, 13
national identity, 8, 18, 118, 167
nationality
 based on nation-state system, 219
 concept of, xiv
 listed as undefined, 211–13
 right to, 9
Nationality Act (Japan), 83, 89, 92, 105, 130, 133
 Article 2.1 of, 107
 Article 2.3 of, 106
 rejection of citizenship, 116
 unconstitutionality of, 116
nationality-based discrimination, 221
National Museum of Ethnology (Minpaku), 122, 129–30, 162, 178, 210
national politics, 38
National Taiwan University, 13, 54, 80
National University of Singapore, 215, 223
nation-based prejudices, 221
nation states, 20–3, 119
 collapse of, xiii
 creation of, xiii
nation-state system, 201, 219
New York University, 75, 91
Ngan Phê, 186
Nguyen Tin Hong Hau, 164, 167
Nguyen Tran Phuoc An, 101
Ningan, in Mudanjiang City, 37
non-governmental organizations (NGOs), 148
 Dream of a Refugee Association, 212
 Stateless Network, 148, 162, 177–8, 193, 195, 223
novel coronavirus pandemic, 178–9, 214–15
 corona border policy, 217
 corona lockdown, 216
 PCR test, 217

Ōdori Heppubān, 137
Ōhira, Masayoshi, 7
Okinawan AmerAsians, 89
Okinawa Social Mass Party, 94
Okinawa's stateless residents, 89
Okuda, Yasuhiro, 91
one-China policy, 37
Osaka, 185
Osaka, Naomi, 220
Ōtsuki Shoten (publisher), 181
overseas Chinese community, in Japan, 7, 10
Overseas Filipino Workers (OFW), xiv

Pacific War, 172
Palestinian refugees, 212
panda diplomacy, 7
Passportology (2016), 169
patrilineal preference system, 92–3
Pelosi, Nancy, 222
permanent resident, xi, 41, 68, 143, 162, 185, 217
Philippines, ix, xii, 89. *See also* Japanese-Filipino children (JFC)
 300-day post-divorce problem, 182–3
 anti-Japanese sentiments, 172
 citizenship of, 104
 as country of emigration, 109
 Japanese residents of, 171–4
 Nikkei-jin Legal Support Center, 172
 zanryu ethnic Japanese of, 171–3, 182
Phontip, Muwangthong, 193
physical education, 216
Plares, Florida Apelin, 108
Potsdam Declaration (1945), 30
public security administration, 184
public transportation, 25
Purple Line ceasefire boundary, between Syria and Israel, 210
Putin, Vladimir, 205

qiaobao, x
qiaosheng (Chinese students returning from abroad), 13

234 INDEX

Qixi Festival (Tanabata festival), 71

Rakhine State (formerly Arakan), Myanmar, 195
re-entry permit, xii, 159
re-entry visa stamps, in Japan, 105
Rees, Andrew, 104–7
Rees, William, 104
reformist economy, of China, 37
refugee camps
   in Bangladesh, 195
   in Beirut, 212–13
   in Hong Kong, 187
   in Philippines, 167
   in Vietnam, 167
Republic of China (ROC). *See* Taiwan
Request for Copies of *Juminhyo* Residence Certificate, 135
rescission of marriage, 182
residence registration, 184, 217
Rohingya ethnicity, 196
Rohingya leader, in Japan, 165–6
Rosette, Cecilia, 104
Russia, 37, 64–5
   certificates of identity, 100
   citizenship of, 205
   invasion of Ukraine, 221–2
   Nansen Passport, 100
Russian Revolution, 94, 100
Ryukyu, 95
Ryukyu Shimpo, 92

Sakagawa, Tomiko, 172
San Diego, 88
San Francisco Peace Treaty (1952), 101, 184
Schengen Agreement, 77
Schengen visa, 77, 168, 169
school education, 16
School Education Act (Japan), 24
sea gypsies, 199
sea nomads, 199
Services for Health in Asian & African Regions (SHARE), 97
sex-trafficking of minors, 114

Shatila refugee camp, 212–13
Shigenobu, Fusako, 101
Shigenobu, Mei, 101
Shinchosha, KK, 160
Singapore, 56, 61, 156, 215–16, 223
Singapore-Malaysia border crossings, 215
Sino-Japanese relations
   normalization of, 7–8, 10
   panda diplomacy, 7
   Peace Treaty, 7
Sino-Japanese War, 17
Six-Day War (1967), 210
socialist market economy, 37
Sophia University, 31
Southeast Asia, Chinese businesspeople in, 56
South Korea, 56
Soviet Union, 204
Spielberg, Steven, 146
stateless alien card, 130–4
stateless Druze bride, life of, 210
Stateless Foreigner, 29
stateless-friendly society, 163
statelessness, issue of, 94, 129
   barriers of, 162
   in Brunei, 142–6
   documentary on, 163–4
   eradication of, 178
   and Great East Japan Earthquake (2011), 209–10
   in the Middle East, 210–12
   nationality and identity conflict, 163
   raising awareness of, 160–1
   and ravages of war, 205–6
Stateless Network Youth (SNY), 178–9
stateless people
   in Brunei, 142–6
   consequences of marrying, 150–3
   discrimination against, 221
   in Japan, 86, 90, 162–3, 210
   lives and minds of, 154–7
   meeting with, 119–22
   Nansen Passport for, 148
   population of, xiv
   reasons for becoming, xiii
   rights of, 94

Rohingya, 165–6
stateless children
　de facto, 91
　de jure, 90–1
　in the Sulu and Celebes Seas, 199
　between US soldiers and Okinawan women, 92
　UNHCR campaign to reduce the number of, xiv
　UN support and protection to, xiii
　world's biggest stateless population, 195–8
stateless servants, of the State, 122–30
stateless society, 221
suisen nyushi (entrance exam by commendation), 32
Syrian Bride, The (film), 210–12
Syrian refugees, 214

Taipei Economic and Cultural Representative Office, 19
Taiwan (Republic of China), ix–x, 19, 22, 120
　economic development of, 7
　entry document, 23
　independence from Chinese rule, 50
　Interior Ministry Citizenship Authorization Certificate, 125
　nationality law of, x
　relationship with mainland China, 37, 51–2
Takizawa, Saburo, 162
Tanaka, Kakuei, 7
Tatebayashi, Gunma, 196
teijusha, 187
Terminal, The (film), 146, 148
terra nullius, 199
terrorism, victims of, 101
Test of English as a Foreign Language (TOEFL), 31
Thailand, 151, 159
　nationality law of, 170
Thammasat University Bangkok Legal Clinic, 192–4
Tilburg University, 177

Tiruru (Okinawa Gender Equality Center), 92
Tokyo Regional Immigration Bureau, 164–5
Tombés du ciel (film), 146
Tomioka High School, in Kanagawa Prefecture, 24–5
Trouw (newspaper), 150
Tsugaru, Yoshitaka, 204
two-China conflict, militancy of, 51

UC Berkeley, 46
Uchinanchu Ryukyuans, 95
Ueno Zoo, 7
United Nations (UN), xiii, 66–9, 79
　Convention on the Reduction of Statelessness (1961), xiv, 148
　Convention on the Rights of the Child (1990), 106
　Convention Relating to the Status of Stateless Persons (1954), xiv, 9
　Disengagement Observer Force (UNDOF), 211
　High Commissioner for Refugees (UNHCR), xiv, 10, 147, 162, 177
　Refugee Convention (1951), 148
　Universal Declaration of Human Rights, 9
United States (US), 76, 79, 81
　citizenship of, 90–1
　military bases, 95
　Treaty of Mutual Cooperation and Security with Japan, 95–8
University of California, Los Angeles (UCLA), 41
University of Tokyo, 16
　Graduate School of Arts and Sciences, 91
　Himeji High School, 101
University of Tsukuba, 32–4, 41, 55, 68
unskilled workers, in Japan, 103

Vatican City, 76–7
Vietnamese citizenship, 189

Vietnamese refugees, 95, 152
	second-generation, 167–70, 186
	undocumented and visa-overstayed workers, 170
Vietnam War, 94
vocational school, 196

waihuiquan (foreign exchange notes), 35
waishengren (provincial outsiders), 2–3
Waseda University, 178–9, 215
	Waseda (University) Festival, 179
White Russians, living in Japan, 100
World War II, 30, 38, 41, 97, 110, 113, 143, 149, 214, 222

xenophobia, 214–15, 220

Yamada, Yumiko, 105
Yamamoto, Rumi, 205
Yiyang, 35

Yokohama Immigration Bureau, 19
Yokohama Overseas Chinese Association, 1, 16, 52
Yokohama Overseas Chinese School, 15, 17, 20, 23
Yokohama's Legal Affairs Bureau, 131
Yokohama-Yamate Chinese School, 16–17
Yoshikawa Eiji Cultural Award, 205
Yugoslavia, xiii, 205–7

zainichi Korean resident, in Japan, 99, 101, 164, 185, 186
zairyu-kado residence card. *See* Certificate of Alien Registration
zairyu residence card, 189, 197
zaitoku
	special stay permit, 151
	visa, 156
Zaw Min Htut, 165–6
Zhou Enlai, 7